Decorative Art
and Modern Interiors

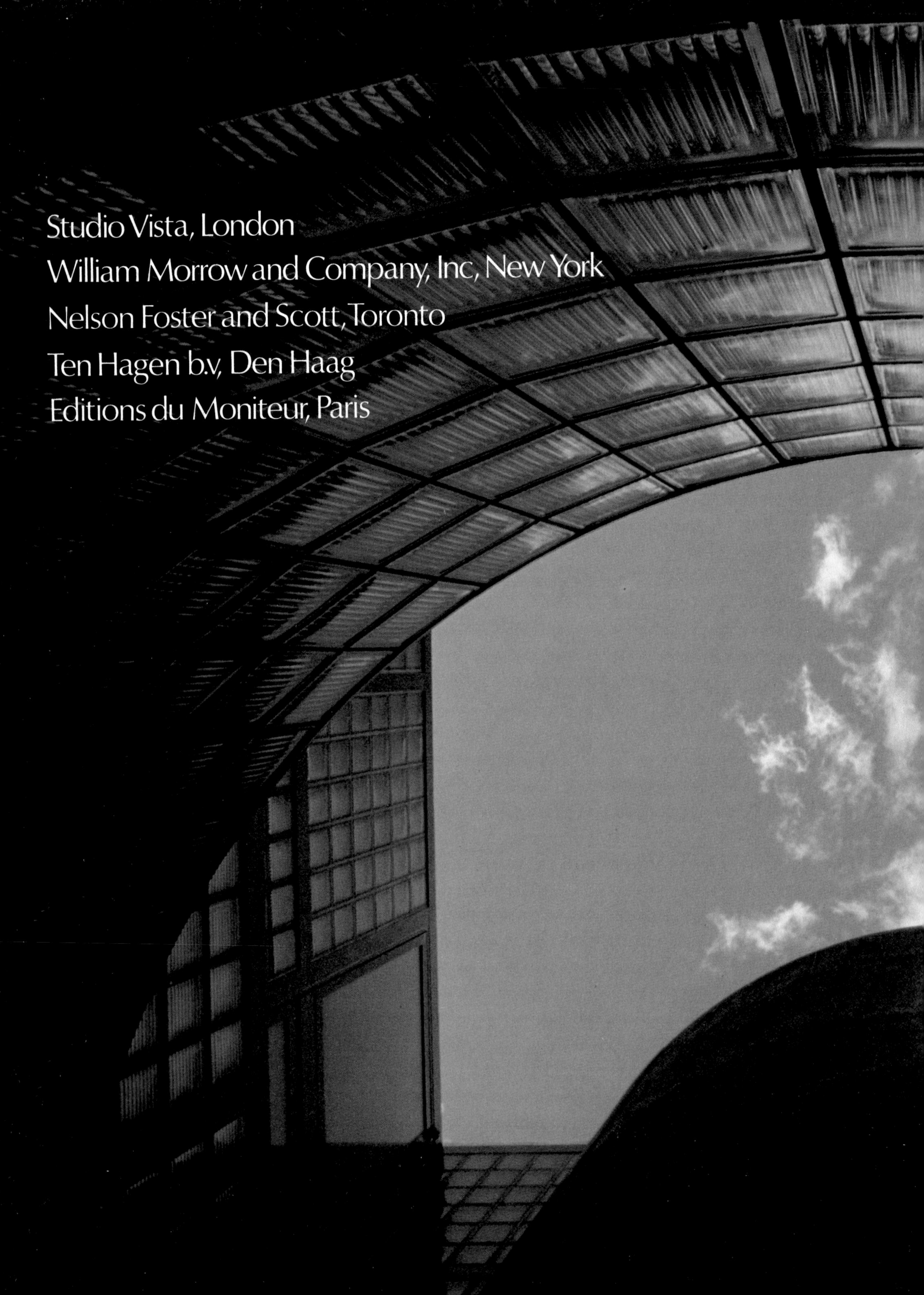

Studio Vista, London
William Morrow and Company, Inc, New York
Nelson Foster and Scott, Toronto
Ten Hagen b.v, Den Haag
Editions du Moniteur, Paris

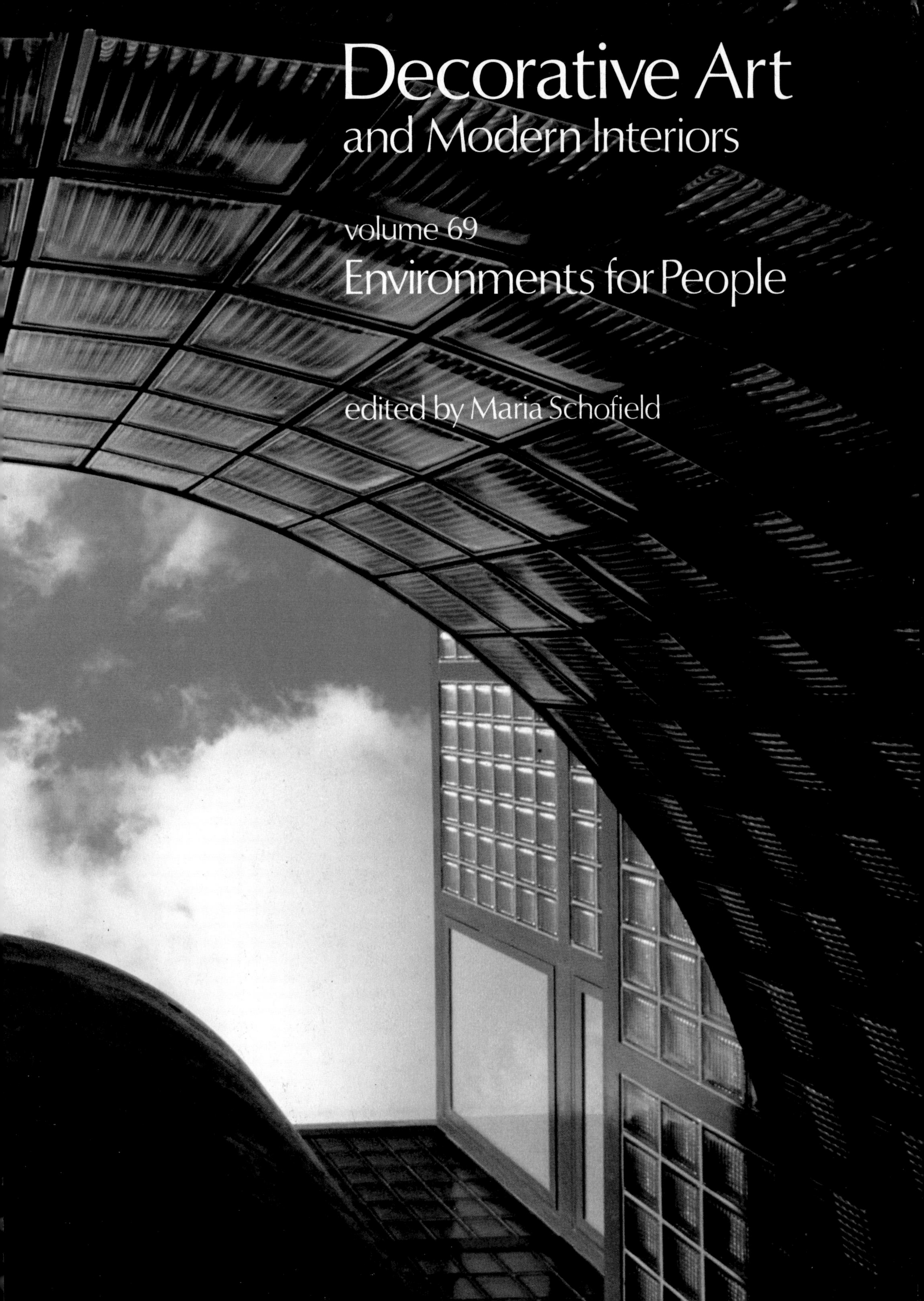
Decorative Art
and Modern Interiors
volume 69
Environments for People
edited by Maria Schofield

A Studio Vista book
first published in the UK in 1980 by Cassell Ltd.
35 Red Lion Square, London WC1R 4SG
and at Sydney, Auckland, Johannesburg,
an affiliate of
Macmillan Publishing Co., Inc.,
New York

Published in 1980 by William Morrow and Company, Inc.
105 Madison Avenue, New York, N.Y.10016

Published in 1980 by
Nelson Foster and Scott, a division
of General Publishing Co. Limited
30 Lesmill Road, Don Mills, Ontario
Canada

Library of Congress Catalog Card Number 80–81603
U.S.ISBN 0–688– 03675–9
U.K.ISBN 0–289–70939–3
Canada ISBN 0919324–48–7

Designed by Alan Bartram
Set in Linotron Optima 9 on 10 pt by
Tradespools Ltd., Frome, Somerset, England
Separations by Colorlito, Milano, Italy
Printed and bound in Italy by SAGDOS Spa, Milano
16 15 14 13 12 11 10 9 8 7 6 5 4 3 2 1

Cover:
The two pools under the inflatable structure at the Swimming Centre, Coal Street Park, Wilkes-Barre, Pennsylvania. Architects Bohlin Powell Brown. Photography Sandy Nixon

Title page:
The Ishihara Residence in Osaka, Japan: view of the sky from the central court. Architect Tadao Ando and Associates. Photography Kazuyoshi Bando

Contents

Acknowledgements

The Editor wishes to thank all architects, designers and manufacturers who supplied illustrations for reproduction. Acknowledgements are also due to the Crafts Council, London, the Glasshouse, London, and Den Permanente, Copenhagen, for their assistance.

Introduction

Among the many factors combining to form our environment, three appear to be all-important: natural conditions, economical considerations, and the way we use our buildings. Climate, soil formation, the quality and duration of natural light physically determine the shape of the spaces in which we live; the function of the building establishes the order of its parts; and economical considerations impose restraints which would be difficult to ignore, no matter how often these are given as reasons to excuse poor ideas or unimaginative building techniques.

Yet, a subtler element also influences the architectural design and, in final analysis, contributes to the appreciation of what is physical, economical or functional. To extract this factor from an architectural idea would require a study of the man, of his inclinations, ingenuity, cultural background, just as much as the natural, economical and functional factors are to be taken into account when studying the building itself.

Cultural traditions, reduced to essential manifestations, are always present in whatever we do, although the way of life changes and new standards are established. Building traditions are evident in the use of man-made materials in spite of the fact that these are available world-wide, so that a house built of concrete slabs around a central courtyard can look unmistakably Japanese even though the traditional Japanese house is not of concrete but of wood. Traditions influence the value we attach to certain situations and help us establish our own sense of priority: the architect translates this into his own idiom.

In effect, the brief for the majority of the projects included in this book reveals a need for an environment capable of relieving the pressures of everyday activities in a variety of situations.

An appropriate example of this is the recent addition of a new building to the Office of Deere & Company in Moline, U.S.A., by Kevin Roche and John Dinkeloo. The original office, set in Illinois open countryside, is one of Eero Saarinen's last works. The new building encloses a large indoor garden directly accessible from the offices at ground level and intersected by a bridge at the upper level.

The Citicorp Centre in New York, by Hugh Stubbins, stands surrounded by Manhattan's first skyscrapers as a symbolic attempt to an architecture that relates to a more human scale, albeit one of grandiose proportions. The Centre comprises a Church, partially built underground, a sunken plaza connected to the city subway, a seven-storey block which includes a three-storey shopping mall and a central atrium, and a soaring 59-storey office tower, clad with aluminium and glass.

Two recent works by Kisho Kurokawa, the National Ethnological Museum in Tokyo and the Kumamoto Municipal Museum, are among the purest expressions of Kurokawa's poetic vision controlled by spiritual discipline. These spaces are ideally intended for meditation, relaxation and leisure, without which people cannot develop harmoniously.

In England, the Sainsbury Centre for Visual Arts in the University of East Anglia, by Foster Associates, has been described as a vast, luminous drawing room where people can meet and study surrounded by a collection of works of art. The Archaeological Museum in Lyon-Fourvière, France, by Bernard Zehrfuss, is a powerful underground structure of concrete built on the site of the Forum of the ancient Lugdunum, which was for two centuries one of the two capital cities of the Roman Empire. Here natural light is only allowed inside through channels which protrude discreetly outside so as not to disturb the historic setting.

Environmental quality is linked to a social experiment in the Correctional Institute at Eagle River, Alaska, by Crittenden Cassetta & Cannon in association with Hellmuth Obata & Kassabaum. The experiment is meant to prove that criminal offenders serving a heavy sentence should need a two-year period of self-imposed discipline, spent in congenial surroundings, before their return to normal life.

A group of five projects relates to travel, sports and entertainment. The National Air and Space Museum in Washington, by Hellmuth Obata & Kassabaum, offers a magnificent setting to a well documented survey of the history of Aviation. The Coal Street Park Swimming Centre at Wilkes-Barre, Pennsylvania, by Bohlin Powell Brown, and the Sports Hall at Nantes, France, by Georges Evano and Jean-Luc Pellerin, exemplify two solutions to different climatic conditions, while the Finnjet Passenger Car Ferry which operates a 24-hour service between Germany and Finland demonstrates the latest methods in commercial shipbuilding. Barton Myers' Citadel Theatre in Edmonton, Canada, is a sensitive combination of the warm and intimate atmosphere of a traditional theatre hall and of the strong, extrovert idiom of the outer shell of steel and glass.

Six examples of domestic architecture, which complete the first section of this book, show different ways of utilizing the site on which the houses stand: the tiny, unpretentious Roundhouse in Greece, by Senkowsky Sakellarios, set in an olive grove; the Mountain Cabin in Colorado by Arley Rinehart, a feat of virtuosity; and the calm, sundrenched Duplex House overlooking San Francisco Bay, by Callister Payne Bischoff.

By contrast, the home of the architect Robert Sobel in Texas, and the Ishihara Residence in Osaka, by Tadao Ando, are enclosed and inward-looking buildings, the former to benefit from a central garden, the latter to exploit to the maximum all available space and light while providing a high degree of privacy.

Continuing the series of articles on *Elements of Architecture*, Professor Pieter de Bruyne writes on the subject of Light. Drawing examples from works of the past and from more recent buildings, the Author examines the role of light in architecture, its deep aesthetic and psychological significance and its value as a poetic element which should be taken into full account from the early stages of a project.

The collection of furnishing and craft objects which concludes the book will perhaps show that a movement in the right direction is beginning to take place, at least in Europe. Cabinetmakers are becoming more aware of the technological advantages offered by industry and are working with designers from the drawing-board stage of a project: this was the theme of a small exhibition of furniture held in May 1979 at Den Permanente, in Copenhagen. Each piece bore the names of the designer and of the cabinetmaker, to indicate the close association between the two. In England, The John Makepiece School for Craftsmen in Wood is becoming a meeting place for visiting master craftsmen from many countries, who give series of lectures accompanied by exhibitions of their own work at the School. One such visit, by James Krenov, coincided with the exhibition of the work of the first graduates from the School, held at the British Crafts Centre in London, where some pieces by the Master were shown alongside the degree work by the students. Also in London, The Glasshouse organized in the Spring of 1980 a series of study-days on practical glassmaking to which museum directors, collectors, gallery owners and publishers interested in modern studio glass were invited to participate. The response to this initiative was unanimous, so that the activity will become a regular event. The actual experience of working with hot glass undoubtedly added a new perspective to the appreciation and understanding of the pieces exhibited in the gallery space adjoining the glass furnace. All in all, this has been a good year, showing encouraging signs of renewed activity.

Maria Schofield

Introducción

Entre los muchos elementos que se combinan para formar nuestro medio ambiente, hay tres que parecen ser de suma importancia: las condiciones naturales, las consideraciones de tipo económico y el modo en que utilizamos nuestros edificios. El clima, las características del suelo y la calidad y duración de la luz natural determinan físicamente la conformación de los espacios en que vivimos; la función del edificio establece el orden de sus partes y consideraciones de tipo económico imponen restricciones que sería difícil no tener en cuenta, aunque a menudo, éstas sean aducidas como excusas para la falta de ideas o para el uso de técnicas de construcción poco imaginativas.

No obstante, hay un elemento mas sutíl que también influencia el diseño arquitectónico y, en fin de cuentas, contribuye a la apreciación de lo físico, lo económico o lo funcional. Al estudiar el edificio en sí mismo el aislar este elemento de una idea arquitectónica, supondría tanto un estudio del hombre, sus inclinaciones, su inventiva y su cultura, como una consideración de los elementos naturales, económicos y funcionales.

A pesar de que las formas de vida cambian y se establecen nuevas normas, las tradiciones culturales, reducidas a sus manifestaciones esenciales, están siempre presentes en todo lo que hacemos. Las tradiciones, en lo que a métodos de construcción se refiere, son evidentes en el uso de materiales artificiales, a pesar de su disponibilidad en todo el mundo, de tal manera que una casa construida de bloques de concreto alrededor de un patio central puede lucir, sin duda ninguna, como japonesa, a pesar de que la casa japonesa tradicional no está hecha de concreto sino de madera. Las tradiciones influencian el valor que atribuimos a ciertas situaciones y nos ayudan a establecer nuestro propio orden de prioridad: el arquitecto traduce esto a su propio idioma.

En efecto, las instrucciones para la mayoría de los proyectos incluídos en este libro, nos muestran la necesidad de un medio ambiente capaz de aliviar las presiones generadas por las actividades cotidianas en diferentes situaciones.

Al respecto, un ejemplo idóneo es la adición reciente de un nuevo edificio diseñado por Kevin Roche y John Dinkeloo a las oficinas de Deere & Company en EE.UU. Las oficinas originales, ubicadas en pleno campo en Illinois, son entre los ultimos trabajos de Eero Saarinen. El nuevo edificio está construido alrededor de un gran jardín interior con acceso directo desde las oficinas en la planta baja y con un puente que lo cruza en el nivel superior.

El Citicorp Centre en Nueva York, diseñado por Hugh Stubbins, se alza rodeado por los primeros rascacielos de Manhattan como un intento simbólico hacia una arquitectura que, no obstante sus proporciones grandiosas, se adapta mejor a lo que podríamos llamar una escala más humana. El Centro comprende una iglesia construída parcialmente bajo el nivel del suelo, una plaza a bajo nivel conectada al Metro de la ciudad, un bloque de edificios de siete pisos que incluye una galería comercial de tres pisos y un atrio central, y una altísima torre de cincuenta y nueve pisos para oficinas, revestida de aluminio y vidrio.

Dos trabajos recientes de Kisho Kurokawa, el Museo Etnológico de Osaka y el Museo Municipal de Kumamoto, están entre las más puras expresiones de la visión poética controlada por la disciplina espiritual de Kurokawa. Estos espacios están idealmente diseñados para la meditación y el recreo, sin los cuales las personas no pueden desarrollarse en forma armónica.

En Inglaterra, el Sainsbury Centre for Visual Arts en la Universidad de East Anglia, diseñado por Foster Associates, ha sido descrito como un vasto y luminoso salón donde la gente puede reunirse y estudiar rodeada de una colección de obras de arte. El Museo Arqueológico de Lyon-Fourvière en Francia, diseñado por Bernard Zehrfuss, es una imponente estructura de concreto bajo el nivel del suelo, construída en el sitio que ocupaba el Foro de la antigua Lugdunum, que por dos siglos fué una de las dos ciudades Capitales del Imperio Romano. Aquí, la luz natural entra sólo por unos canales que sobresalen de tal manera de no perturbar el ambiente histórico del lugar.

En el caso del Instituto de Correción de Eagle River, en Alaska, diseñado por Crittenden Cassetta & Cannon en conjunto con Hellmuth Obata & Kassabaum, la calidad del medio ambiente se liga a un experimento social. El experimento fue diseñado como prueba de que los criminales que han estado cumpliendo una pesada condena, necesitan un período de dos años de autodisciplina en un ambiente adecuado antes de volver a la vida normal.

Un grupo de cinco proyectos tiene por tema viajes, deportes y espectáculos. El Museo Nacional del Aire y del Espacio en Washington por Hellmuth Obata & Kassabaum, ofrece un magnífico escenario para una muestra bien documentada de la historia de la Aviación. El Centro de Natación de Coal Street en Wilkes-Barre, Pennsylvania, diseñado por Bohlin Powell Brown y el Hall de Deportes de Nantes por Georges Evano y Jean-Luc Pellerin, ejemplifican dos soluciones para diferentes condiciones climáticas, mientras que el transbordador Finnjet que ofrece un servicio de veinticuatro horas al día, entre Alemania y Finlandia es un ejemplo de los métodos más recientes utilizados en la construcción de barcos comerciales. El Citadel Theatre, diseñado por Barton Myers en Edmonton, Canada, es una combinación discreta del ambiente íntima y cálida de un teatro tradicional y el idioma poderoso y extrovertido de la caparazón exterior de vidrio y acero.

Los seis ejemplos de arquitectura doméstica que completan la primera parte de este libro, muestran diferentes maneras de utilizar el espacio en el cual la casa se situa: la casa-redonda en el medio de un olivar en Grecia, pequeña y sin pretensiones diseñada por Senkowsky Sakellarios; la cabaña montaña en Colorado por Arley Rinehart, una proeza de virtuosismo; y la casa Duplex con vista a la Bahía de San Francisco, tranquila y bañada de sol, diseñada por Callister Payne Bischoff.

Como contraste, la casa del arquitecto Robert Sobel en Texas y la Residencia Ishihara en Osaka por Tadao Ando, son edificios encerrados y orientados hacia el interior; el primero para aprovechar un jardín central y el segundo para explotar al máximo el espacio y la luz disponibles, proveyendo al mismo tiempo de un alto grado de soledad.

Continuando la serie sobre *Elementos de Arquitectura* el Profesor Pieter de Bruyne escribe acerca de la Luz. Tomando ejemplos de trabajos del pasado y de edificios más recientes, el autor examina el papel de la luz en la arquitectura, su significado profundamente estético y psicológico y su valor como elemento poético que debe ser tomado en consideración desde las primeras etapas de un proyecto.

La colección de mobiliario y artesanía con la cual se termina el libro, puede tomarse como indiccaión de la buena orientación del diseño, por lo menos en Europa. Los ebanistas están cada día maś conscientes de las ventajas tecnológicas ofrecidas por la industria y están trabajando junto a los diseñadores desde las primeras etapas del diseño de un proyecto: éste es el tema de una pequeña exposición de muebles llevada a cabo en Mayo de 1979 en Den Permanente, Copenhagen. Cada pieza contenía los nombres del diseñador y el ebanista para así subrayar la estrecha colaboración entre ellos. En Inglaterra, la John Makepeace School for Craftsmen in Wood se está convirtiendo en un lugar de encuentro de Maestros artesanos de muchos países, que dan ciclos de conferencias compañadas por exposiciones de sus propios trabajos en la Escuela. Una de estas visitas, la de James Krenov, coincidió con la exposición de los trabajos de los primeros graduados de la Escuela llevada a cabo en el British Crafts Centre en Londres, donde algunos trabajos del Maestro se expusieron en conjunto con los trabajos de los estudiantes. También en Londres, la Glasshouse organizó en la primavera de 1980 una serie de jornadas de estudio sobre los aspectos prácticos de la producción de objetos de vidrio a las cuales fueron invitados a participar directores de Museos, coleccionistas, dueños de Galerías de Arte y editores interesados en objetos modernos de vidrio. La respuesta a esta iniciativa fue unánime, por lo cual, esta actividad se realizará en el futuro en forma regular. El tener acceso a la experiencia directa del trabajo con vidrio caliente, sin duda, añadió una nueva perspectiva para la apreciación y comprensión de las piezas expuestas en la parte de la Galería contigua al horno del vidrio. En resumen, este ha sido un buen año que ha mostrado signos alentadores de renovadas actividades.

Maria Schofield

はしがき

我々の環境を形成する要素は、たくさんあるが、その中で自然の状況、経済的配慮、および建物の使用目的の三つが、もっとも重要であるように思われる。気候、土壌層、天然光線の質と照射時間が、我々が住む空間の形態を、物理的に決定し、その建物の機能が、各部分の建築様式を決め、経済的配慮が、無視し難い制約を生み出すのである。もっとも、この経済的配慮は、想像力に欠けた建築技術や、ありふれたアイデアに対する言い訳に、しばしば用いられるものであるが。

しかし、これほど本質的ではないが、建築デザインに影響を及ぼし、終極的には、何が物理的で、経済的で、機能的であるかを評価するのに役立つものがある。この要素を建築学的アイデアからひき出すためには、人間自体の、また、人間の傾向、創意、文化的背景などを研究する必要があり、これはちょうど、建築物自体を研究するときに、自然、経済、機能の各要素を考慮しなければならないのと同じである。

もっとも本質的なものにまで昇華された文化的伝統というものは、生活様式が変化し、新しい規準が確立されようとも、常に我々の行動の中に存在するものである。人工の材料は、世界中どこででも手に入れることができるが、その使い方の中に、建築物の伝統というものが見られるものである。たとえば、日本の典型的な家は、コンクリートではなく、木でできているが、中庭のある家は、それがコンクリート板でできていても、まぎれもなく日本的に見える。伝統というものは、我々がある状況に下す価値観や、何に優先権を置くかを決めるときにも、影響を及ぼすものであり、建築家は、これによって、自分独自の作風を創り出すのである。

この本に収められている大部分の作品を見ると、種々様々な状況の中での日常生活の圧迫を、解きほぐすことのできる環境の必要性がわかってくる。

この事実を適格に表わしている例として、米国モリーンにあるケビン　ローチ (Kevin Roche) とジョン・ディンケルー (John Dinkeloo) によるディーア社 (Deere & Company) の増築された建物が、あげられる。元来の建物は、イリノイ州の広々とした田舎に建っており、エーロ・サーリネン (Eero Saarinen) の最後の作品の一つである。新築された建物の中央には、大きな屋内庭園があり、一階の各部屋から直接、行かれるようになっている。二階では、各棟をつなぐ渡り廊下が、この中庭を横切っている。

ヒュー・スタビンズ (Hugh Stubbins) によるニューヨークのシティーコープ・センターは、マンハッタンの超高層ビルに囲まれてそびえているが、巨大な建物にもかかわらず、より人間に密着した建物にしようという試みを象徴しているかのようである。このセンターには、一部分地下になっている教会、市の地下鉄につながる地下広場、三階建てのショッピング・アーケードや中央アトリウムのある七階建の区域、59階建てのオフィス・タワーなどがあり、外装は、アルミニュウムとガラスである。

黒川紀章の最近の二作、大阪の国立民族博物館と熊本県立博物館は、まさに、同氏の鍛え上げた精神にコントロールされた詩的概念を表現しているものである。これらの空間は、沈思黙考、リラックス、レジャーを意図したものであり、これなくしては、調和のとれた人間には、なれないものである。

イギリスの東アングリア (East Anglia) 大学にある視覚芸術のセインスベリー・センターは、フォスター社 (Foster Associates) の作であるが、広大な、陽当たりの良い客間として知られ、芸術作品に囲まれて、会合したり勉学したりできるのである。フランスのリヨンにあるベルナール・ゼルフス (Bernard Zehrfuss) の手による考古学博物館は、2世紀の間ローマ帝国の二つの首都のうちの一つであった古代ルグタナンのフォーラムの敷地に建てられたコンクリート造りの、頑丈な地下建築である。太陽の光は、歴史的背景をこわさないために、遠慮深げに外に通じているトンネルを通してのみ、屋内にさしこむようになっている。

クリテンデン・カセッタとキャノン (Critenden Cassetta & Cannon) がヘルムス・オバタとカサバウム (Hellmuth Obata & Kassabaum) の協力を得て、アラスカのイーグル・リバーにある驕正所で、ある社会的実験をしたが、これは、環境の性質に関連したものであり、重罪の刑事犯罪者は、普通の生活に戻る前に、2年間の自発的鍛練と自然のままの環境の中での生活が必要であるというものであった。

次の五つの作品は、旅行、スポーツ、娯楽に関係したものである。ヘルムス・オバタとカサバウムによるワシントンにある国立航空宇宙博物館は、航空の歴史についての豊富な実証材料を伴った調査を展示するのに、すばらしい舞台装置を提供している。ボウリン・パウエル・ブラウン (Bohlin Powell Brown) によるペンシルバニアのウィルクスバレにあるコール街公園水泳センターとジョルジュ・エヴァノ (Georges Evano) とジャンニル・ペレリン (Jean-Lue Pellerin) によるフランスのナントのスポーツ・ホールは、二つの異った天候条件の、それぞれの解決法を示している。一方、ドイツとフィンランドの間を、24時間営業で運航しているフィンジェット・カーフェリーは、商業用船舶の最新の造船法を示している。カナダのエドモントンにあるバートン・マイヤーズ (Barton Myers) の城郭劇場は、伝統的な劇場の持つ暖い、親しみやすい雰囲気と、外側の鋼鉄とガラスの強じんな外向的雰囲気との微妙な組合わせを表現している。

この本の最初の部分を占めている住居建築の六つの例は、それぞれの敷地の異った使い方を示している。センコウスキー・サケラリオス (Senkowsky Sakellarios) によるギリシャの小さな円形家屋は、オリーブの林の中に建てられており、アーリー・ラインハート (Arley Rinehart) によるコロラドの山小屋は、まさに芸術の権化であり、キャリスター・ペイン・ビショフ (Callister Payne Bischoff) によるデュプレックス・ハウスは、サンフランシスコ湾を見下ろす静かな陽当りの良い邸宅である。

これとは対照的に、テキサスにある建築家ロバート・セイベル (Robert Sabel) の家や、安藤忠雄の設計による大阪の石原邸は、高い塀で囲まれた、閉鎖的な感じのする建物であり、前者は、中央庭園に特徴があり、後者は、高度なプライバシーを保ちながらも、できるだけのスペースと光線を利用している。

シリーズ「建築の諸要素」は、今回は光についてピエテル・ド・ブライン (Pieter de Bruyne) が書いているが、彼は、過去および最近の建築から例をとって、建築における光の役目、その深い審美的心理的な特徴、および詩的要素としてのその価値を調べ、光は建築の初期の段階から、十分考慮しなければならないものであると述べている。

この本の最後を占めている家具と工芸品のコレクションは、この正しい方向への動きが、少くともヨーロッパでは、はじまっていることを示している。家具師は、工業が提供している技術上の長所に注目しはじめ、設計の段階からデザイナーと協力して仕事をしている。このことは、1979年5月コペンハーゲンのデン・ペルマネンテで開催された家具の小展覧会のテーマであった。各部分には、家具師とデザイナーの名前が刻まれていたが、これは、この二人の密接な協力関係を示すものである。イギリスの「木工師のためのジョン・メイクピース学校」は、多くの国々からの技工長が、自分の作品の展覧会を開き、講演をし、様々な人と会う場所となってきている。ジェイムス・クレノフ (James Krenov) が、ここを訪問したとき、たまたまこの学校の第一回卒業生の作品展が、ロンドンの英国クラフトセンターで開かれており、技工長の作品が、学生の卒業作品と一緒に展示されていた。ロンドンのグラスハウス協会は、1980年の春、実際的なガラス制作の研修日を組織し、現代スタジオガラスに興味のある美術館長、収集家、画廊経営者、出版者などを、招待した。これに対する反応は絶大で、この催物は、定期的なものになるだろうと思われる。熱いガラスに実際に取り組んでみてはじめて、ガラス炉の隣りの画廊で展示されている作品を、新しい見方で鑑賞し、理解することができるようになるのである。今年は、これまでの作品を見直すのに良い年である。

マリア・スコフィールド

Environments for People

The Sainsbury Centre for Visual Arts University of East Anglia, England

Architects
Foster Associates

Photography
Ken Kirkwood
John Donat

The brief for the Sainsbury Centre was developed in consultation with the University of East Anglia, the University Grants Committee and Sir Robert and Lady Sainsbury, who had decided to donate their large and varied collection of art to the University. The original buildings for the new university were designed by Sir Denys Lasdun and in his masterplan future growth was planned along the Yare Valley. A network of roads with drainage and services was already constructed in readiness.

The architects for the new building in consultation with Lasdun, decided to locate the centre along this planned line of growth. The fact that the Centre would thus be next to the Science buildings was in sympathy with the Sainsbury's wish for their gift to be of benefit to the broadest cross-section of the student population. Preliminary research into gallery buildings in Europe and in the United States was widely conducted, particularly from the user viewpoint. As well as an Art Gallery, the new building had to contain the School of Fine Arts, the Senior Common Room and a new Restaurant open to the public as well as the university.

The various functions were all housed in one linear shed. In order to create an area completely free from columns, and thus a more flexible space,

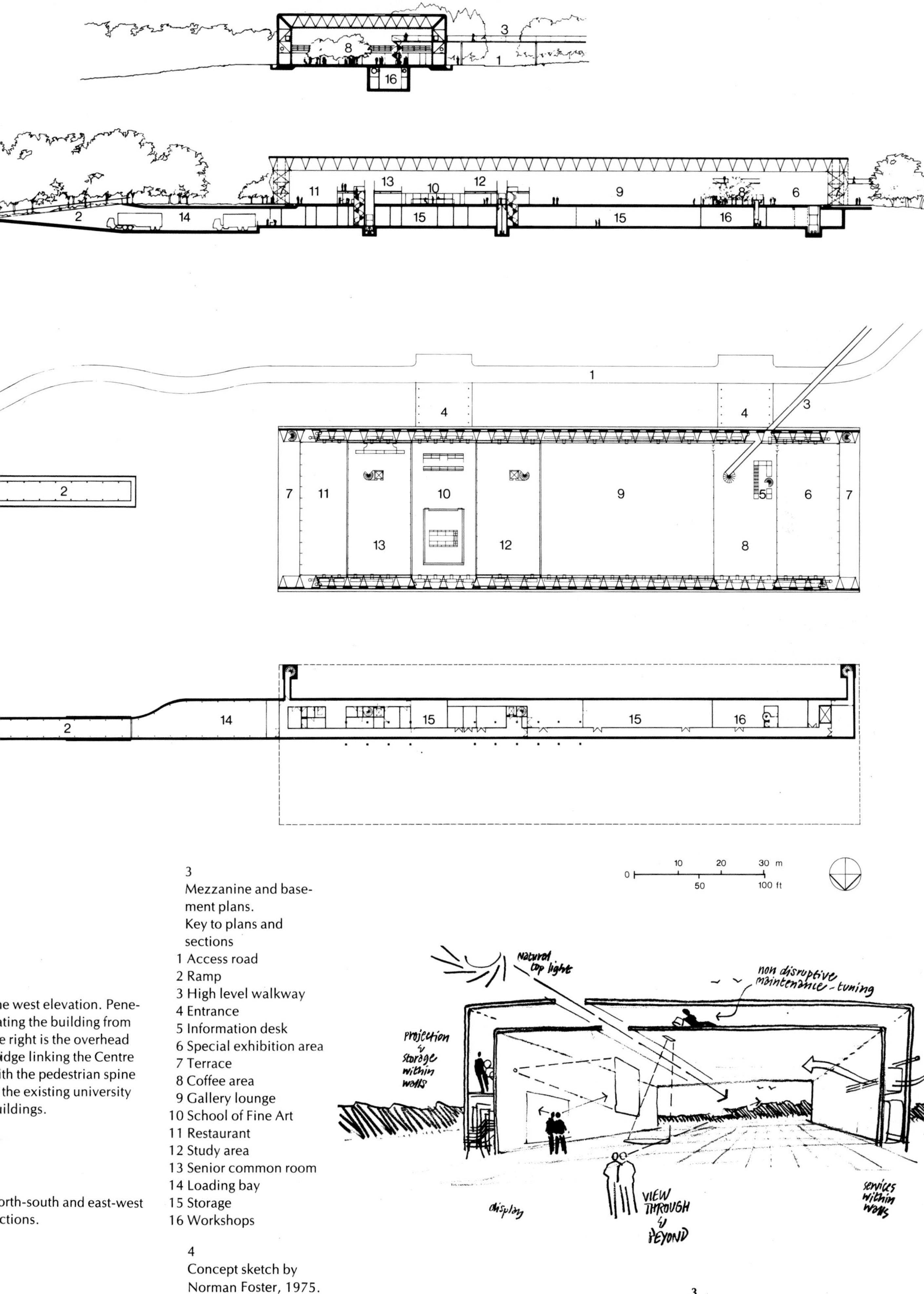

…e west elevation. Pene-…ting the building from …e right is the overhead …idge linking the Centre …th the pedestrian spine … the existing university …ildings.

…orth-south and east-west …ctions.

3
Mezzanine and basement plans.
Key to plans and sections
1 Access road
2 Ramp
3 High level walkway
4 Entrance
5 Information desk
6 Special exhibition area
7 Terrace
8 Coffee area
9 Gallery lounge
10 School of Fine Art
11 Restaurant
12 Study area
13 Senior common room
14 Loading bay
15 Storage
16 Workshops

4
Concept sketch by Norman Foster, 1975.

5
Detail of gable corner showing three of the four types of cladding panels: solid, glass and curved.

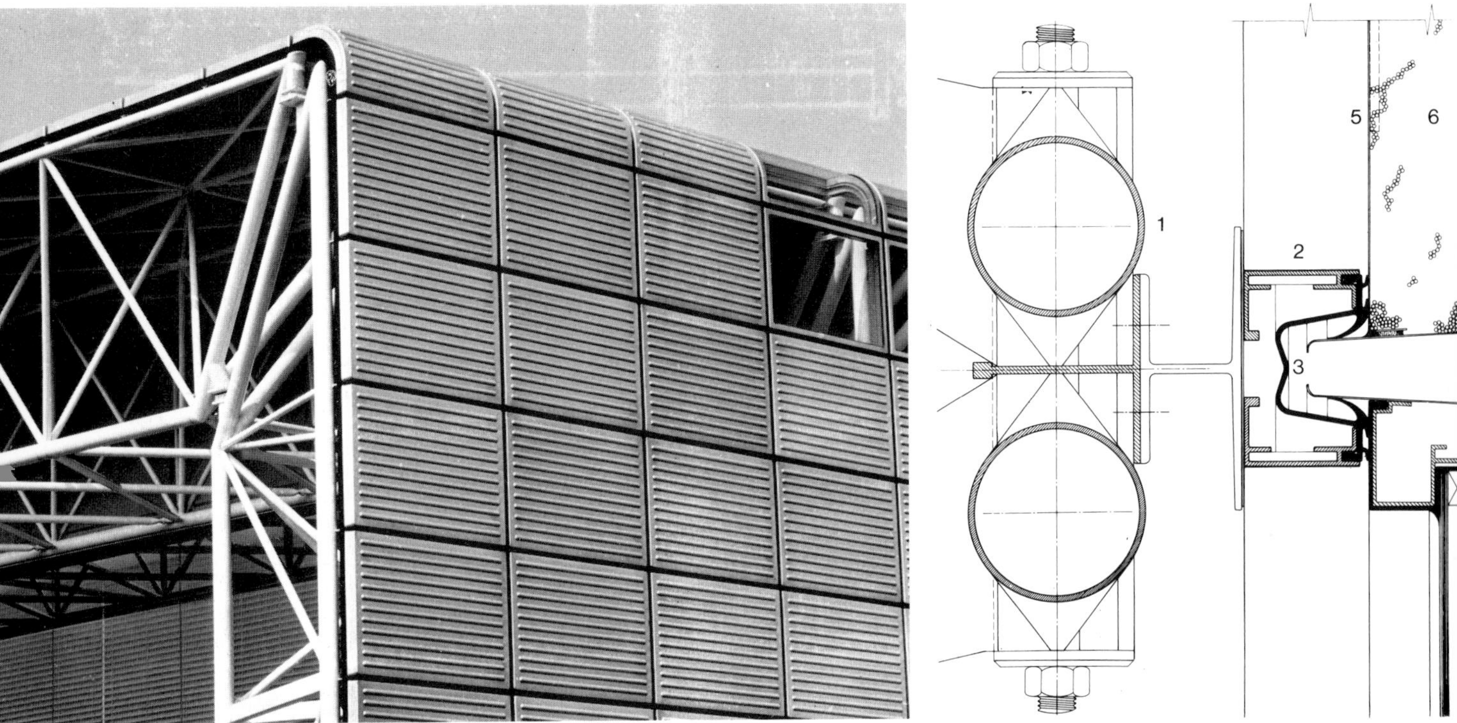

7
Typical cladding panel junction
1 Tubular steel frame
2 Enamelled extruded aluminium sub-frame
3 Neoprene ladder gasket
4 Aluminium outer skin
5 Aluminium inner skin
6 Insulation core
7 Double glazed unit

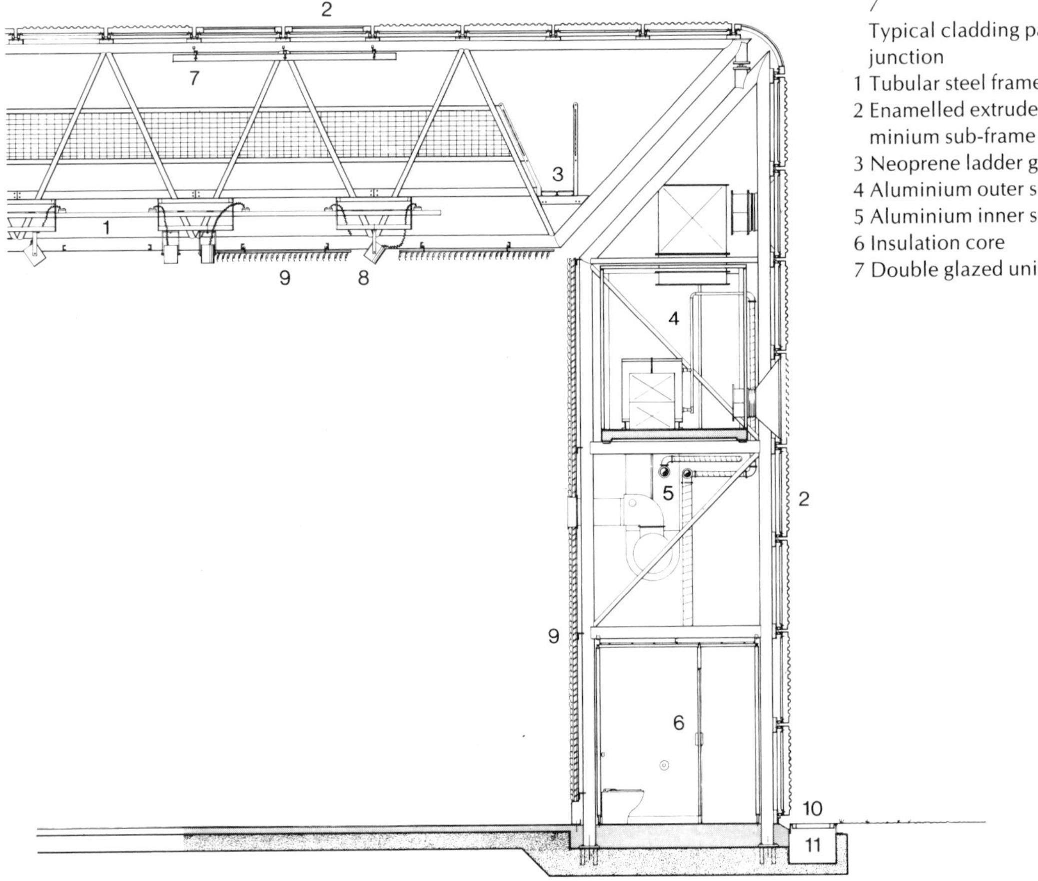

6
Section through external wall
1 Tubular steel truss
2 Interchangeable vacuum formed aluminium panels: glazed, solid or louvred
3 Access catwalk
4 Plant
5 Air distribution zone
6 Services: plant, darkroom, toilets, stores
7 Solar controlled aluminium louvres
8 Artificial lighting
9 Adjustable aluminium louvres
10 Cast aluminium perimeter grille
11 Gutter

etail of inner corner of
e west elevation. Note
e interplay of reflection
nd transparency which
nimates the rigid structure
f the building. Behind the
ass curtain wall is the
pecial exhibition area.

skeleton frame 133m (436ft) long and spanning 5m (110ft) was constructed from thirty-seven ıbular steel trusses supported on similar lattice owers. All building components were pre-abricated and assembled on site.

Internally the clear height is 7.7m (25ft), which llows sufficient room for mezzanine floors and the isplay of tall sculpture. The whole structure rests n continuous concrete strip footings with an ntegral floating ground slab. Extra foundation pads re provided for the existing and for future internal tructures.

The outer cladding to the steel framework is esigned to be completely flexible. There are four ifferent types of panels: glass, solid, grilled, and a urved panel to turn the corner between wall and oof. The solid panels are a sandwich construction vith a vacuum-formed outer skin of highly reflec-ive, superplastic anodised aluminium (the first pplication of this material in the building industry) and a foam filling 100mm (4in) thick, to give a high insulation value. Each panel measures 2.4m (8ft) wide by 1.2m (4ft) high and is locked into a continuous net of neoprene gaskets by means of six bolts. The panels can be easily interchanged in a matter of minutes. The neoprene sections also serve as rainwater channels, directing water into a continuous cast-aluminium grille at the base of the outer wall. Banks of perforated aluminium louvres, backed with acoustic wadding where necessary, form the internal lining to the structure. Louvres on the ceiling are adjusted automatically to regulate the internal lighting levels and, together with the interchangeable external panels and a highly flexible system of electric display lighting, create what Norman Foster refers to as a 'highly tunable' light control system.

At either end of the shed is a sheer glass curtain wall of full height panels of glass with minimal neoprene joints to allow completely unobstructed views of woods at one end and of a lake at the other.

The 2.4m (8ft) wide space created between the outer skin and the internal louvres is a service zone containing lobbies, cloakrooms, store rooms, photographic darkrooms, mechanical and electrical plant. This allows maintenance to take place without disturbing the internal areas, particularly in the ceiling zone where catwalks give access to the display lighting which can be adjusted independently of the exhibition below.

The design of internal spaces, the nature of the enclosing wall with its adjustable, highly reflective skin and its well insulated panels, combined with the design of the ventilation system, have created an alternative to air conditioning and its associated high installation and running costs. The building draws its main heat supply from the central high temperature water distribution system of the campus. This feeds a ducted warm air heating installation which has provision for fresh and recirculated air mixing and dust filtration. Air discharge is usually from long-throw side wall diffusers with individual room control by concealed thermostats. The decision not to use air conditioning was in keeping with the spirit of creating a relaxed environment rather than a hermetically sealed vault for works of art.

An overhead glass-sided bridge links the existing pedestrian spine of the university buildings with the new block. The bridge sails over the sloping lawns and penetrates the envelope at a 45 degree angle before culminating in a spiral staircase which brings the visitor down into the entrance conservatory, where are the main reception desk and a coffee bar. To one side is a special exhibition area overlooking the lake and to the other is the main exhibition area, which is referred to as the 'living area' because of its groups of easy chairs with low tables and books encouraging visitors to relax and talk amongst the exhibits; a major departure from the usual hushed atmosphere of art galleries. The

9
Interior of 'living area' looking west. Note the informal seating arrangement to the right, the coffee area in the conservatory in the background and the overhead bridge used as a surveillance point.

The Sainsbury Centre for Visual Arts
University of East Anglia
Foster Associates

10
View of the special exhibition area from the exterior terrace at night. The linear rhythm of the external blinds and the ceiling blinds interlock to create an insubstantial lacy effect of shimmering light.

11
Details of roof construction: a network of catwalks housed in the depth of the steel trusses allows access for changing the external cladding panels and adjusting light fittings.

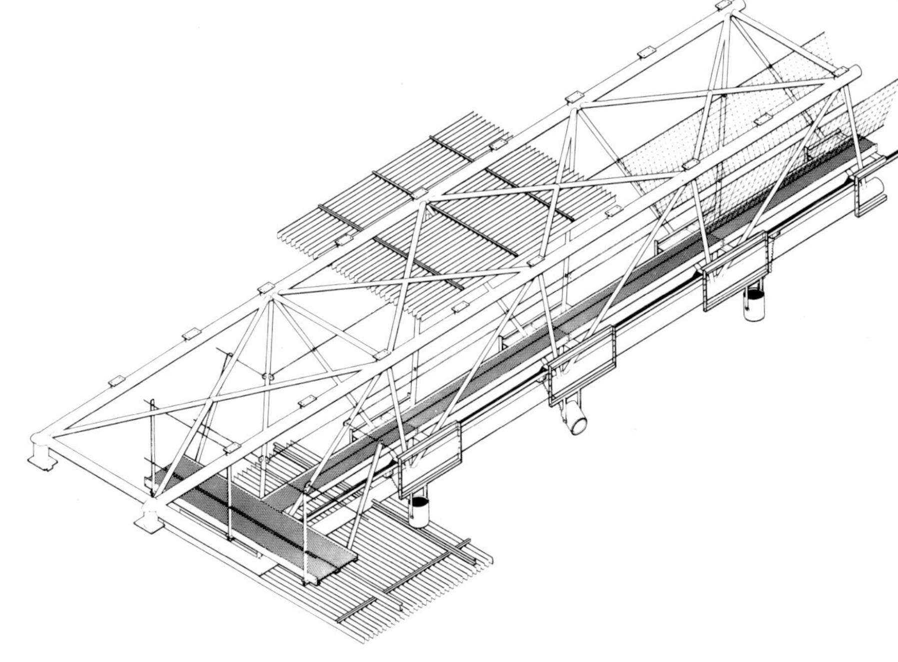

tail of spiral staircase.

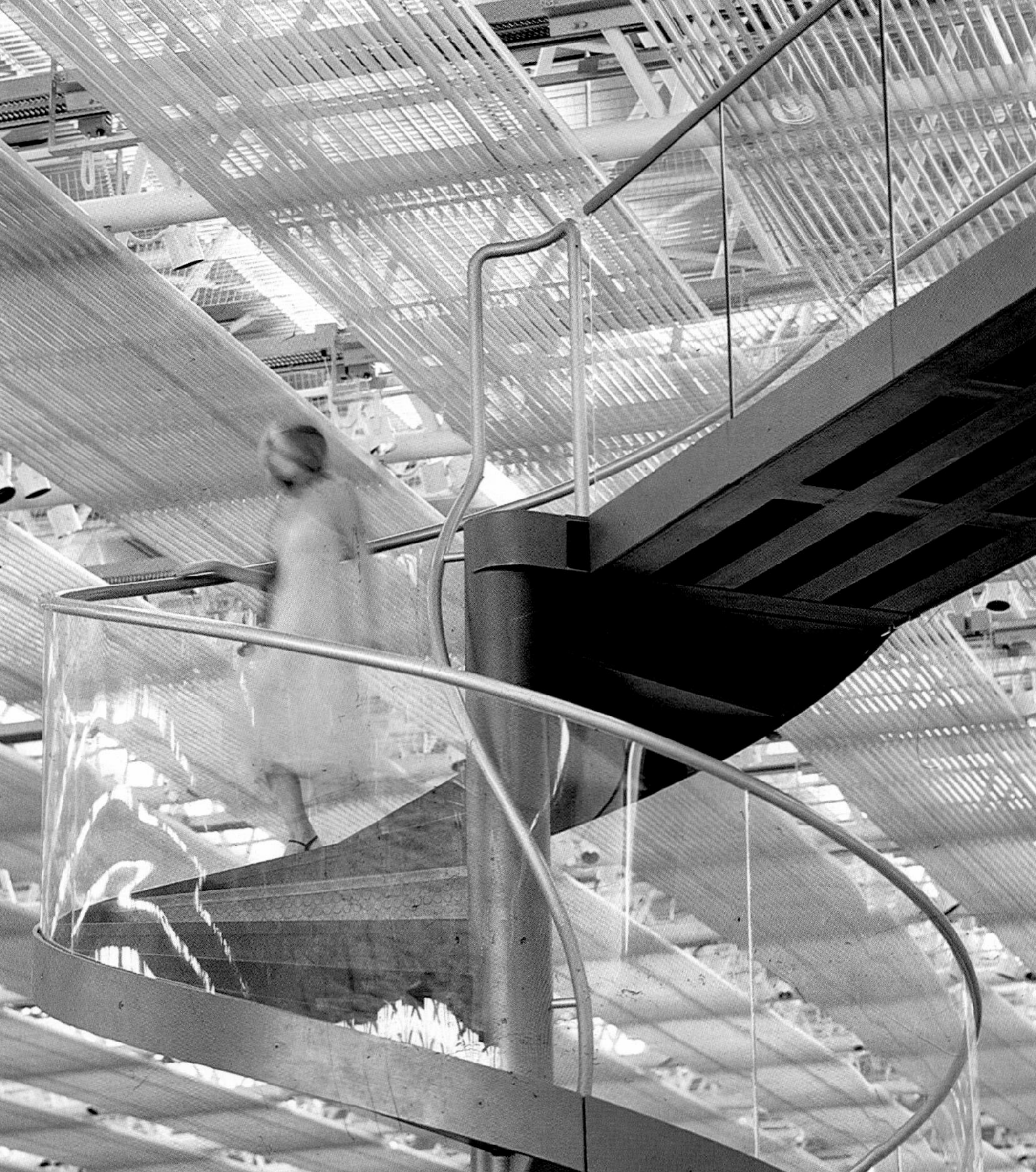

'living area' is separated from the School of Fine Arts by the reserve study area which has a mezzanine floor. Together with the entrance bridge, the use of mezzanine floors provides the security staff with convenient vantage points allowing surveillance of a wide area, thus reducing the number of staff required.

Another two-storey internal structure with kitchens on the ground level and the Senior Common Room at mezzanine level separates the school from the restaurant. All the internal spaces are connected by a passage which runs along the north side of the building and individual spaces can be closed off when necessary.

All the ground floor areas are served by a basement spine running the full length of the building. A ramp to the west connects underground loading docks to the access road. The basement contains store rooms for works of art and workshops and along its length are the staircases and lifts which connect all three levels. The plan is arranged so that the main gallery becomes a thoroughfare between the main university buildings and the School of Fine Arts, Restaurant and Senior Common Room.

There are five different types of display cases, which can be individually air conditioned. Each case has a 0.60m (2ft) square stove-enamelled steel base and a top of optically clear Perspex, which contains no colouring to filter out ultraviolet light as this function is provided by the building envelope.

13
Detail of 'living area' with louvres closed. Note the adjustable nozzles supplying warm air.

14
The senior common room on the mezzanine; in the centre is the lift of toughened glass and tubular steel.

15
At night the exhibition area is more introspective, but the highly polished marble floor reflects individually lit display cases, continuing the main theme of the architectural concept, based on transparency and reflection.

16
Seating area in the 'living area'. Students and visitors are encouraged to linger and talk.

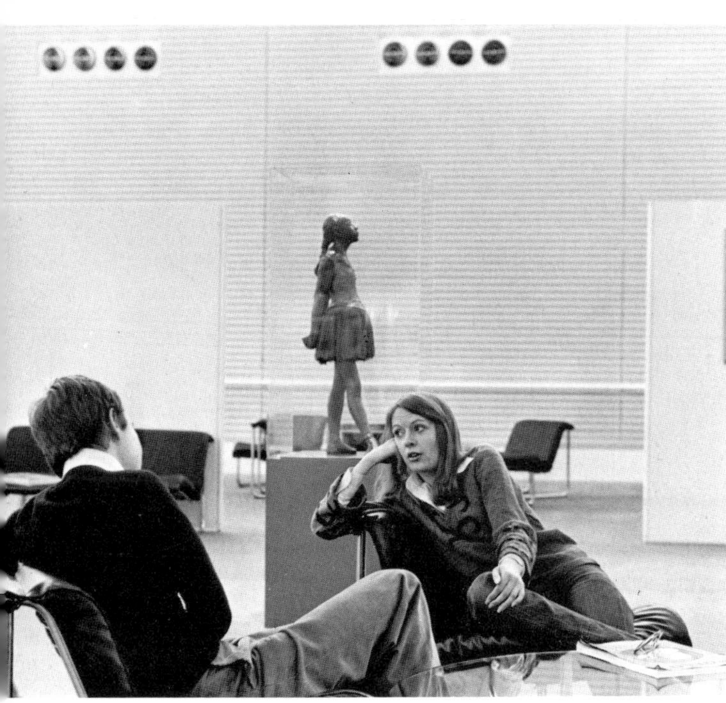

17
The sleek north elevation.

18
View of the east elevation at night with the dramatically lit access ramp descending to the basement loading bay.

The two passenger lifts at the Sainsbury Centre represent a unique collaboration of Foster Associates, Marryat and Scott, lift manufacturers, James Clark and Eaton, glass specialists, and Tennant Panels Ltd, automobile manufacturers. The lift cars are constructed from welded tubular steel, complementing the space frame of the main structure, and both the car and the lift shaft enclosure are clad with toughened glass, creating an almost transparent lift installation. An aluminium grille on top of the lift car with its own lift control panel simplifies cleaning the internal glass areas. Each lift is operated by a single hydraulic ram enclosed in a deep steel-lined bore hole below basement level, thus avoiding the need for lift plant at high level.

The Archaeological Museum Lyon-Fourvière, France

Architect
Bernard Zehrfuss

Photography
Dahliette Sucheyre

An archaeological museum which would bring together several scattered collections of Gallo-Roman remains has been constructed in the Roman forum on Fourvière Hill, Lyon, where two amphitheatres have been excavated. To reduce the impact of a large new building on such a sensitive area, the architect Bernard Zehrfuss decided to construct the bulk of the 5000sq.m (54,300sq.ft) of exhibition space underground.

From a storage area on the lowest level, the main section of the building extends upwards through two exhibition levels to emerge one storey above ground, where the restoration workshops, plant rooms and the curator's flat are situated. To the left of the main block is a secondary section containing lifts and stairs and exhibitions primarily of mosaics. Its structure is traditional and comprises five levels, three of which connect with the main museum. All levels in the museum are linked by a continuous ramp which is large enough and strong enough to allow access on all floors for machinery used in positioning the heavy stone exhibits.

The ground conditions made excavation a comparatively easy process. After the side of the hill had been removed a 15m (49ft) high and 60cm (2ft) thick retaining wall of in-situ concrete was erected

19
External view of museum. The planted stepped tiers cover the bulk of the museum with only a few windows and a single storey structure visible.

20
Section showing the main concrete structure.

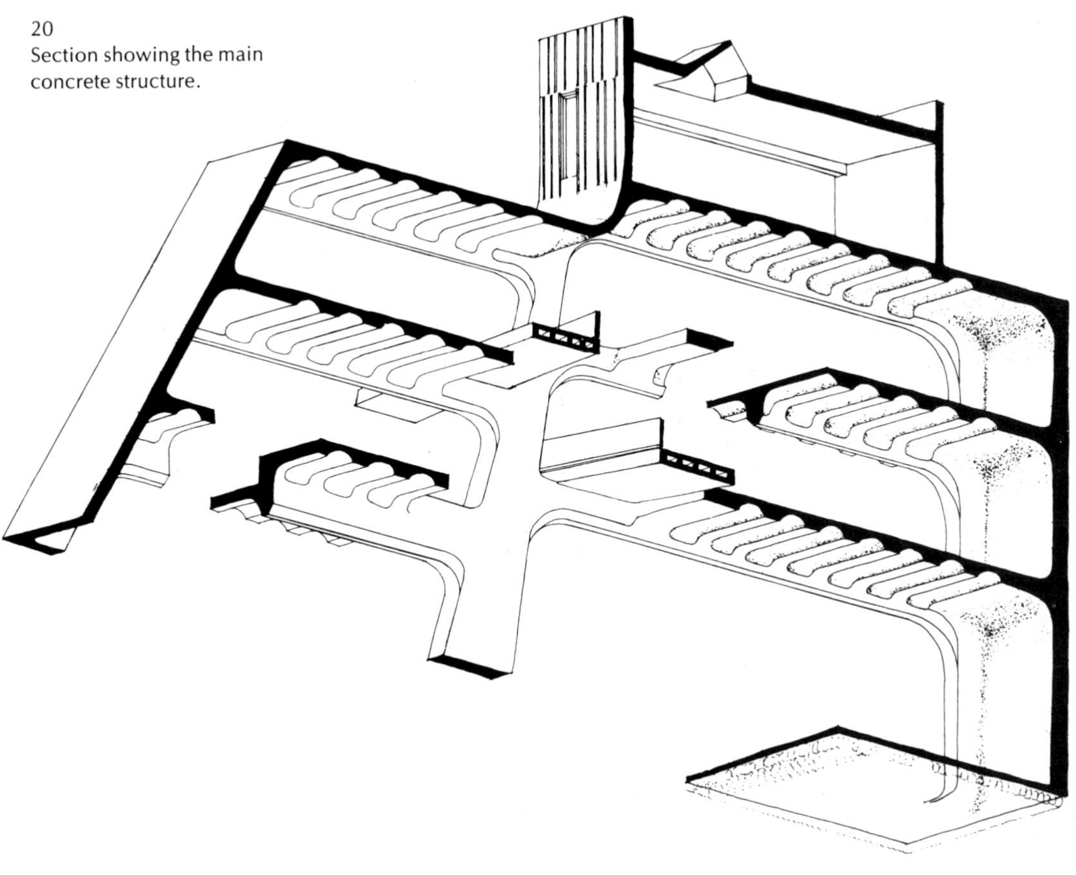

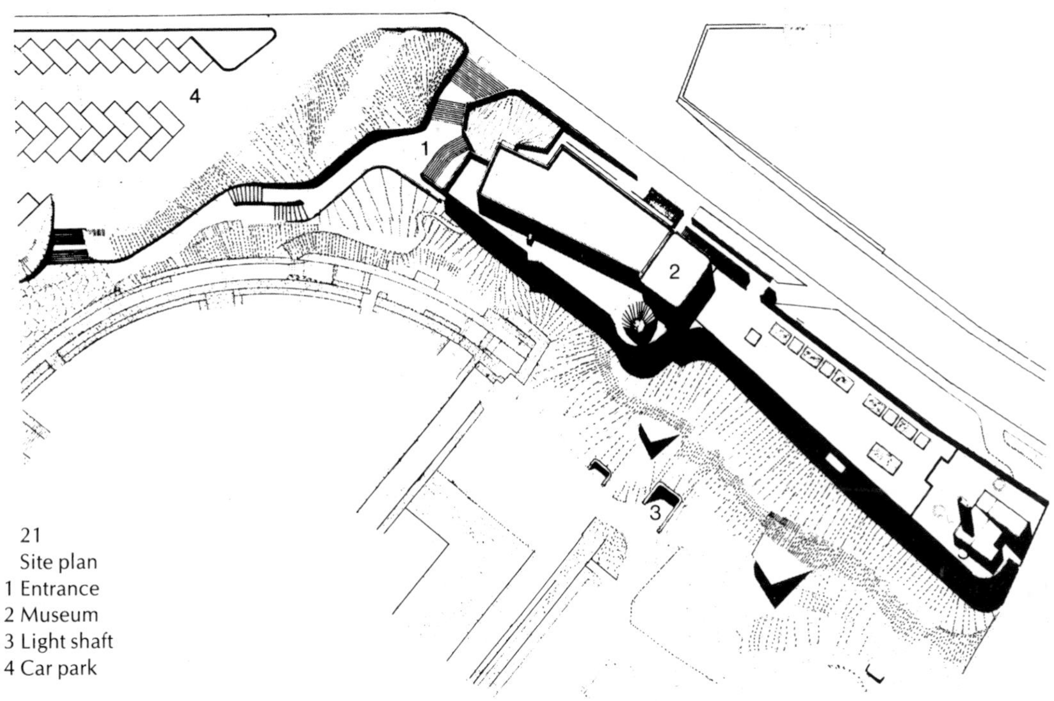

21
Site plan
1 Entrance
2 Museum
3 Light shaft
4 Car park

The Archaeological Museum
Lyon-Fourvière, France
Bernard Zehrfuss

22
Exhibition hall with ramp leading to a higher level. Both exhibition floors slope creating a flow of space which is further liberated by the absence of load-bearing walls.

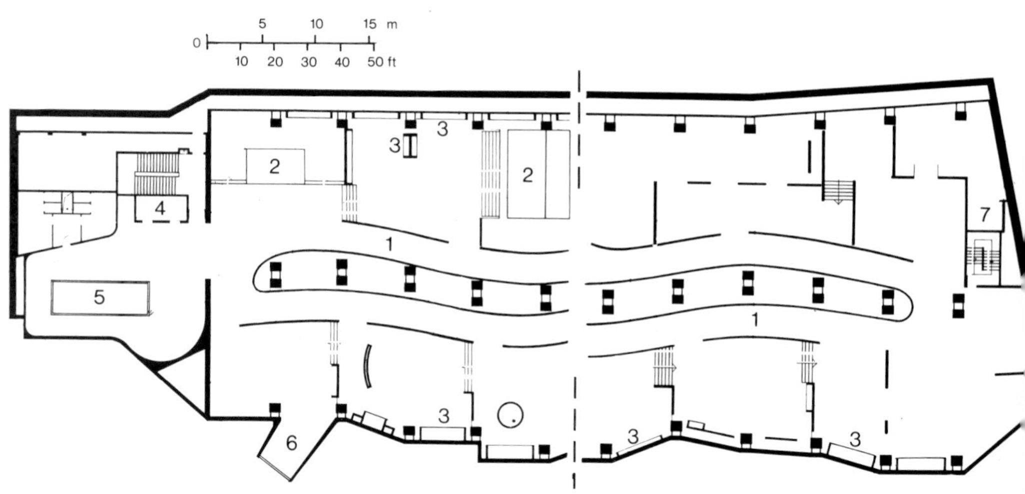

23
Plan of exhibition level
1 Ramp
2 Mosaic
3 Display case
4 Lifts
5 Void above mosaic floor below
6 Light shaft
7 Goods lift

24
Mosaic in exhibition hall. Each one of the portal frames had to be designed by computer because of the complexity of the structure. Columns along the back retaining wall are vertical but the inclination of the others varies: the outer columns incline to follow the gradient of the hillside and the twin central columns are neither parallel to each other nor to those on the outer or inner walls.

25
Section
1 Street level
2 Conservation department
3 Ramp
4 Exhibition hall
5 Storage

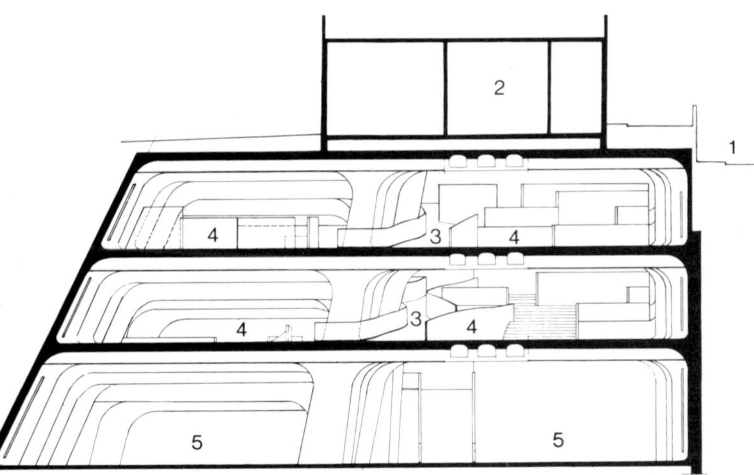

on three sides, and designed both to retain the earth and to release the build-up of water pressure by channelling ground water away into the Roman drain which once served the amphitheatres. The wall is in twenty-three 4.5m (15ft) wide sections; sixteen along the rear wall, three on the left hand side and four on the right, each anchored into the hillside with ties ranging from 12m (39ft) to 17m (56ft) in length. The structure incorporates concrete land drains, 50cm (1ft 8in) wide, a waterproof membrane of heat-bonded sheet plastic and an inspection gallery, 1.2m (4ft) wide, built along the

The Archaeological Museum
Lyon-Fourvière, France
Bernard Zehrfuss

26
Spiral stair between exhibition levels.

entire length of the retaining wall to give early warning of any failure in the construction.

Two rows of ten triple portal frames on a constant longitudinal grid of 6m (20ft) comprise the main structure. The rear wall is straight for seven sections of the grid and oblique for four and the external wall is cast in a series of horizontal steps following the natural contours of the hill, so that the width of the building varies along its length. The outer columns of the portal frames are set in from the retaining and from the outer wall. Short beams connect the twin columns in the centre and the outer columns with the walls, to take up horizontal stresses. Each column measures 1m × 35cm (3ft 3in × 1ft 2in) and continues down to a reinforced concrete foundation pad. Beams are a constant thickness of 80cm (2ft 7in) but vary in height from 1.35m (4ft 5in) to 2.25m (7ft 5in) to carry the exhibition floors of prefabricated reinforced concrete coffered sections 5.25m (17ft 3in) long and 1.49m (4ft 11in) wide covered with an in-situ screed.

The sloping ramp was cast in-situ while the reinforced concrete balustrade is prefabricated in adjustable formwork to allow for the differing gradients. The cavernous structure, while appropriate for an underground building, often appears oppressive; this is perhaps inevitable when the floors are required to support loads of up to 1500kg/sq.m (307lb/sq.ft). Air conditioning ducts are housed in the space between the central columns of the portal frames and between the outer columns and walls.

All internal surfaces are left in their natural state, so a high standard of workmanship was demanded on the concrete works, all concrete being pumped into the formwork, not poured, to achieve a greater degree of control.

ne of two laminated glass ndows which allow amatic views of the man amphitheatres. atural light also pene-tes the underground ucture through several ht shafts which are aled by transparent plas- domes concealed in the ternal planting.

gallery window from tside.

The Home of the Architect Toronto, Ontario, Canada

Architects
A.J. Diamond and Barton Myers

Photography
Yukio Futagawa
Karl Sliva
Barton Myers

A long and narrow site in Yorkville Village, Toronto, gave Barton Myers the opportunity to plan a new home for his family which he hopes will bring new vitality to an inner city area. The site measures 7.6m × 38.1m (25ft × 125ft) and the city authorities waived the normal requirement for a 6.1m (20ft) set back from the road and granted permission to maintain the existing building line.

Toronto experiences a climate of extremes, with a long, cold winter from November to April, when the mean temperature is −3.8°C (25°F) and a warm summer from June through September with a mean temperature of 23.8°C (75°F) and peaks of 32.2 to 33.8°C (90 to 93°F). At first, the architect planned to build a house around an open courtyard but in considering the long winter and the problem of urban pollution he decided to roof this over, to exploit the winter sun.

The two-storey house, 21m (70ft) deep and 6.1m (20ft) wide, is divided into three sections: on the street front are the garage and entrance hall, with the daughter's and guests' bedrooms, bathroom and study above. The hall leads into the central, double-height living area where the space flows vertically up to the exposed steel trusses supporting the glazed roof, which curves from front to rear of

9
he street facade. The new ouse remains sympath-tically in scale with its eighbours while being adically different in most ther respects.

30
Central space. The stairs to the upper level are on the right. Awnings can be unfurled along the bottom members of the roof trusses to shade the interior.

The Home of the Architect
Toronto, Ontario, Canada
A. J. Diamond and Barton Myers

31
Stairs with the kitchen visible through the door on the right.

32
Section.

33
Plans of first and second levels.
Key to plans and section
1 Garage
2 Entrance
3 Hall
4 Dining area
5 Living area
6 Kitchen
7 Master bedroom
8 Dressing room
9 Bathroom
10 Bridge
11 Study
12 Bedroom

34
Living area on the lower level looking through to the central space.

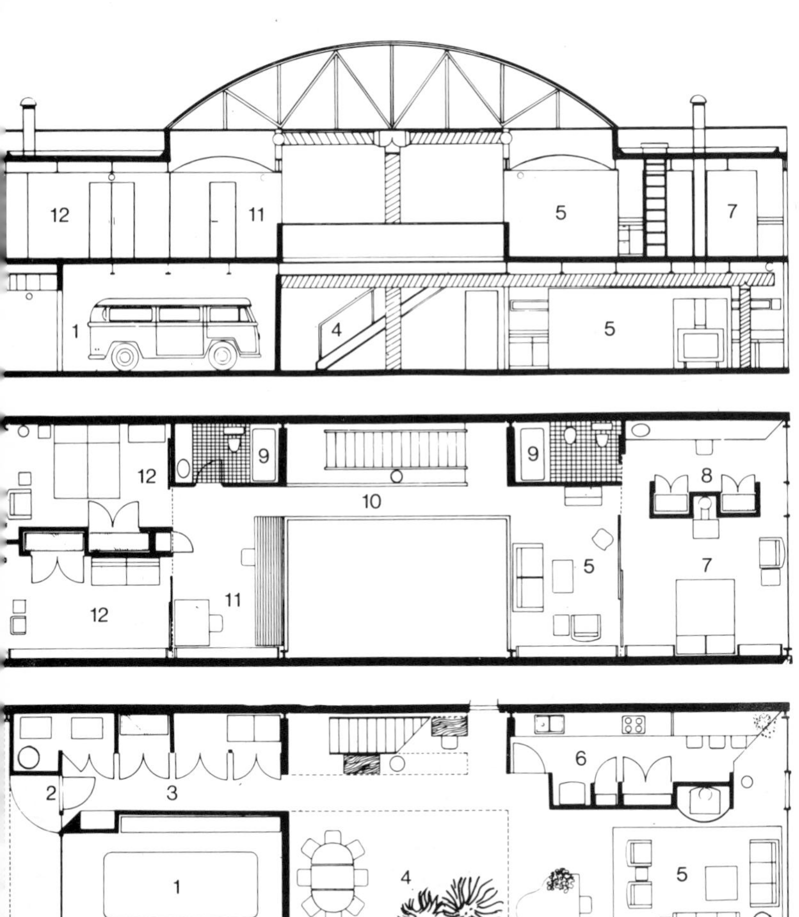

the house, and horizontally through the ground floor of the rear two-storey section containing the kitchen and sitting area, and out to the garden. On the first floor of this section is the master bedroom with adjoining bathroom, dressing room and lounge. A bridge connects the master bedroom suite with the study. Two roof decks which serve as outdoor gardens and platforms for cleaning the glazed roof are reached from the bedroom areas by ladders. This plan is a vast improvement over that of the neighbouring houses because the courtyard brings light directly into the centre of the house, the gloomiest part of the traditional terrace house.

Between two parallel, solid walls of concrete block, internally insulated and dry lined to form a fire barrier, a steel frame has been constructed. To make the interior space as flexible as possible the metal-stud, dry-lined partitions are all non load-bearing and easily removeable, and open web steel joists have a clear span between the blockwork walls. The joists support ribbed metal decking on which is poured a concrete slab to form the first floor and the flat roofs. Four rigid steel frames brace

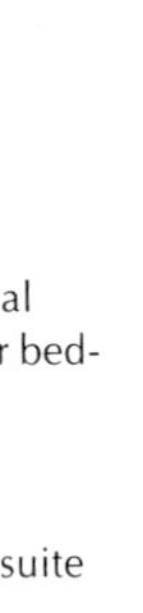

35
View across the central space from the master bedroom to the study.

36
The master bedroom suite seen from the bridge.

37
Evening view of the house from the garden, clearly illustrating the structure of the house: open web steel joists spanning between blockwork walls and supporting exposed ribbed metal decking. Also note the glass clipped direct to the steel end frame which braces the structure.

the structure along the length of the house. The frames at either end serve also as window frames, the glass being clipped directly to the structural steelwork.

The main feature of the house is its 12.2m × 5.1m (40ft × 20ft) glazed roof. After studying several alternatives the architects chose to use an industrial system which was economical and had been rigorously tested in many commercial situations for greenhouses. Barton Myers was impressed with the sophisticated technology developed for the benefit of agriculture: thin sections, standard components, clear vinyl air ducts to eliminate shadow. Problems such as condensation, ventilation and shade in hot weather had been already solved in the systems he examined.

Double glazing was found not to be justified in terms of initial capital cost versus a higher running cost, but the extensive area of single glazing, together with the lightweight structure, make solar gain a serious problem in the summer months. Air conditioning has not yet been installed so until the proposed cooling coils and condenser arrive the Myers have to rely on natural ventilation to cool the house. Louvres in the curved gables of the roof and vents along the north and south eaves encourage through ventilation. Canvas is suspended from the bottom section of the trusses to combat excessive heat gain from solar radiation. Although the natural ventilation and shading has proved adequate, air conditioning is still a necessity to combat dirt from the polluted air. In winter, heating is provided by a forced hot air system run from a gas boiler.

Continuing the industrial nature of the exposed roof trusses and glazing, hot air ducts, water pipes and lighting conduits are all frankly exposed.

The Coal Street Park Swimming Centre Wilkes-Barre, Pennsylvania, USA

Architects
Bohlin Powell Brown

Photography
Sandy Nixon
Mark Cohen

A city park has been created on what was formerly 32 acres of slag heaps. A 240m (800ft) long pedestrian spine, with car parks at either end, links two local neighbourhoods and connects with all the major functions within the park. These include playing fields for softball, baseball, American football, soccer and hockey, an ice-rink, children's play area and a swimming centre.

The swimming centre consists of a bath house containing changing rooms and toilets, a wading pool and a competition pool with a section for diving. The building complex also houses a snack bar, which serves the entire park. This is linked to the bath house by an outdoor dining area which consists of a series of bays facing towards the pool but with openings in the rear wall overlooking the pedestrian spine and children's play area. The bays are separated by concrete block walls and can be sheltered from the sun by yellow canvas awnings slung from a steel frame. Materials used in the construction of the bath house are in-situ and pre-cast concrete, concrete blocks and steel. All concrete is left exposed and steelwork is painted.

The bath house is situated so that it shelters the pedestrian mall from the prevailing westerly wind. The visitor approaches the building up a long ramp

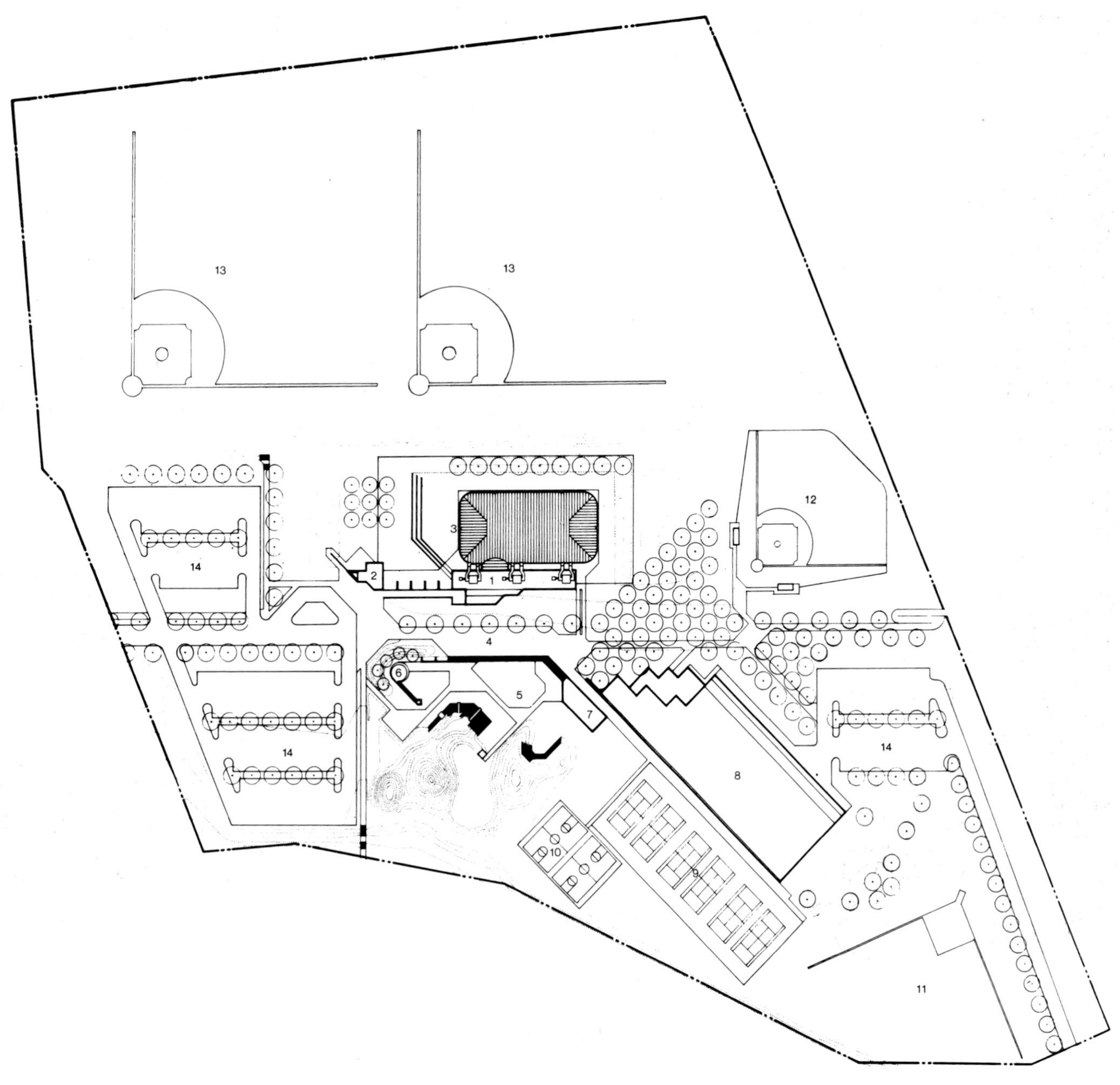

nked on one side by a red and blue steel ndrail. This handrail passes into the fully-glazed trance hall and sweeps round the perimeter fore terminating on the face of the concrete ception desk. Industrial lighting fixtures are partlly concealed by the profile of the rail and are ed at closer centres, to increase in rhythm as the il approaches the desk. Large-scale graphics rther help to emphasize the circulation pattern.

To increase the use of the centre from a possible ree months per year to all year round, an inflatble structure, 30m × 60m (100ft × 200ft) has been signed to cover both pools.

38
The swimming centre seen from the south-east with the children's play area in the foreground.

39
Master plan of the city park
1 Bath house
2 Snack bar
3 Air dome over pool
4 Pedestrian spine
5 Children's play area
6 Spray pool
7 Shelter and toilets
8 Covered ice rink
9 Tennis courts
10 Basketball courts
11 Softball field
12 Junior baseball field
13 Baseball fields
14 Car parks

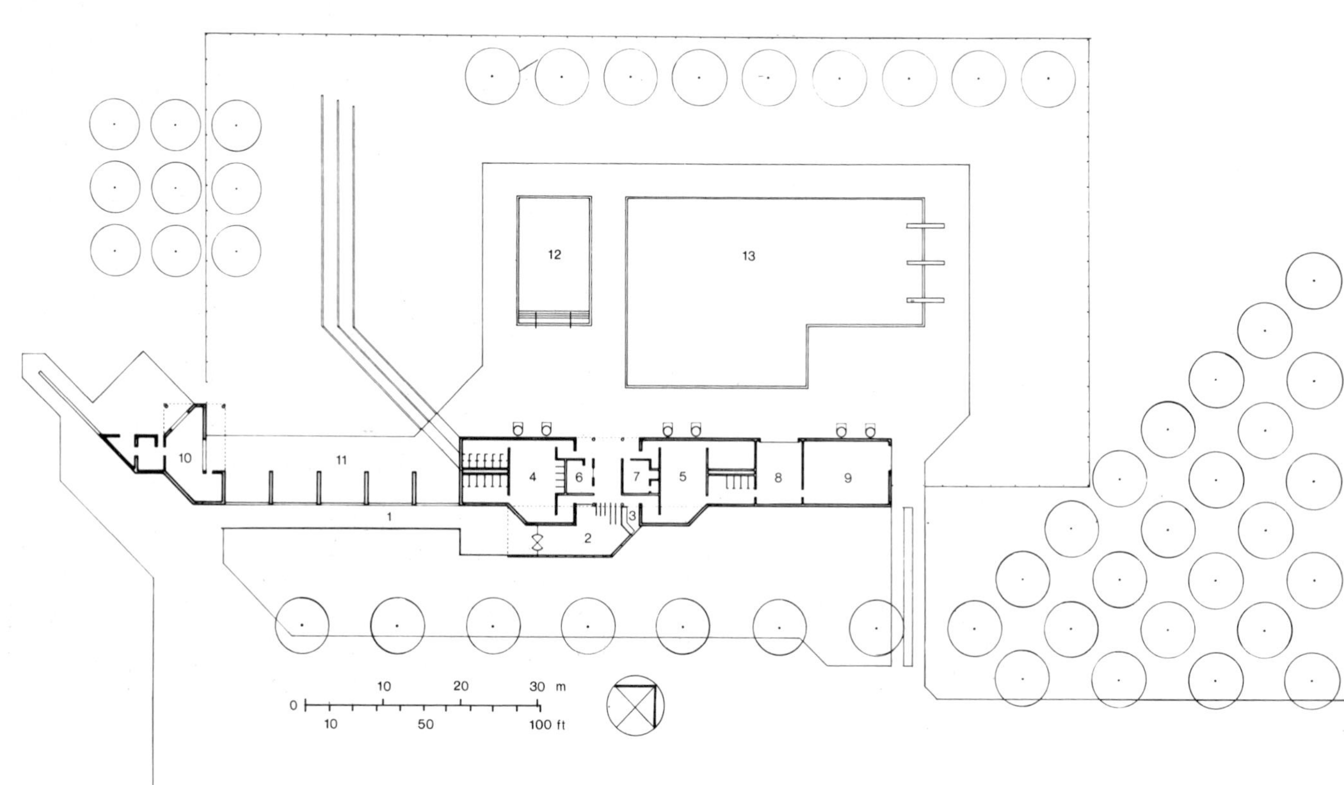

1
2
3
4
5
6
7
8
9
10
11
12
13
10 20 30 m
0
10 50 100 ft

The Coal Street Park Swimming Centre
Wilkes-Barre, Pennsylvania
Bohlin Powell Brown

e entrance hall; the re-
ption desk is in the
ntre and the entrance to
changing rooms on the
t.

n of bath house and
ol
mp
trance hall
ception desk
omen's changing
om
en's changing room
fice
st aid
me storage
ol equipment
ack bar
en-air eating area
ading pool
mpetition pool

e swimming pool is co-
red with a translucent
-supported structure to
tend its use throughout
e year.

verpage

neral view of the two
ols.

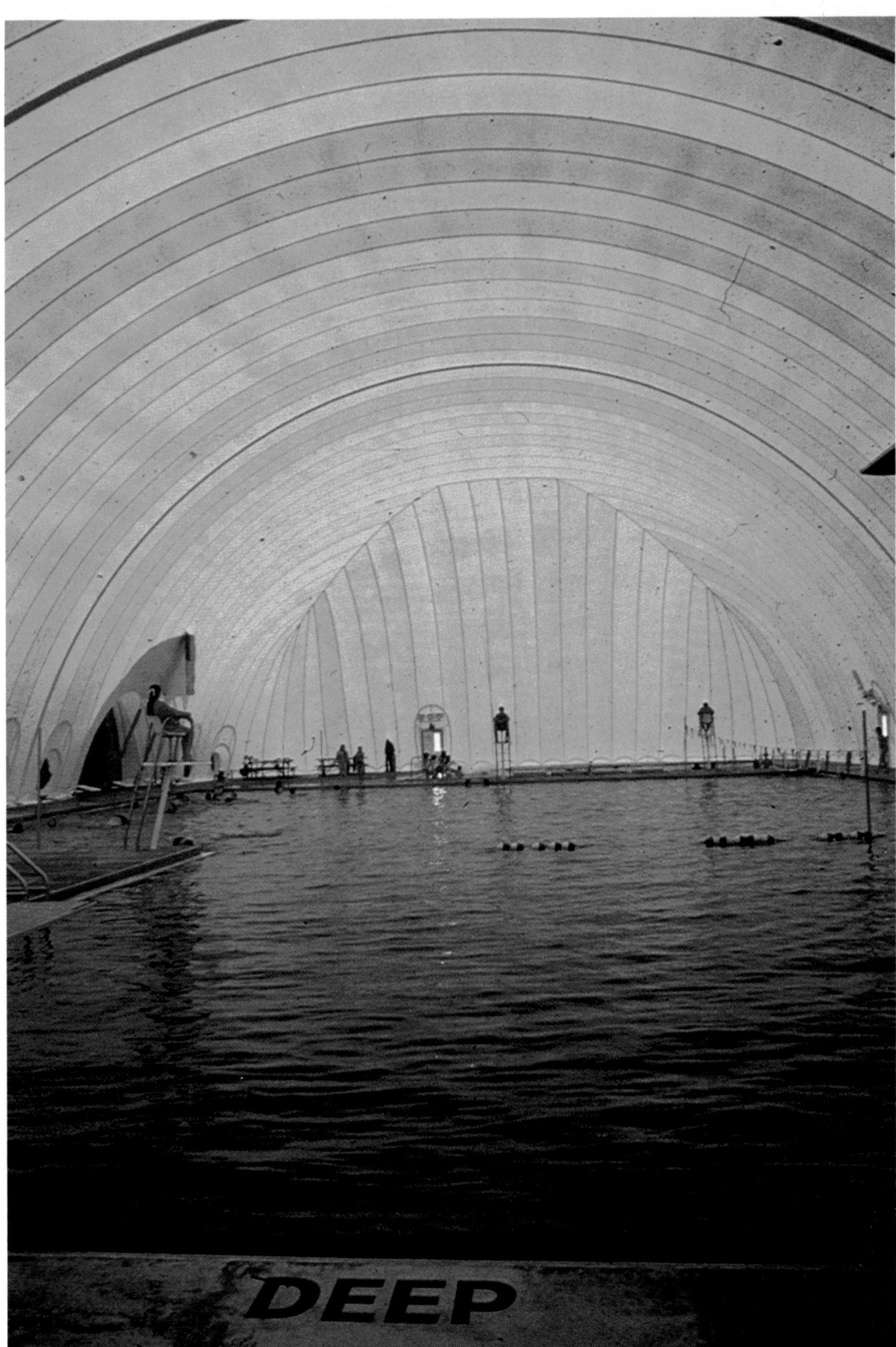

Heating and pressurization equipment which serves both the air-supported structure and the bath house is placed on the bath house roof. Large round ducts, grouped in pairs of supply and return, swoop down to the pool surround to connect with the fabric of the air structure. Connection is made at the base to minimize the chances of the fabric tearing in a high wind. The interiors of the ducts are painted red and expanded metal screens are recessed into their openings to prevent children climbing up inside.

Two arcs of red steel, fixed to the concrete facade of the bath house, anchor the air structure to the bath house and, along with guy-ropes, form the catenary framed entrance to the covered pools.

The pressure in the bath house is equalized with that of the inflatable to avoid the formation of airlocks between the two structures. Thus, from the entrance lobby, the visitor can look straight into the pool enclosure.

The pools are surrounded by rising grass-covered banks which protect the bathers from winds in summer and provide inclined sun-bathing areas.

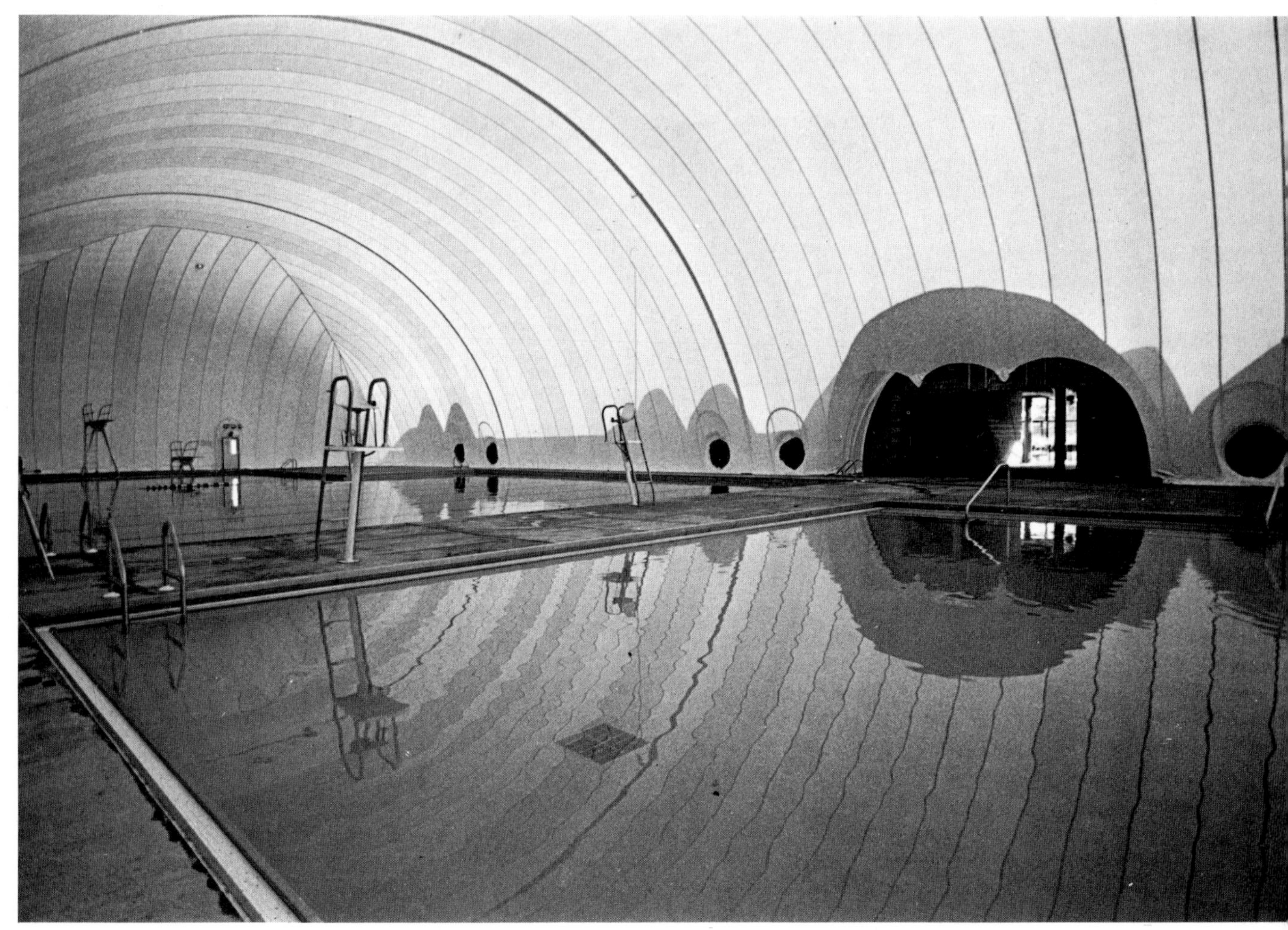

44
View of the pool looking towards the changing rooms. On the far side of the pool can be seen the duct openings and the entrance from the bath house.

45
Area between the wading pool and the main pool. The inflatable structure has a translucent elegance totally in harmony with its watery surroundings.

The Coal Street Park Swimming Centre
Wilkes-Barre, Pennsylvania
Bohlin Powell Brown

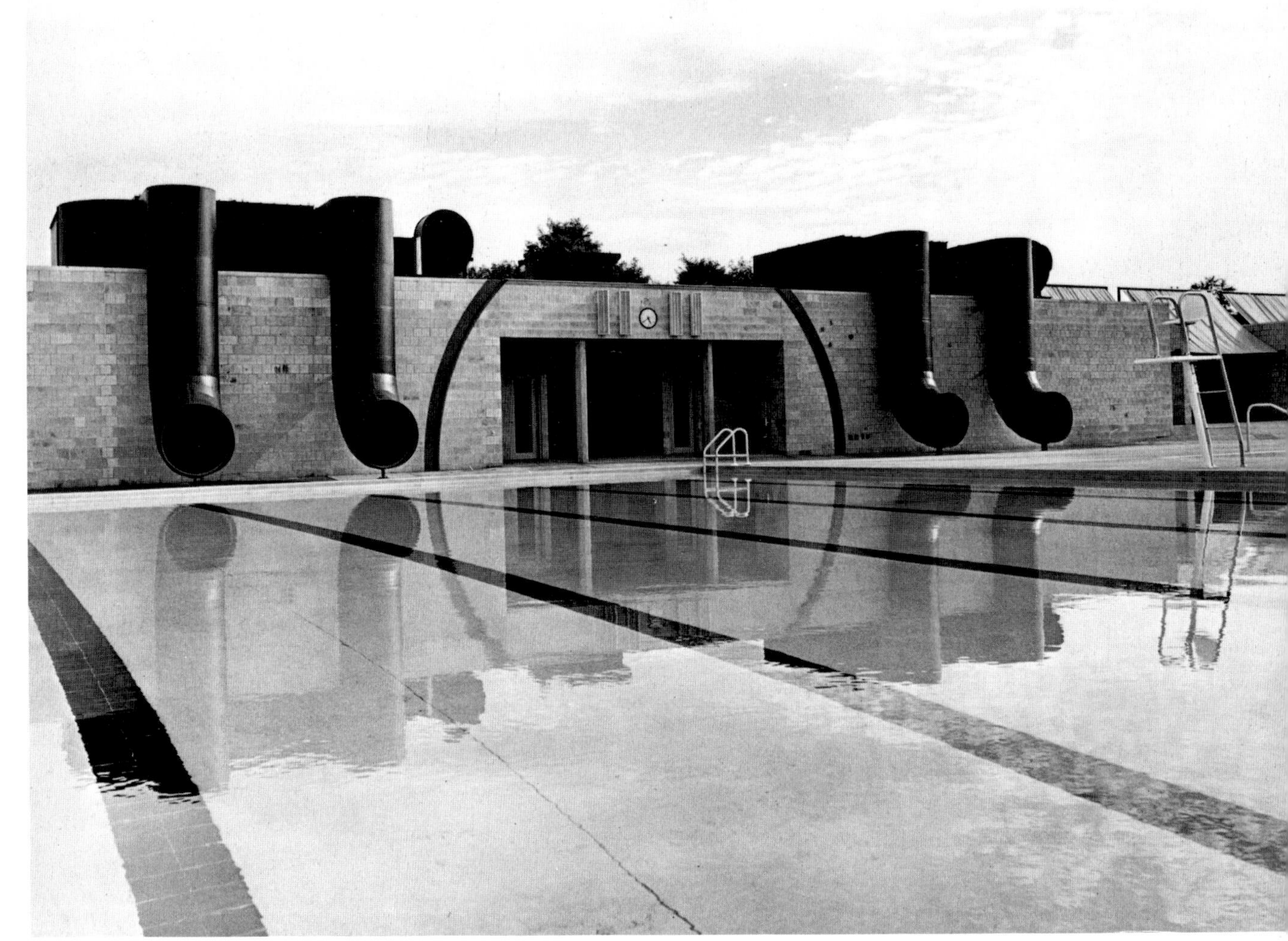

46
Looking across the pool to the bath house; the open-air eating area is on the right.

47
The colourful supply and return ducts acquire a playful quality in the months that the pool is uncovered.

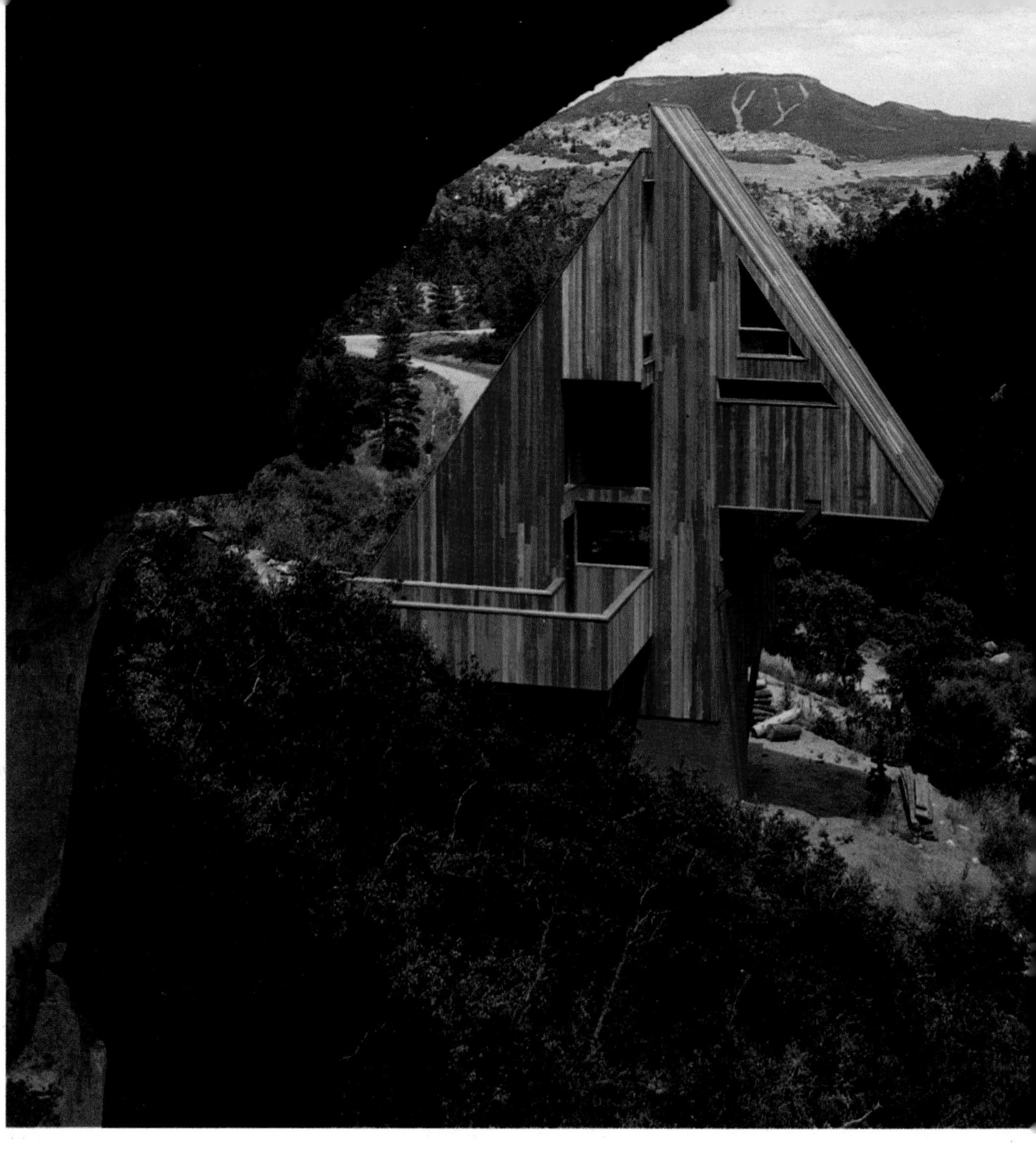

A Mountain Cabin
Perry Park, Colorado, USA

Architects
Arley Rinehart Associates

Photography
Richard Henri
Richard Springgate

The restrictions of a steeply sloping site with minimal support conditions, and a desire to disturb the landscape as little as possible, resulted in an award-winning design for a mountain cabin, by Arley Rinehart Associates.

Four 406mm (16in) diameter caissons, anchored 2.44m (8ft) into bedrock, support a central wedge form which contains a two-storey living area. Two smaller wedge forms are cantilevered from the main unit: their roof load and the floor cantilevers are supported by steel braces from the caissons.

A bridge gives access to a mezzanine in the main unit; opposite the entrance door are the kitchen and bathroom. From the mezzanine, a short flight of steps leads to the living area below and a centra spiral staircase connects with three bedrooms, contained in the two upper levels of the house.

The house is constructed of 100mm × 150mm (4in × 6in) timber studs for the walls and 100mm × 200mm (4in × 8in) joists for the roof, with a 13mm (½in) plywood skin on both sides to form a stressed skin structure. Exterior roof and wa surfaces are clad in tongue-and-groove redwood boarding and the interior ply surface is left expose and painted white. A thick fibreglass quilt betweer the two layers of plywood insulates the house. The

8
iew of the entrance front.
ole access is via a bridge
hich lends a defensive
uality to the cabin appro-
riate for a mountain re-
eat in such a wild setting.

9
ans of entrance, second
nd third levels.

0
ections.
ey to plans and sections
ridge
ntrance
athroom
itchen
reakfast bar
ving room
edroom
ore
rows nest

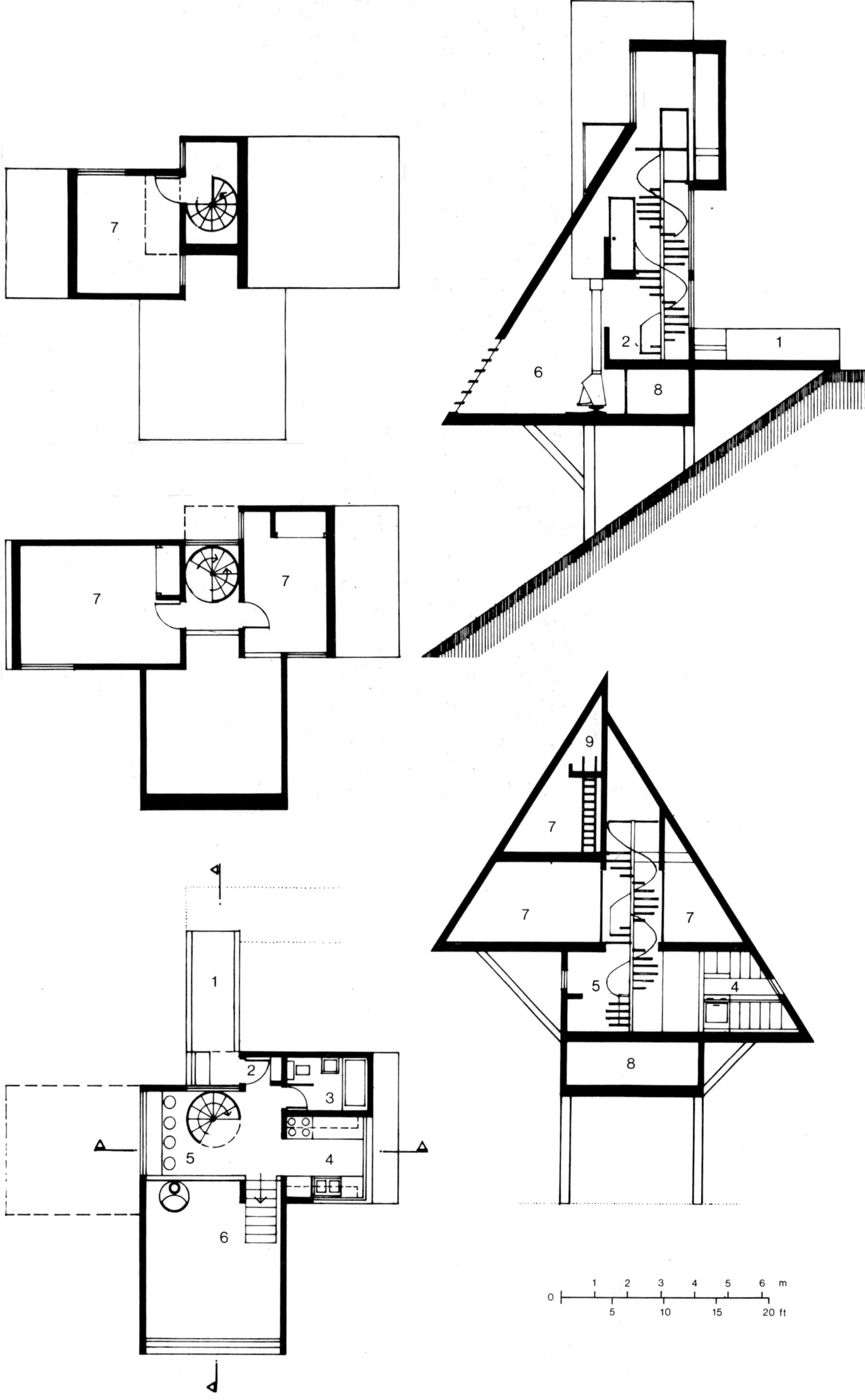

A Mountain Cabin
Perry Park, Colorado, USA
Arley Rinehart Associates

king up from the living
a to the breakfast bar
entrance level and the
rooms above. A drama-
soaring space has been
ated at the centre of the
ding where the canti-
ered wedges intersect.

cabin seen against the
ghbouring crags almost
ears to be part of the
ural terrain.

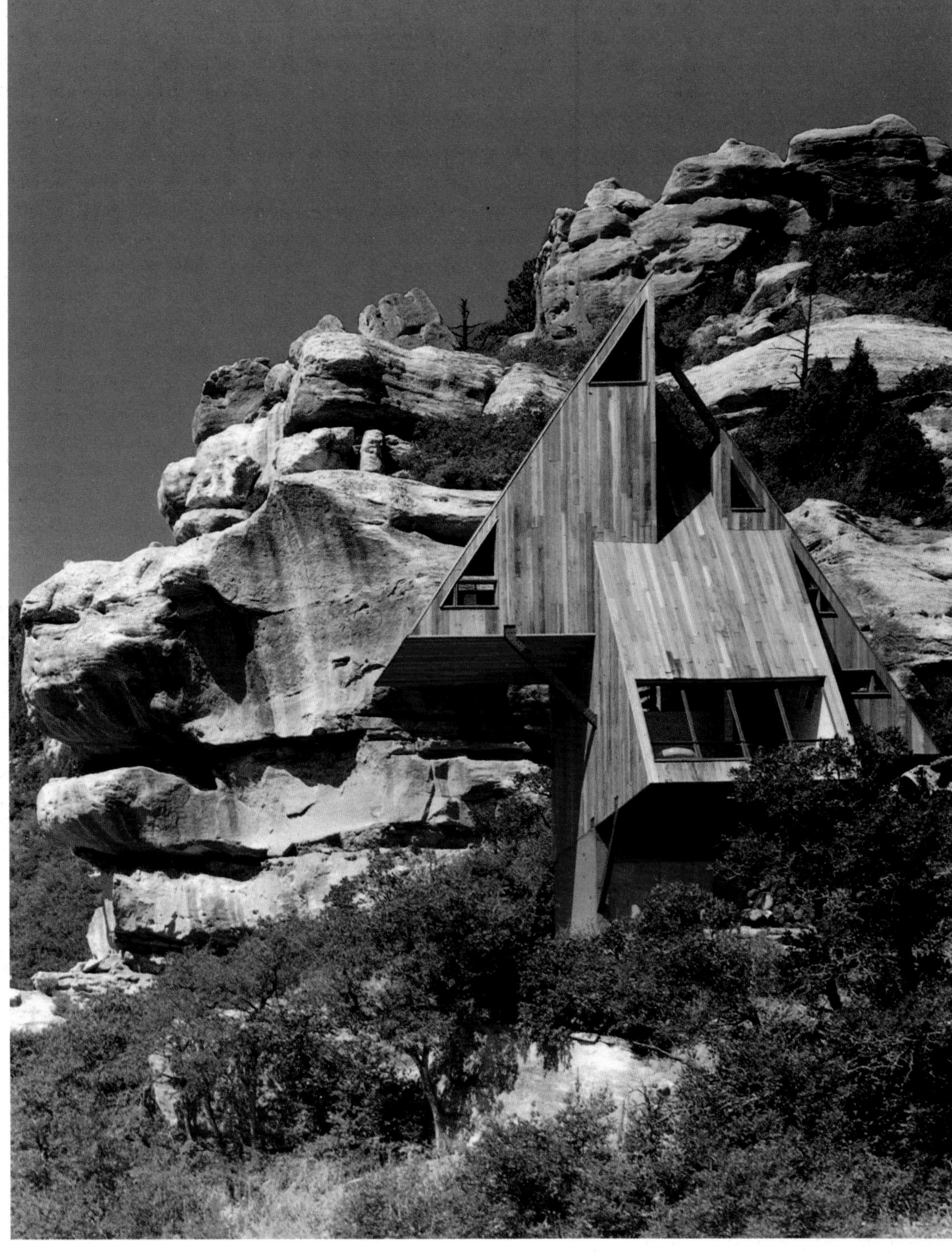

very nature of a stressed skin structure, where the entire wall area acts as a structural element, is compatible with the demands of a highly insulated structure with small windows. Electric underfloor heating is thermostatically controlled in each room to achieve further economy of energy in unoccupied spaces.

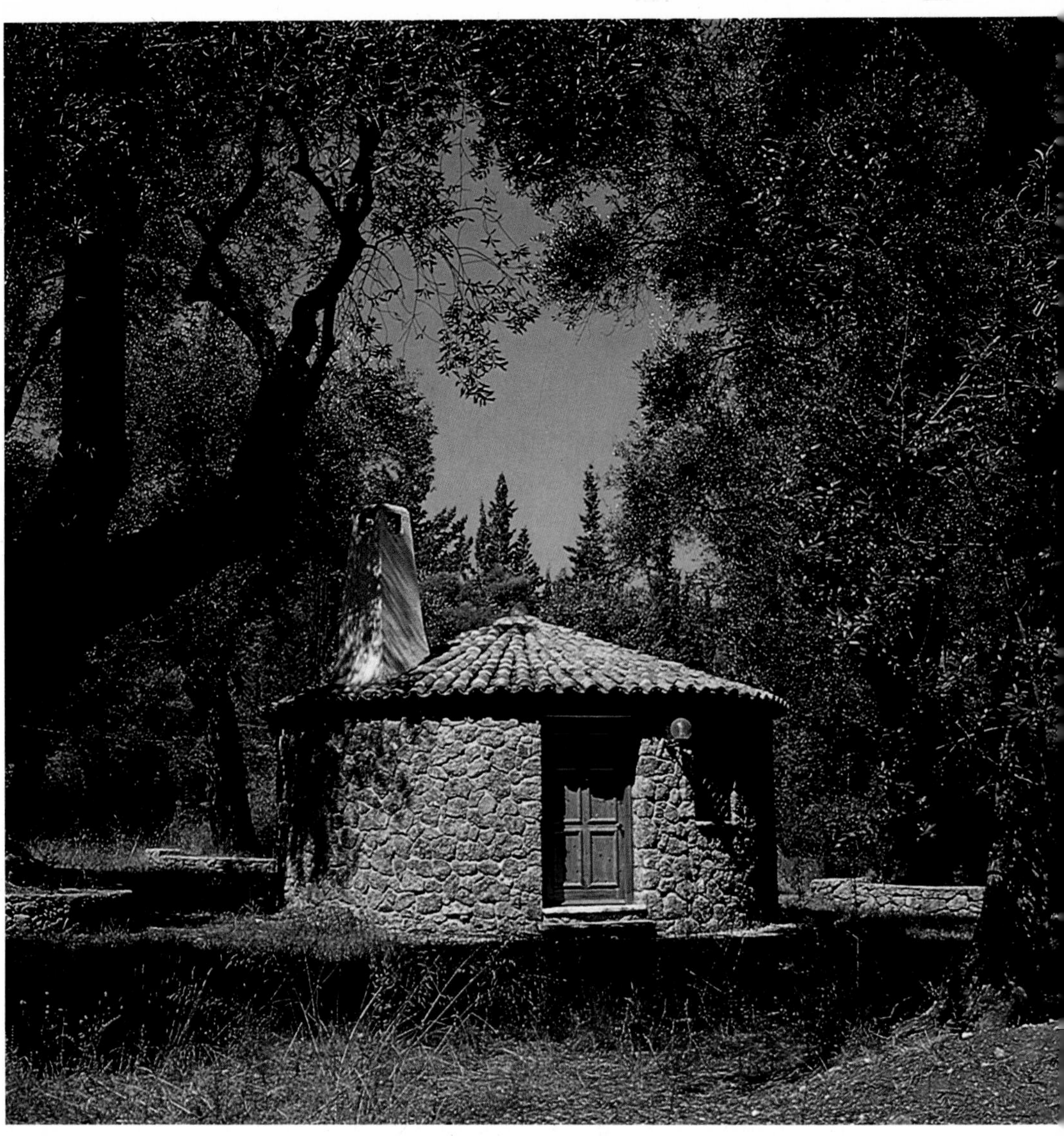

The Roundhouse
Agia Pelagia, Corfu, Greece

Architects
H.E. Senkowski and E.T. Sakellarios

Photography
N. Desyllas

This miniature dwelling is one of five holiday homes built on a family estate in the southern part of the island of Corfu. The estate has a total area of 40 acres approximately, and a seafront of 450m (1498ft). The roundhouse is set about 50m (166ft) inland and is surrounded by olive trees which abound on the island.

Apart from an accretion containing a shower room, the plan of the house is a circular single space, designed mainly for the use of one member of the family. Some personal touches are evident in the design of the fireplace and of the built-in bed; otherwise the method of construction follows the traditional style of indigenous architecture, using local materials.

The circular load-bearing wall is of stone, craft[ed] by a local mason. The surmounting timber roof consists of round beams radiating from a cylindri[cal] connecting piece placed at the highest point of th[e] roof and supported by the roof beams. The roof tiles, salvaged from the demolition of old building[s] are of the Byzantine type. The stone slabs of the floor came from the village of Sinies, in the northern part of the island. The roof beams, the boarding and the built-in cupboards are of Greek mountain pine.

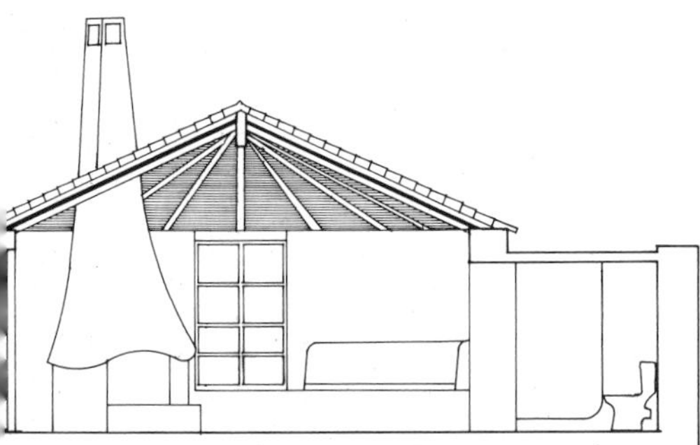

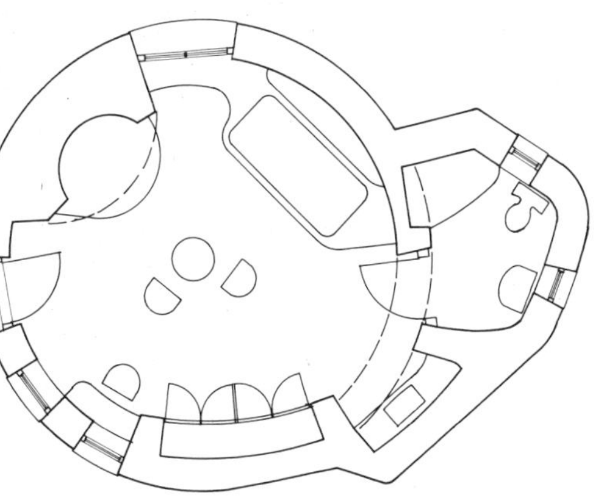

53
Exterior view.

54
Section and plan.

55
View of interior showing the fireplace, writing desk and part of the bed ranged around the wall.

56
View of the kitchen recess. In the centre stand the only items of free-standing furniture: a bamboo chair and a rustic table, the top of which is a single piece of olive wood.

The Sports Complex Nantes, France

Architect
Georges Evano and
Jean-luc Pellerin

Photography
Dhaliette Sucheyre

The second stage of an extensive sports complex in the municipality of Nantes has recently been completed. The project is part of a national plan to provide French cities with modern sports facilities and has been programmed in three stages.

The first phase, begun in 1971, includes a large sports hall with a training ground of 53m × 33m (174ft × 108ft) and a capacity for 5000 spectators, 4000 seated and 1000 standing. This can be increased to 6500 spectators by utilizing adjoining areas normally reserved for special gymnastic displays. Also included in the initial phase are changing rooms, showers, radio and television broadcasting rooms, administrative offices and meeting rooms, a medical and social centre and staff lodgings. The second phase, begun in 1977 and completed in the summer of 1979, includes rooms for training and warming-up and three playing fields of 1140, 980 and 775sq.m (12,270, 10,548 and 8342sq.ft) with adjoining changing rooms and showers. The third phase is still in the planning stage and will include a hall, 44m × 24m (144ft × 79ft) with space for 1500 spectators, 1000 seated and 500 standing, and an entertainment centre.

The architects wanted to design a building whic

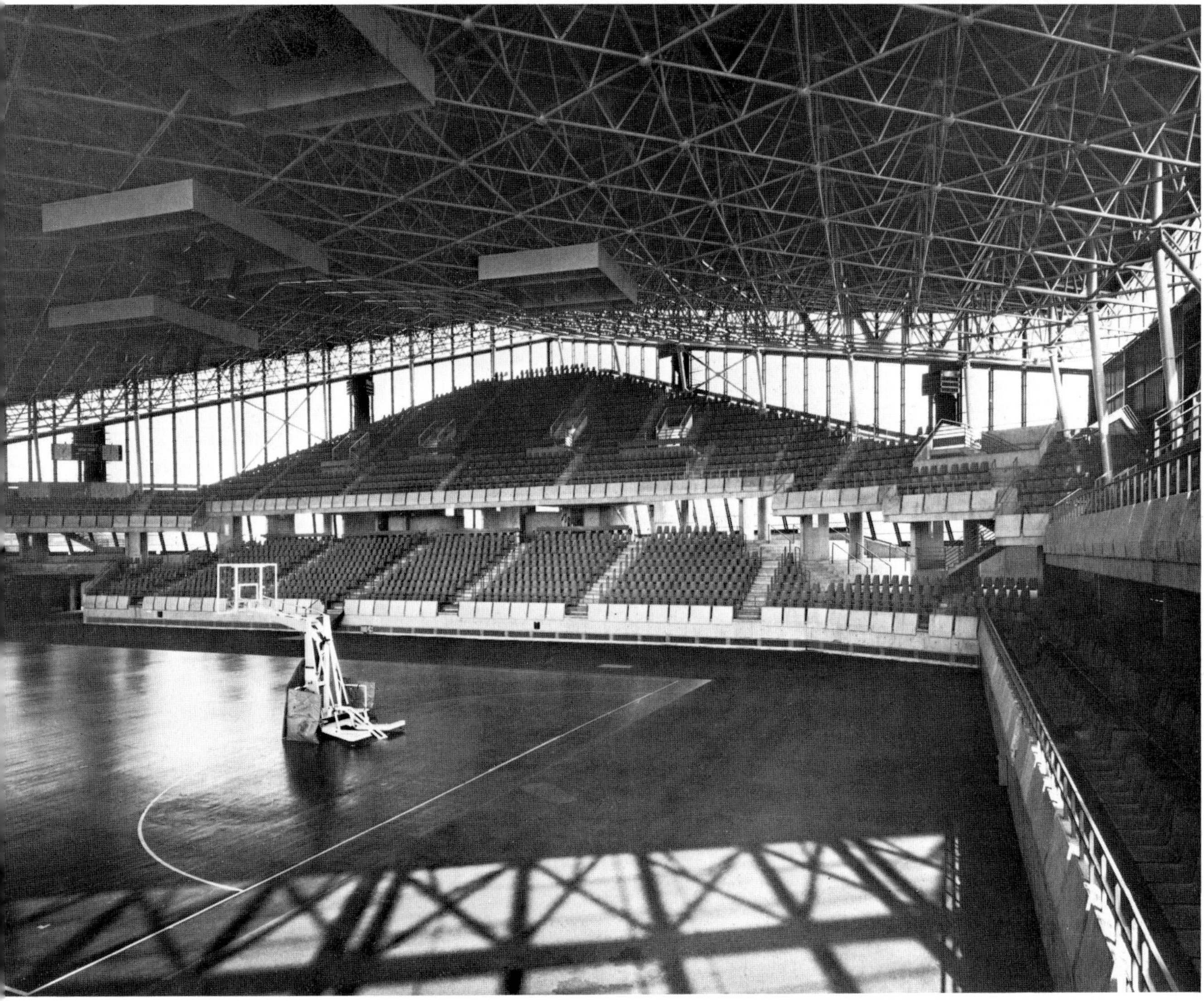

ew of the sports complex
om the Loire.

58
The main arena. The primary circulation space is visible below the upper tier of seating.

59
Preliminary design sketches of the building's form showing how the hexagonal shape on plan evolved to concentrate spectators on the long sides of the main arena bringing them closer to the athletes.

SUR LA LOIRE ET LA
LE (PROMENADE PÉRIPHÉRIQUE
ERTURE SUR L'EXTÉRIEUR)
APPÉE SUR LA SALLE)
NIVEAU SPORTIFS.
PLATEAU
ACCES FUTUR
DE PLAIN PIED (SPECTATEURS)
VOLUME PRINCIPAL.
PRISME DE VERRE RÉFLÉCHISSANT
(NOIR BRILLANT)
VOLUMES D'ACCOMPAGNEMENT
AMORCE DU SOCLE
(COULEUR VIVE.)
EXTENSION 2ème TRANCHE
SOCLE DU PRISME

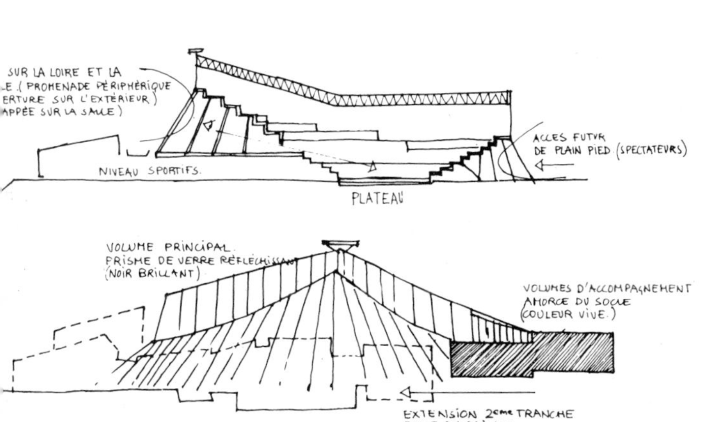

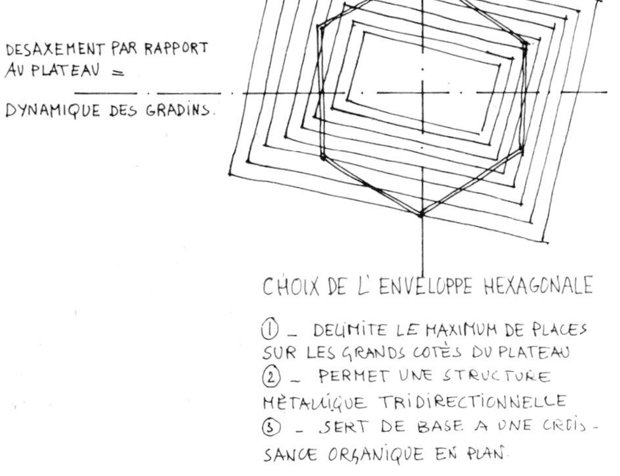

DESAXEMENT PAR RAPPORT
AU PLATEAU =
DYNAMIQUE DES GRADINS.
CHOIX DE L' ENVELOPPE HEXAGONALE
① _ DELIMITE LE MAXIMUM DE PLACES
SUR LES GRANDS COTÈS DU PLATEAU
② _ PERMET UNE STRUCTURE
MÉTALLIQUE TRIDIRECTIONNELLE
③ _ SERT DE BASE A UNE CROIS-
SANCE ORGANIQUE EN PLAN.

The Sports Complex
Nantes, France
G. Evano and J.-L. Pellerin

60
Plan of the completed phases I and II
1 Public entrance
2 Main arena
3 Subsidiary sports halls

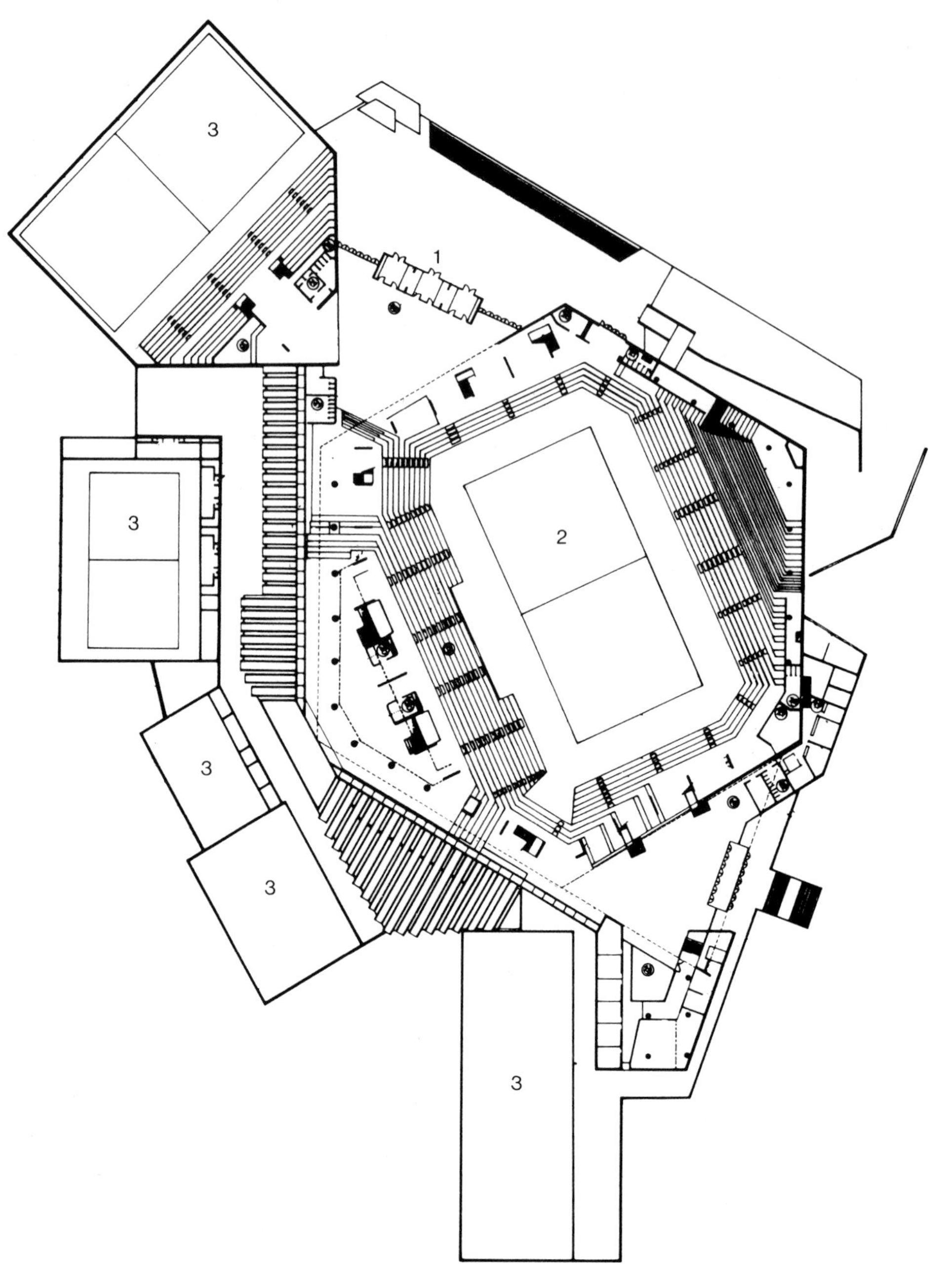

would become a recognisable landmark, standing out from the surrounding banal office blocks. The large scale of the main stadium and the amenity of the site, which borders the river Loire, provided them with a very good opportunity to achieve their purpose.

One of the major problems was to ensure good visibility for each member of the crowd of 5000. This was obtained by adopting an hexagonal plan for the seating around the oblong arena. Spectators are seated on steeply raked tiers which are concentrated in tapering wedges on the long sides of the arena.

Covering the hall is a space frame 2.5m (8ft 2in) deep constructed from tubular steel equilateral triangles with 3.3m (10ft 6in) sides. This form of structure allows a clear span of 80m (262ft) with no intermediate supports obstructing vision lines. The rigid frame is supported on thirty-six inclined tubular steel posts of varying height placed immediately behind the rear row of seats and with movable joints at the bottom and top junctions.

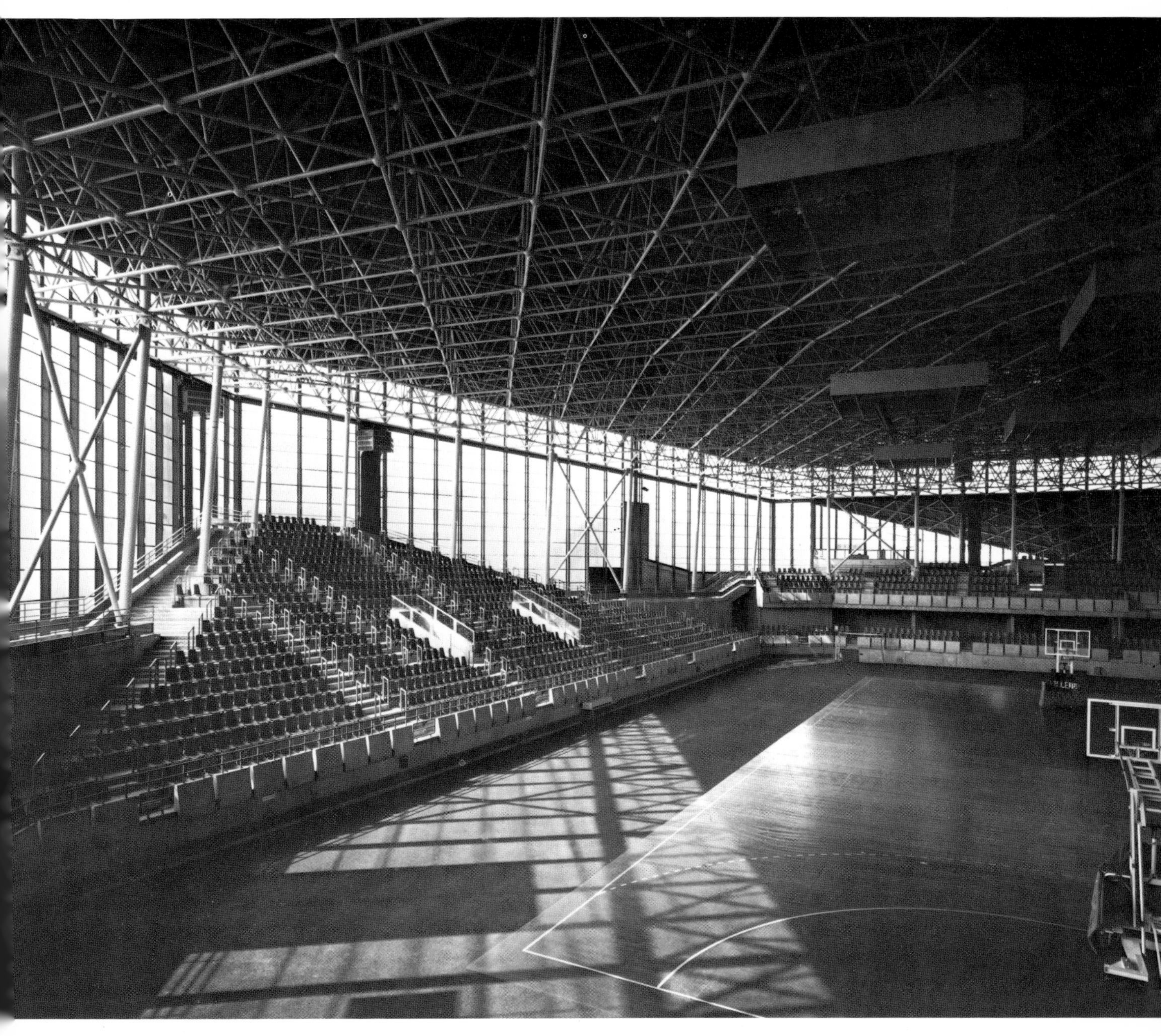

61
The main arena. The tubular steel perimeter supports are articulated to allow for movement in the space frame. Circulation runs between the columns and the external curtain walling.

62
One of the sports halls built in the second phase.

63
Corridor to the changing rooms and second phase sports halls.

A further requirement for the hall was abundant natural light which floods into the buildings from curtain walling, tinted to avoid glare and excessive solar gain, extending around the perimeter of the building. A measure of acoustic control is effected by the design of the stepped concrete seating areas which act as louvres directing noise out of the hall into the peripheral circulation areas. However, the level of resonance remains sufficient for the hall to be used for other activities such as conferences and large meetings. Circulation areas are designed to allow spectators and sportsmen free movement around the building independent of each other and also to allow for the addition of the third phase of the project.

The National Air and Space Museum Washington, USA

Architects
Hellmuth Obata & Kassabaum

Photography
Barbara Martin

Across the Mall in Washington, opposite the cool neo-classical National Gallery of Art stands the National Air and Space Museum, opened to the public in July 1976. The ten million people who visited it in its first year testify to its unequivocal success. Construction was begun in 1972 on the monumental building, which measures 209m × 69m (685ft × 225ft). However, there is still only room to display a fraction of the Smithsonian Institute's comprehensive collection of air and space craft.

The Mall facade is in seven bays; four solid blocks clad in pink Tennessee cedar marble, a finish stipulated by the Fine Arts Commission to match the National Gallery of Art, alternating with three bays of bronze glass curtain walling, which form the main exhibition areas. The glass and steel construction of the glazed bays is remarkably similar in technique to aircraft construction. Each bay is 35m × 37m × 19m high (115ft × 120ft × 62ft) and is supported by five tubular steel L-shaped trusses, triangular in cross-section, 3m (10ft) deep along the roof and 2.5m (8ft 4in) wide vertical pylons. The roof is glazed with square transparent acrylic panels and the walls are double-glazed in bronze-tinted glass. The trusses have been

65
Site plan: the National Air and Space Museum is the latest public building set in Washington's neo-classical grid

1 National Air and Space Museum
2 Hirshhorn Museum
3 Smithsonian Institution
4 National Museum
5 National Gallery of Art
6 Jefferson Drive
7 Independence Avenue

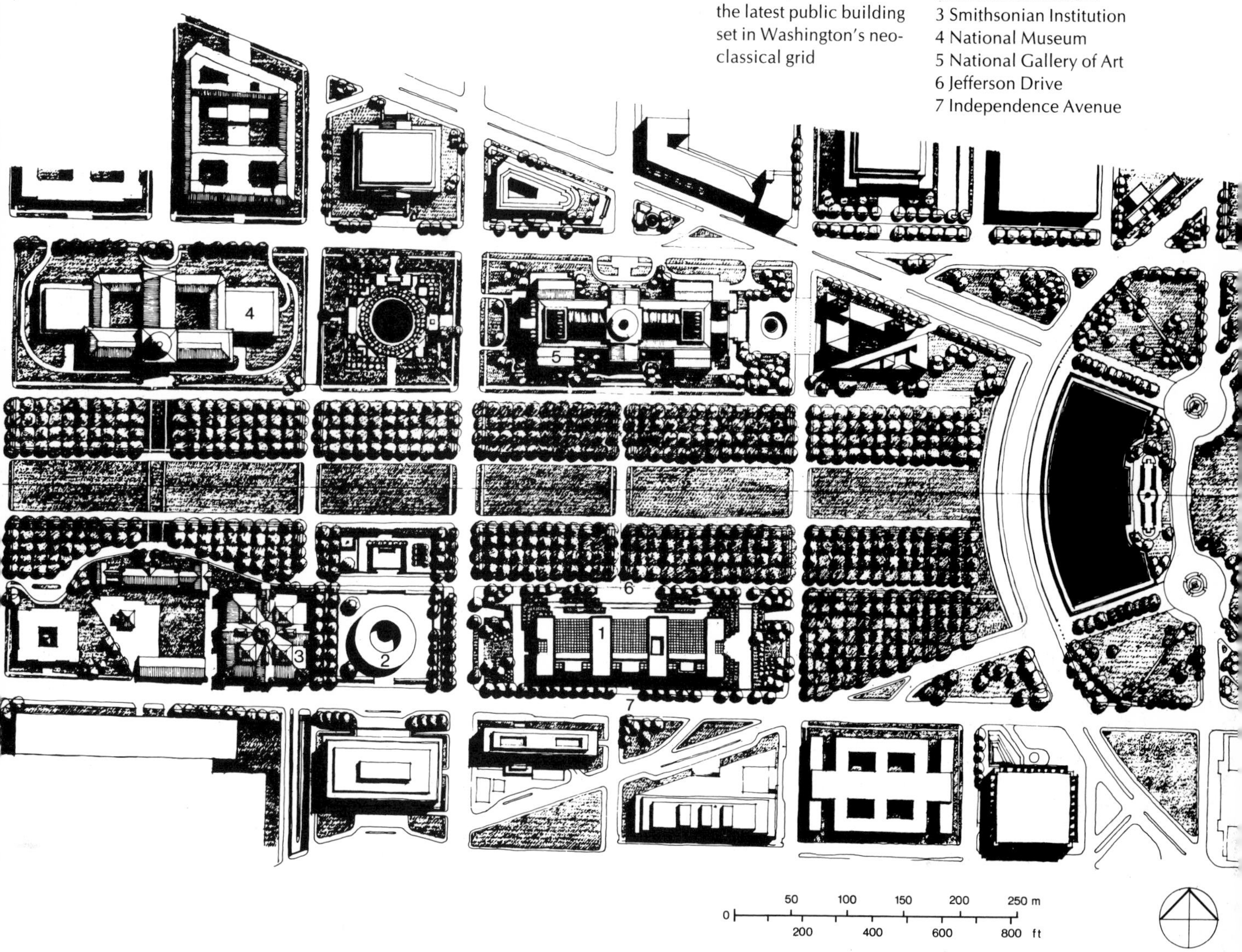

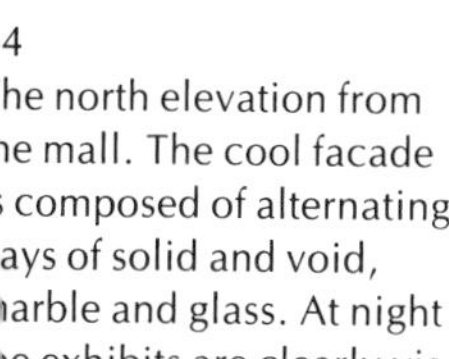

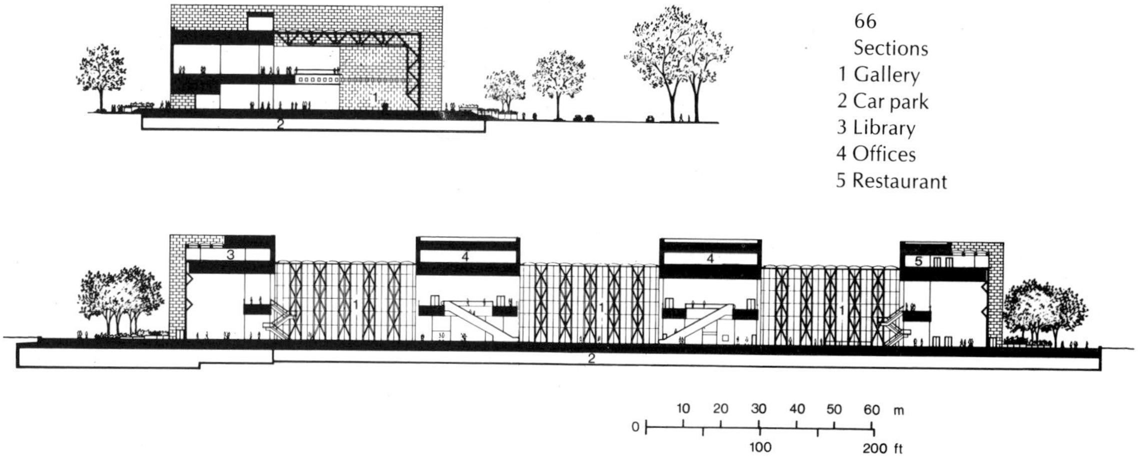

4
he north elevation from ne mall. The cool facade composed of alternating ays of solid and void, arble and glass. At night e exhibits are clearly visle floodlit inside the useum.

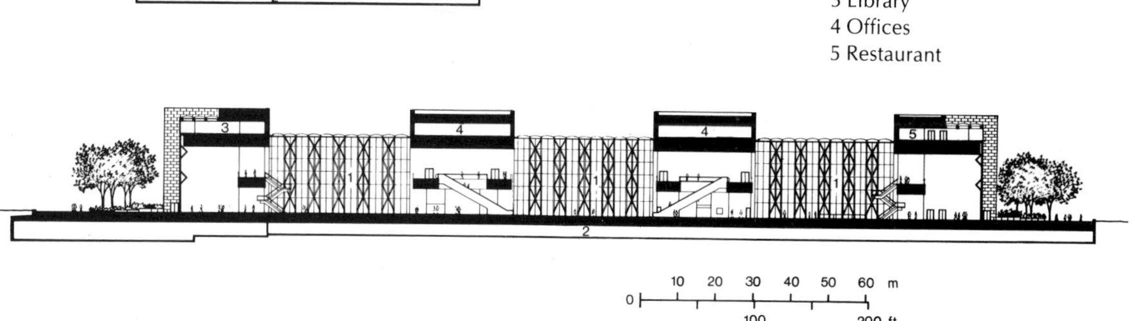

66
Sections
1 Gallery
2 Car park
3 Library
4 Offices
5 Restaurant

The National Air and Space Museum
Washington, USA
Hellmuth Obata & Kassabaum

designed to provide a uniformity of appearance in both horizontal and vertical sections and their open structure allows the maximum daylight into the exhibition halls. They were also designed to carry heavy suspended loads, the exhibits themselves, and the structural engineers have developed a matrix of loading coefficients to enable the museum staff to determine the precise loading on a single truss with alternative placings of exhibits.

Contrary to their solid appearance, the marble clad blocks are a form of lightweight structure. Marble panels 1.5m × 0.8m × 30mm thick (5ft × 2ft 6in × 1¼in) are fixed to a steel frame of vertical angles at 0.8m (2ft 6in) centres. This allows the facade to expand and contract more easily than in the more conventional method of imbedding marble veneer in precast concrete panels, which requires large expansion joints. Steel framing, being lighter, permitted the use of slab foundations instead of piles, thereby reducing construction costs. A thermal insulator and vapour barrier was sprayed onto the inside face of the marble and an internal skin of metal stud and dry wall finish was built. The cavity thus formed contains mechanical and electrical services. Marble has also been used on the walls of the large open exhibition halls, at all entrances and, as an aggregate, in areas of external concrete paving. The underground car park for 550 vehicles is constructed of in-situ concrete.

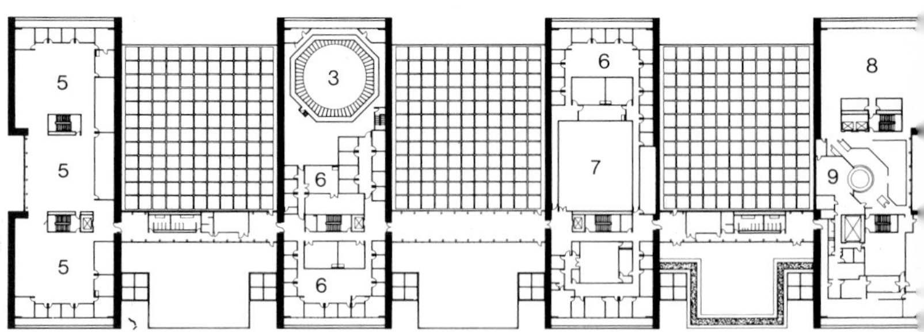

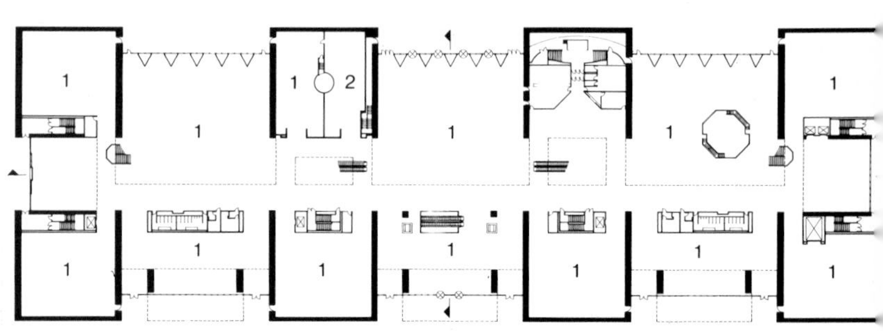

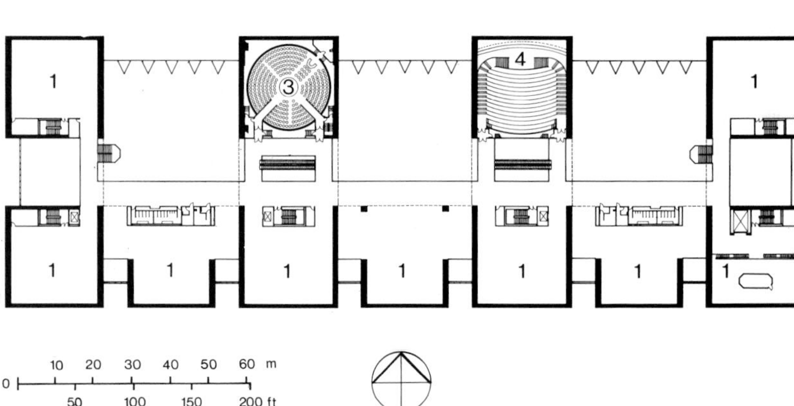

67
Plans of first, second and third levels
1 Gallery
2 Store
3 Spacearium
4 Auditorium
5 Library
6 Offices
7 Cooling tower
8 Restaurant
9 Kitchen

68
Lindbergh's *Spirit of St. Louis* hovers above the Wright brothers' *Kitty Hawk Flyer* in the central *Milestones of Flight* gallery. The delicate spruce struts of the *Flyer* almost disappear when seen against the framework of tubular steel trusses.

The National Air and Space Museum
Washington, USA
Hellmuth Obata & Kassabaum

etail of the wall structure the Hall of Air Transpor- tion.

e Space Hall. A section the floor has been low- ed to accommodate the wering rockets on dis- ay. The staircase leads to e second level.

The National Air and Space Museum
Washington, USA
Hellmuth Obata & Kassabaum

71
The *Apollo to the Moon* gallery on the second level.

72
Circulation spine on the first level.

The museum has a very simple layout with two lines of galleries on two levels, all directly accessible from one long central corridor. At first floor level the spine forms a balcony to the three main exhibition spaces. The central gallery, which is set on the same axis as the National Gallery on the opposite side of the Mall, houses the only permanent exhibition: *Milestone of Flight*; the other galleries are occasionally rearranged. The aircraft are suspended from the trusses so they appear in

flight when viewed against the background of sky seen through the glazed roof. The first floor balconies allow closer inspection of the exhibits displayed in the central gallery, ranging from the world's first powered, manned, heavier-than-air flying machine, the Wright Brothers' *Kitty Hawk Flyer*, to *Gemini IV*, the space craft from which astronaut Edward H. White became the first American to float weightless in space.

To the west is the Hall of Air Transportation and to the east the Space Hall where the largest objects are displayed. Visitors can enter the *Skylab* orbital workshop, which is identical to the unit launched in 1973. The 16m (52ft) tall cylinder had to be separated into four sections to squeeze it into the building. Rockets and missiles stand in a 5.5m (18ft) deep pit but, even so, the 22m (71ft) high *Jupiter C* rocket almost touches the roof.

Twenty smaller galleries, each approximately 23sq.m (75sq.ft) cover general aviation, the aircraft

The National Air and Space Museum
Washington, USA
Hellmuth Obata & Kassabaum

73
Contrasting eras in the *Milestones of Flight* gallery. The *X-15*, holder of the world altitude and speed records, flies above the Wright brothers' *Flyer* and the *Apollo 11 Command Module*, used on the first manned moon landing.

74
The central exhibition hall from the viewing gallery illustrating the clearly expressed common axis with the National Gallery of Art on the other side of the mall.

Vorld Wars I and II, air traffic control, balloons I airships, and air/sea operations. In the *Apollo he Moon* gallery the museum presents the tory of the American manned space flight pro-mme which culminated in the historical landing the moon by Armstrong and Aldrin while Mike lins, the present director of the museum, circled Moon orbit. The emphasis is on audio-visual sentation techniques and sterile exhibition thods have been avoided. The appropriate osphere is also created by several murals.

he museum also contains the National Air and ce Agency's collection of over five hundred major works of art, and a theatre seating 485 people with a curved screen 15m × 23m (50ft × 75ft) equipped with 70mm projection equipment. A film, *To Fly* introduces the audience to various experiences of flight in a balloon, a biplane, a jet display team, and a hang-glider. The Albert Einstein Spacearium similarly attempts to simulate flight into space as well as illustrating the celestial sphere by projecting images onto its 21m (70ft) diameter aluminium dome.

The third floor houses offices, the Smithsonian Institute's aerospace research and reference library and public and private dining areas.

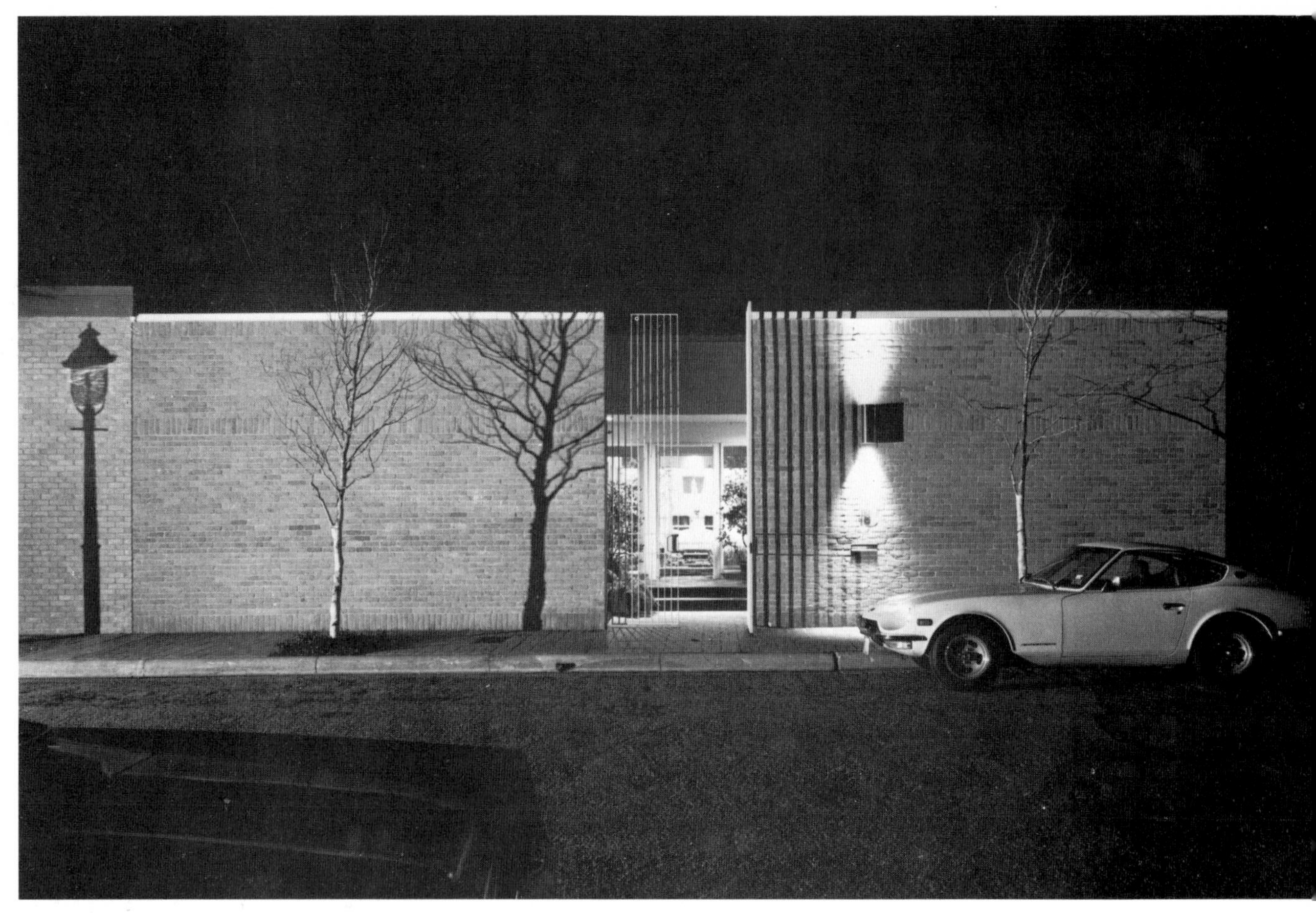

The Home of the Architect Houston, Texas, USA

Architect
Robert Sobel

Photography
Alexandre Georges

Enclosed within two streets in Houston is a small residential estate begun in the 1960s and now completed. On either side of a private drive, plots of land have been allocated to the houses which, although individually designed and built, are all of brick and either one or two storey in height. At the centre of the estate is a communal swimming pool and a recreational pavilion. A service road runs behind each row of houses.

One of the more recently completed projects was designed by the architect Robert Sobel as a home for himself and his wife. The house is entirely inward looking, as are all the homes on the estate, with rooms arranged round the perimeter of the s and looking onto a central courtyard planted wit holly trees and ornamental shrubs. All the princi areas, such as the entrance hall, living room, dining room and master bedroom, have fully glazed walls with sliding doors opening directly onto the atrium, creating a flow of space around central garden. Light control and privacy are secured by a system of shutters along the living and bedroom sides adjacent to the central court.

Services are at the four corners of the main cou with the kitchen and master bedroom looking ont their own small planted areas. Flanking the en-

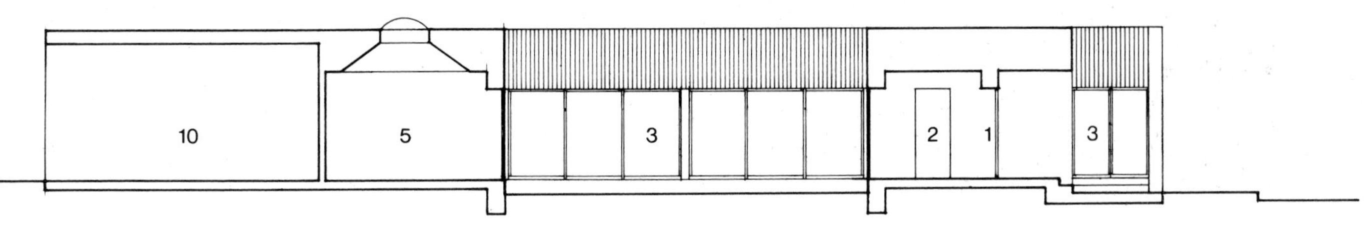

e entrance elevation. A
t in the high wall leads
a small entry courtyard.

76
Plan of the house, section and site plan
1 Entrance
2 Hall
3 Courtyard
4 Living room
5 Dining room
6 Kitchen
7 Master bedroom
8 Bathroom
9 Bedroom
10 Garage

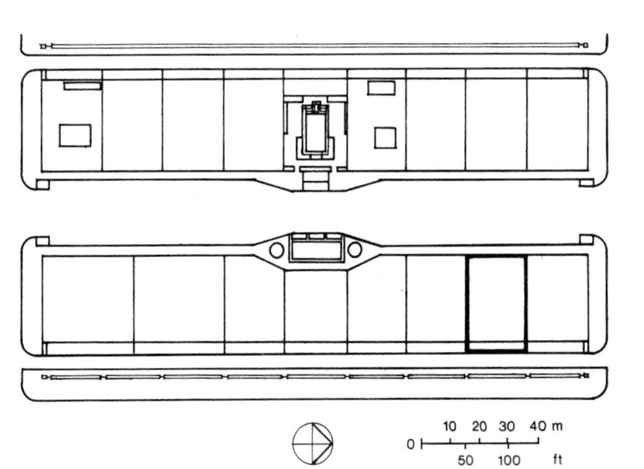

The Home of the Architect
Houston, Texas, USA
Robert Sobel

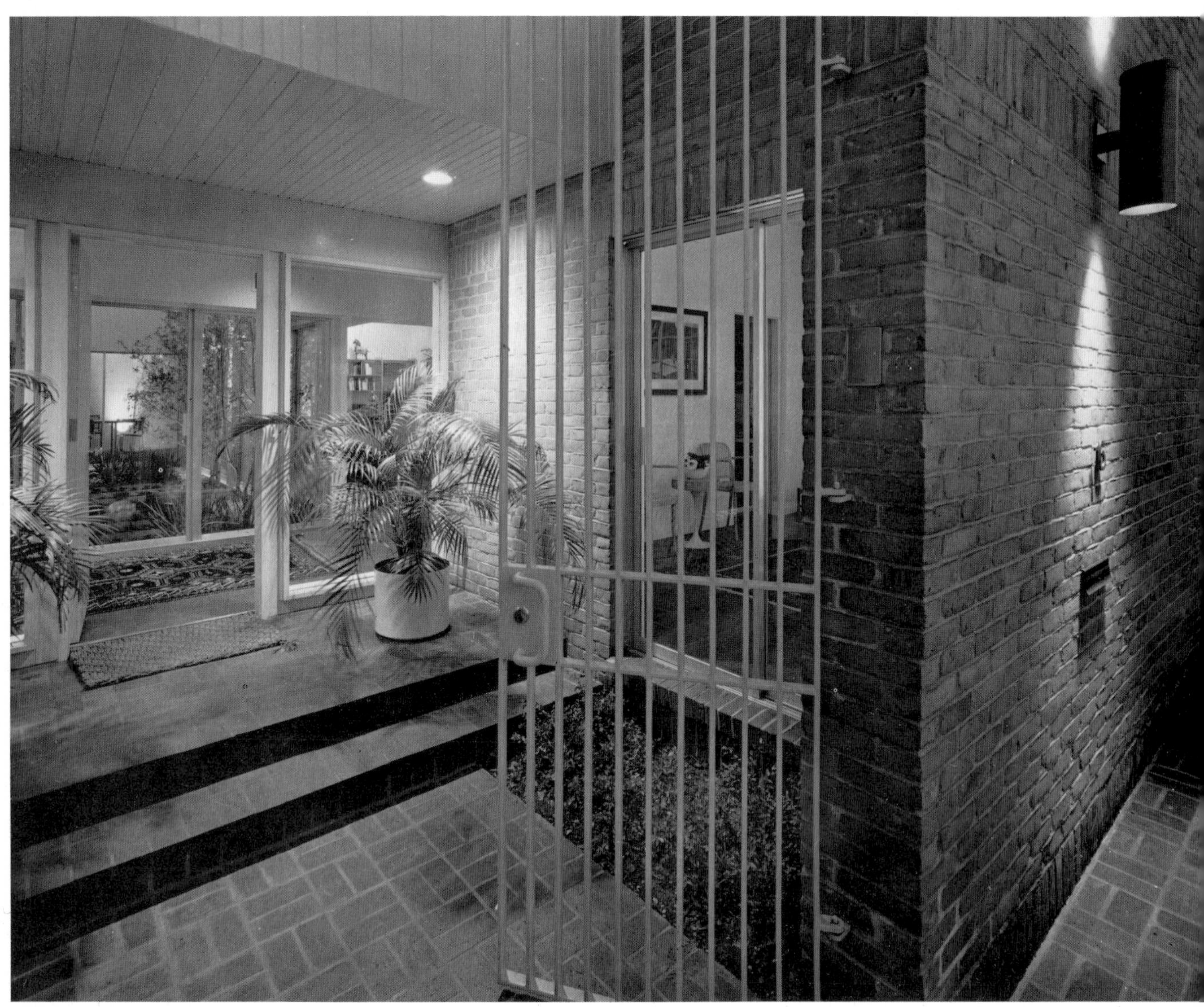

trance are two guest bedrooms which have sliding glass doors onto the main entrance courtyard. Thus, all interior spaces relate directly to an enclosed exterior space.

The essentially open plan is united by the use of simple common finishes: all interior walls and ceilings are painted white and all floors are paved with brindle brick pavers. To further unite interior and exterior, the bricks run out into the central garden and down the entrance steps.

The house is of timber frame construction with brick external cladding. Internally, ceilings are generally at 3m (10ft) with flow and return ducts f the all-electric air conditioning system concealed in downstands around the perimeter of the principal rooms. To emphasize the importance of the dining area which, placed as it is on the axis of th main entrance is the culmination of the internal aspect first seen by the visitor, the dining room ceiling rises in a pyramidal form to a skylight.

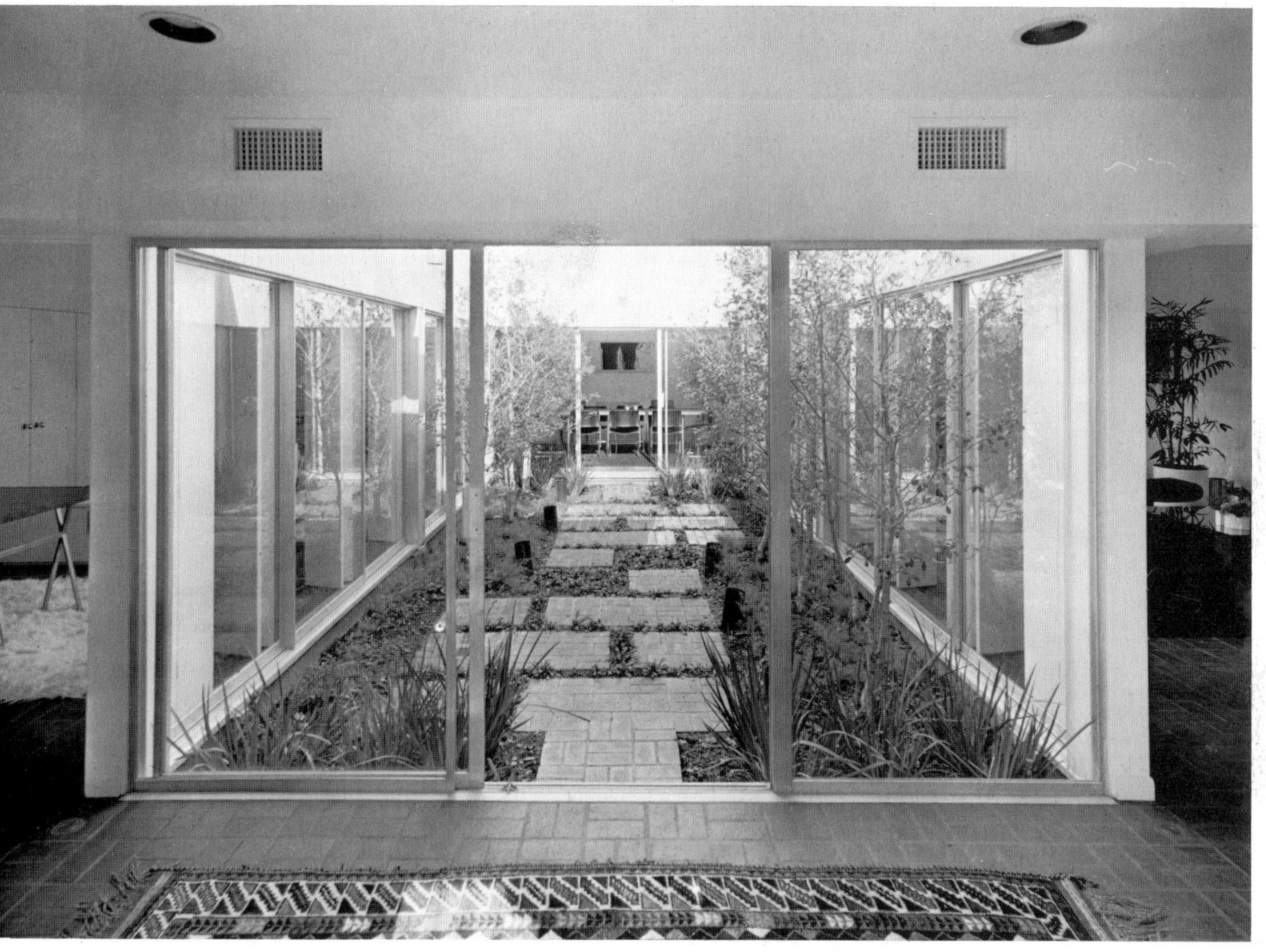

77
The main entrance. The courtyard serves a double purpose: first as a formal space for greeting visitors and secondly as the contact with nature for the two flanking guest bedrooms. A canopy partially covers the courtyard, protecting the entrance door.

78
View from the hall along the axis of the house to the dining room beyond. The master bedroom is on the left and the living room on the right. The spaces flow around the central courtyard which allows the rooms to relate to the external elements and to each other.

The Home of the Architect
Houston, Texas, USA
Robert Sobel

79
View into the living room from the hall. Careful artificial lighting ensures that the courtyard is also the focal point of the house at night.

e master bedroom. Brick
vers flow from the bed-
om into the courtyard,
iting inside and outside.

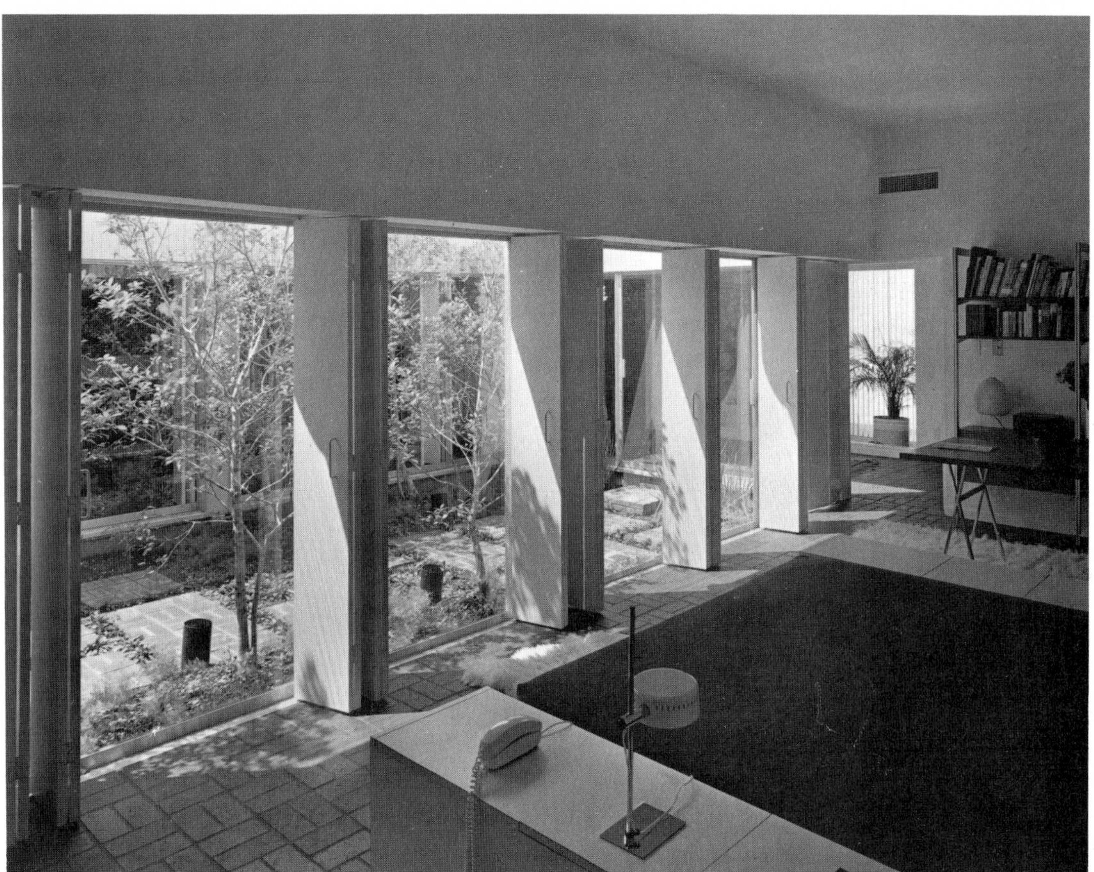

e master bathroom look-
, onto one of the much
aller courtyards which,
spite its size, is ex-
mely effective in bring-
, light and air into the
ep plan of the house.

The Home of the Architect
Houston, Texas, USA
Robert Sobel

e south entrance. The w building is surrounded carefully preserved sting trees and can only appreciated at close arters.

rth-west corner of the seum. The restored for- cations of the castle und the museum on all es, the modular grid of new building overlay- the geometry of the cient half-buried walls.

The Kumamoto Municipal Museum
Kumamoto Prefecture, Japan
Kisho Kurokawa

89
Exhibition hall on the second level.

90
View of the museum interior. Natural light from the roof is supplemented by elegant suspended spotlights. Each structural module has an octagonal stainless steel air conditioning duct suspended from the diagonal bracing members.

A variety of modular systems are used for displaying the exhibits and their unobtrusive colours have been chosen to focus attention onto the exhibits themselves. Exhibit storage rooms on each level are connected by large elevators. The building also contains a special exhibition space and a planetarium.

Kurokawa has designed a series of buildings each produced by the repetition of a standard cell; Kumamoto Museum is the most recent example of this method. Here the reinforced concrete post and beam structure is constructed on a 10m (32ft 10in) square grid. On the exterior the most striking feature of the building is the capitals of the columns which step concentrically outwards to form nodes expressing the possibility of future growth. The rhythm of the columns clearly expresses the module on which the building is constructed and gives the elevations a calm, classical feeling: a temple to learning in a sacred grove. Internally the circular capitals connect the top of the round columns with a network of horizontal beams. These brace the structure below the intricate roof which is a composition of quarter pyramids with

windows in one or both of their vertical faces. The roof is formed from tilted concrete slabs and finished externally with tiles made from sheet copper. Natural light from the roof is supplemented by artificial lighting controlled by photosensitive cells. In the exhibition area the air conditioning ductwork has been treated as a piece of gleaming sculpture with ducts made from insulated stainless steel plate forming an octagon in each module. Separate air conditioning units are fed by a dual system of low pressure steam pipes from a boiler which burns a heavy, cheaper grade of oil, and chilled water pipes which dissipate heat through three cooling towers.

All interior finishes are an unobtrusive grey and the exterior of the building is clad in grey porcelain tiles. Concrete columns and beams are painted with mirror finish polyurethane paint on both exterior and interior.

The Kumamoto Municipal Museum
Kumamoto Prefecture, Japan
Kisho Kurokawa

91
View from the physics and engineering hall to an exterior exhibition terrace.

92
North pedestrian entrance. A network of paths leads through the trees to the remaining section of Kumamoto Castle.

The National Ethnological Museum Suita, Osaka Urban Prefecture, Japan

Architect
Kisho Kurokawa

Photography
Tomio Ohashi

On the site of the World Exposition held at Osaka in 1970, a major cultural centre has been created. The Japan Folk Arts Museum and the International Art Museum have recently been joined by the National Ethnological Museum, designed by Kisho Kurokawa. The site slopes towards the east and is bounded on the north side by the now well-established Expo '70 Japanese garden. Five Expo' pavilions formerly stood on the site and removing their foundations proved to be a major problem in the early stages of the building programme. Approaching from the east, where seminar rooms cantilever out from the facade to emphasize the main entrance, the massing of the building gives a clear indication of its plan: a central square four-storey block, with circular towers, containing lifts, stairs and services rising from each corner, and, on three sides of this block, two-storey pavilions containing the subsidiary exhibitions.

The public space is planned on two levels with the large entrance hall and adjoining shop and restaurant on the ground floor and the exhibition concentrated on the first floor. One of the cantilevered seminar rooms forms a porch to the main entrance lobby which leads into a side aisle of the entrance hall. A glazed barrel vault covers the two

tail of the south facade. aluminium clad circu- service tower projects ove the corner of the in block.

onometric.

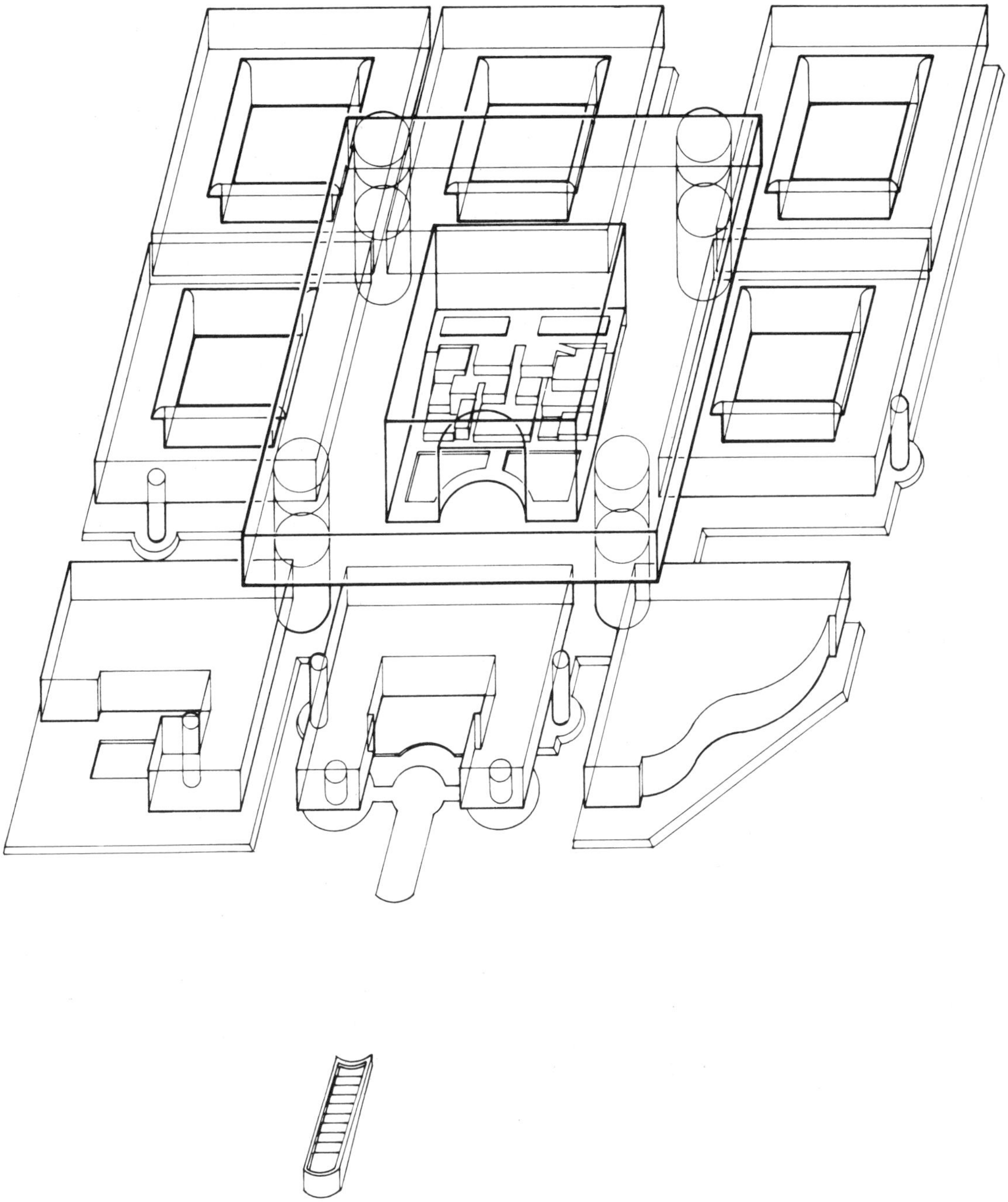

storey 'nave' of the hall pouring light onto the polished granite pavement. A pond on the exterior of the building extends into the entrance hall itself. The highly polished granite floor and columns and the surface of the pool contrast with the natural Indian sandstone face of the walls below the barrel vault. The exposed stage-ceiling system in this area has an infill of diecast aluminium strips laid in a free pattern reminiscent of the ripples in the pool below, with totally concealed downlighters and air conditioning grilles. The major part of the ground floor is occupied by large storage areas and associ-ated workshops and the main plant rooms for the mechanical and electrical services. Storage space is located directly beneath the exhibition area and connected to it by two lifts. Layering the two different functions makes future extension of the space relatively simple.

The National Ethnological Museum
Suita, Osaka Urban Prefecture, Japan
Kisho Kurokawa

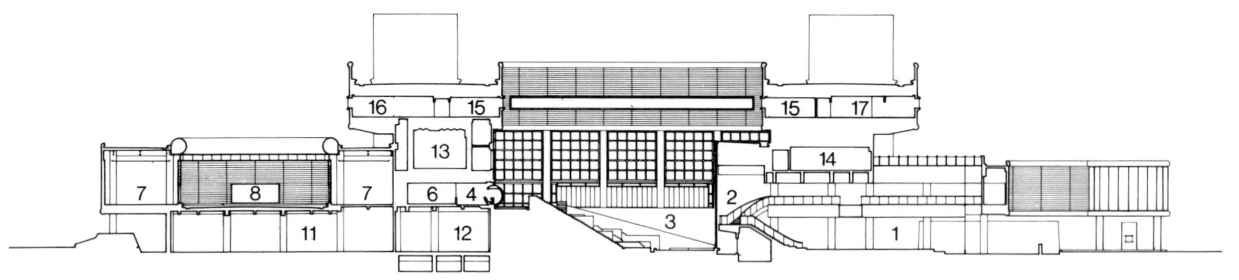

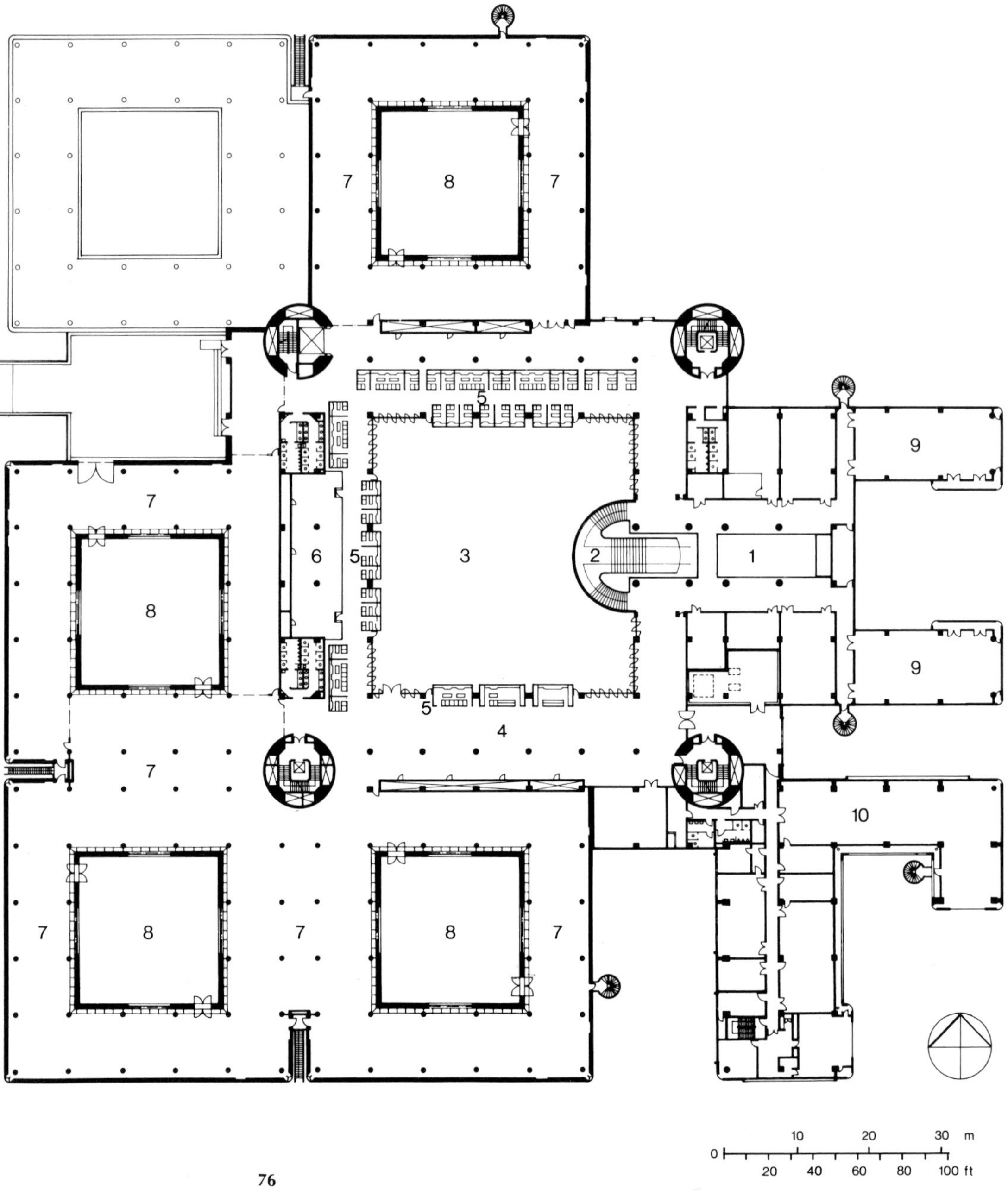

95
East-west section and plan
1 Entrance hall
2 Main staircase
3 Central courtyard
4 Introduction space
5 Videotheques
6 Videotheque control
7 Exhibition space
8 Courtyard
9 Seminar room
10 Administration
11 Store rooms
12 Plant rooms
13 Photographic studio
14 Data storage
15 Instructors' rooms
16 Laboratories
17 Research rooms

96
The entrance hall show
Kurokawa's varied and
skilful use of materials
textures and his manip
lation of both natural a
artificial lighting.

From the hall the visitor climbs the main staircase to the exhibition on the first floor. The staircase projects into the central courtyard so that the half-landing becomes an ambiguous zone being neither entirely outside in the courtyard nor entirely inside the building. Capsules thrust into the courtyard at first floor level. These are the 'videotheques' which provide summary introductions on video equipment to the various sections in the museum. Finishes in this central area are mostly metallic: the videotheques are made from aluminium sheet; the ceiling tiles are perforated aluminium; columns are clad in aluminium, while the floor is covered with industrial sheet rubber.

The museum is managed as a joint study facility for the National University and must take into consideration the needs of the research scholar as well as those of the ordinary museum visitor. Therefore the area around the central courtyard is planned as a general introduction to the adjoining specialised exhibitions and the visitor is left free to choose between the nine regional displays which are housed in four individual blocks. Each block has a courtyard 20m (66ft) square at its centre, used for the display of large pieces of sculpture from different civilizations. On each face of the courtyard is a glazed opening which can be totally closed off by lowering an internal steel shutter. Round the top of the courtyard walls runs a tube of clear plastic which allows light into the internal space. The level of illumination can be adjusted by means of electrically controlled flaps. A further block will be added to the north-west corner to complete the symmetry of the building.

7
iew of the central courtard from the main stair-ase. On the landing the sitor stands in the open ourtyard yet still within e building envelope.

8
he videotheques; har-ony of curved with ctilinear forms in the troduction space.

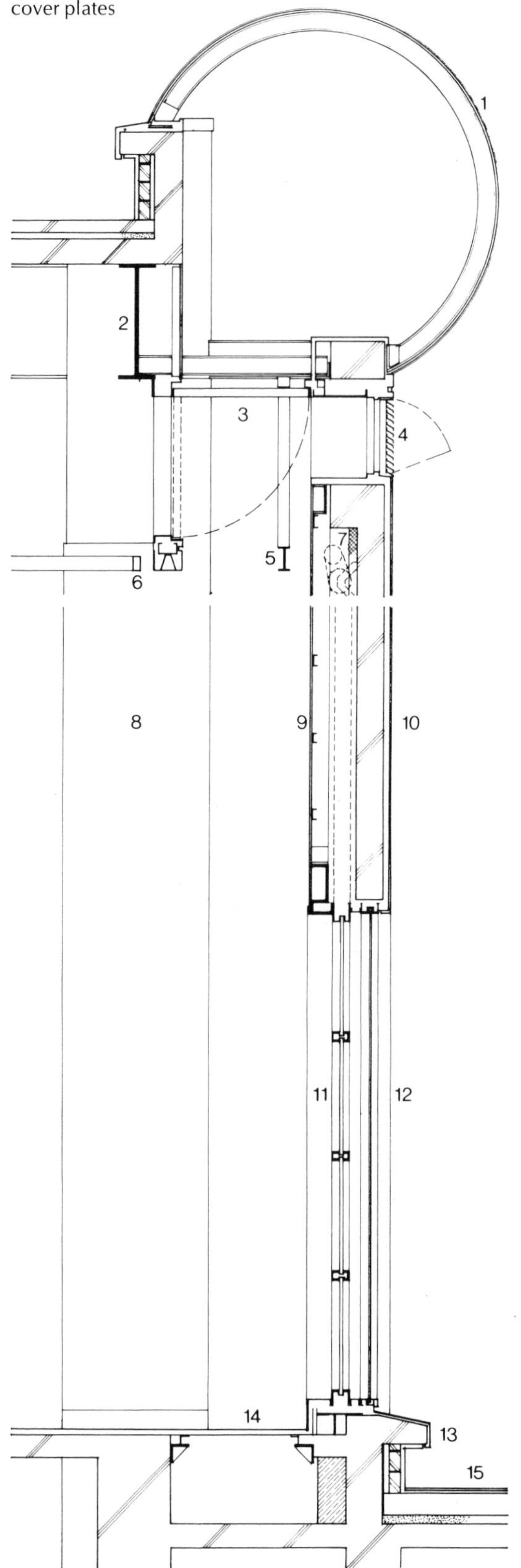

99
Section through the courtyard wall of an exhibition pavilion
1 Transparent plastic sheets formed from thermosetting resins in a steel framework with aluminium cover plates
2 Main structural steelwork
3 Electrically operated steel panels controlling the level of natural illumination in exhibition hall
4 Electrically operated smoke exhausts
5 Suspension steelwork for display panels
6 Exposed stage ceiling
7 Rigid insulating panels of foamed resin
8 Main structural column
9 Fire resistant plywood internal lining with hemp cloth covering
10 Tile cladding
11 Steel security shutter
12 Aluminium sliding doors
13 Aluminium coping
14 Floor of exhibition hall
15 Courtyard

All exhibition space relates to the outside, to Nature, through the courtyards which act as intermediary zones. Kurokawa greatly admires the seventeenth-century Katsura Detached Palace in Kyoto, extended in a series of pavilions placed on the diagonal. Each of these pavilions is for Kurokawa a 'jiga', a capsule space and the Buddhist word for self and identity. The pavilions are connected by an 'engawa' which is a continuous

erandah formed by projecting the eaves. The ngawa' serves several functions: an external cor-dor connecting internal rooms, an area for greet-g guests, a zone where nature and architecture eet. A courtyard is such a space, as is the half-nding on the main staircase of this museum. The hilosophy of 'engawa' relates closely to the Japan-e concept of 'ma', which means timing, silence, oundary zone, void. In Noh drama when an expression of tragedy or grief is changed to one of joy there is a moment of immobility in which change is indicated, a moment of profound meaning. This moment is known as 'ma'. It also occurs in ancient Japanese court music, the Gagaku, when the musician or singer is allowed to improvise in the intervals between discordant sounds. The courtyard also incorporates some of the complex philosophies connected with the tea ceremony.

100
Sculpture in the courtyard of an exhibition pavilion representing Aztec gods.

The National Ethnological Museum
Suita, Osaka Urban Prefecture, Japan
Kisho Kurokawa

101
Exhibition hall. A wide range of lighting effects can be achieved by adjusting light fittings from catwalks in the exposed stage-ceiling.

102
Open display cases. The display system allows close contact between the exhibit and the visitor.

The space of the tea-room is minimal so that by limiting space the participants in the spiritual ceremony can comprehend the vastness of Nature. The act of enclosing the courtyard liberates the space, enabling it to signify all the qualities of the world of Nature; the part is always greater than the whole and the greater coexists with the lesser in mutual contradiction and inclusion of each other. Antagonist coexistence of forms and materials are found throughout the building: the curved forms of the videotheques with the rectilinear building structure, polished materials with rough unfinished materials.

The building is laid out on a tartan grid: a grid o 5m (16ft 5in) × 7.5m (24ft 7in) laid over a grid of 7.5m (24ft 7in) square. Where the smaller grid intersects are the four towers, each 10m (32ft 10in in diameter, which contain the lifts, stairs and vertical service ducts. External walls are placed 1.25m (4ft 1in) outside the larger grid. On the first floor the 5m (16ft 5in) grid marks the zones between the different spaces which flow into each other creating a feeling of free movement amongst the exhibits.

Finishes used on the building are almost universally of a grey colour: aluminium diecast borders t

e facade, grey cladding tiles, stainless steel, ater-polished or jet-burner-finished granite, grey arble and grey cast stone. In the twilight colours erge into a greyness, architecture loses its three-mensional qualities and the boundaries between iildings and Nature vanish. The grey tone, known 'Rikyu' grey, stems from the traditions of the tea eremony. Sen no Rikyu (1521–91) was a master of e tea ceremony and encouraged the use of simple a ceremony rooms. Rikyu grey is created by ixing red, blue, yellow, green and white together id can have various hues depending on the mix.

In the exhibition space the use of grey and black finishes serves to focus attention on the exhibits themselves. The display cases are built from a standard system of matt-black aluminium sections and glass, and are designed to allow maximum openness and close contact between the exhibits and the visitor. The exhibits stand on an aluminium grid 3.2cm (1¼in) square which also serves as a scale by which to measure the specimens. The system is totally flexible and all displays are laid out in harmony with the main structural grid on a smaller overlay grid of 1.25m (4ft 1in) and angular displacements of 45 and 90 degrees. Lighting is mainly housed in the concentrated exposed stage-

The National Ethnological Museum
Suita, Osaka Urban Prefecture, Japan
Kisho Kurokawa

103
Display cases built from standardized components. Vertical panels are suspended between two of the enclosed cases.

104
Escape stair from the main exhibition level. Square projecting tiles break up the smooth surface of the tile cladding creating a textured facade which changes with the varying sunlight.

ceiling system.

Above the introduction space, on the second floor, are the computer room, library and photographic studio and the third floor contains offices, laboratories and seminar rooms. The teaching staff have rooms on this floor around the quiet central courtyard.

The central four-storey block is designed as an independent combination steel and reinforced cor crete frame structure with load bearing walls on th ground floor acting as ties. The two-storey exhibition pavilions have steel frame structures. Heat for the building is supplied by an air-thermal-source heat pump and heat is stored in thermal storage tanks. The storage tanks are particularly important because some zones must have mechanically controlled temperature and humidity twenty-four hou a day. In some of the storage rooms on the ground floor and the film storage room on the third floor, the air conditioning system has to operate betweer the extremely fine limits of plus or minus 1 degree Centigrade and plus or minus 3 per cent humidity. A gas boiler provides auxiliary heat.

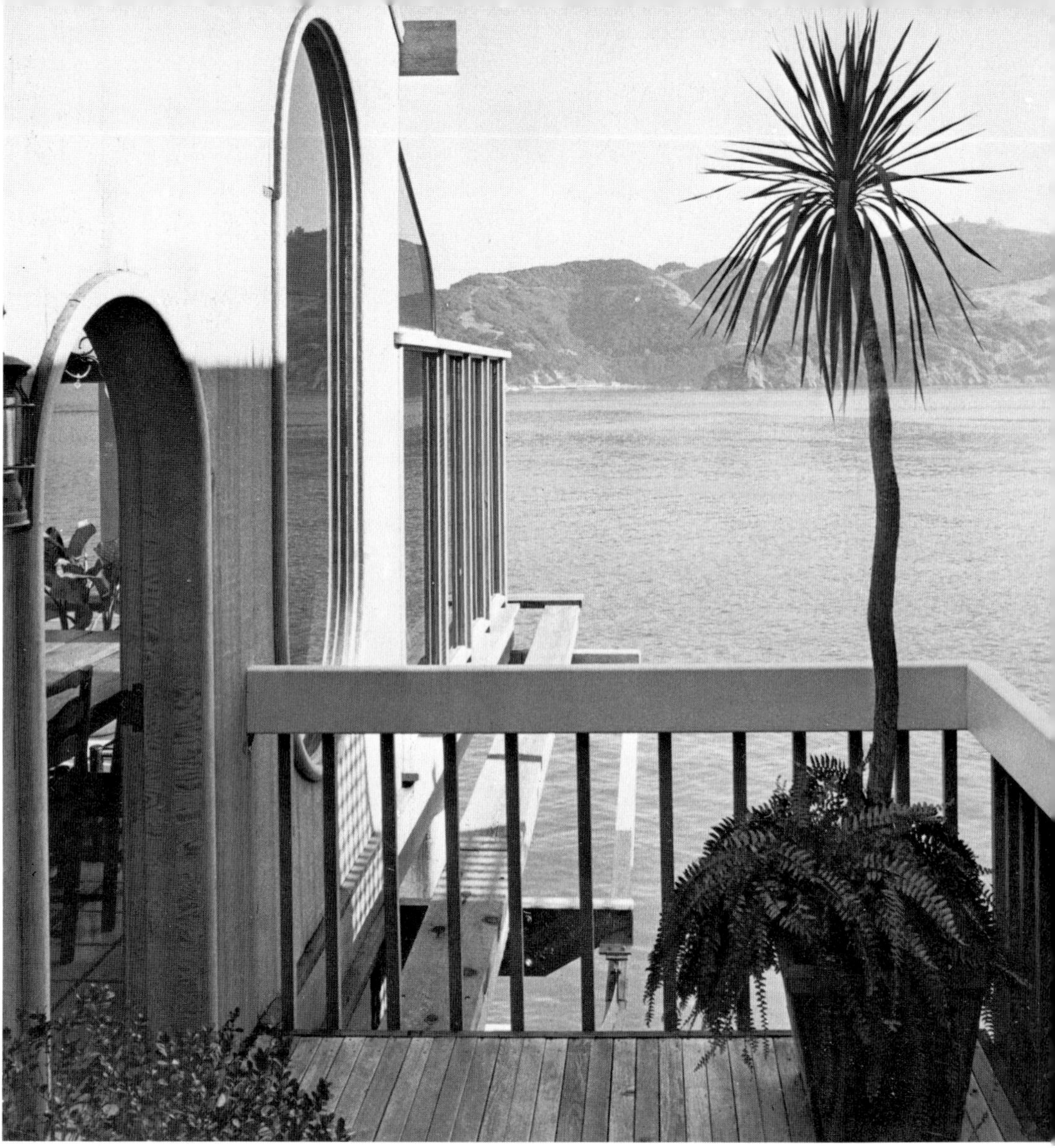

A Duplex House
Tiburon, California, USA

Architects
Callister, Payne and Bischoff

Project Associate
Joseph O. Newberry

Photography
Carla de Benedetti

The village of Tiburon clings to the base of a Californian cliff which drops steeply into San Francisco Bay. Houses jut out from the waterfront road and their foundations are often well beyond the water edge.

This house was designed and built for two separate families. One unit is a mirror image of the other, separated by a 2.5cm (1in) gap for acoustic privacy but using a common foundation system. The site for the house was a particularly challenging one: the cliff is unstable along this stretch of coastline and the edge of the public road required support. To give the house a secure footing, reinforced concrete piers 60cm (2ft) in diameter were constructed up to 2.4m (8ft) deep into the bedrock, six of them below the high-water mark. A network of 30cm (1ft) wide by 60cm (2ft) deep concrete ground beams connect the pier heads on the slope of the cliff and consolidate the earth. Circular concrete columns 45cm (18in) in diameter rise from the submerged piers to support a series of laminated timber beams which carry the timber framework of the house. The road is at the uppermost level of the site, so the garages have been placed at the top of the house. Descending two external flights of stairs down either side of the

5
ew from the entrance
cony out across San
ncisco Bay. The house
ends over the water; a
tion of the supporting
ucture can be seen
ough the balustrade.

6
tion.

107
Plans: (above) street level and mezzanine (below) main level and lower level.
Key to plans and section
1 Entrance
2 Solarium
3 Hearth room
4 Kitchen
5 Sun deck
6 Master bedroom
7 Bathroom
8 Dressing room
9 Bedroom
10 Workshop/mechanical
11 Lower deck
12 Gallery/study
13 Garage
14 Entrance gate
15 Fern garden

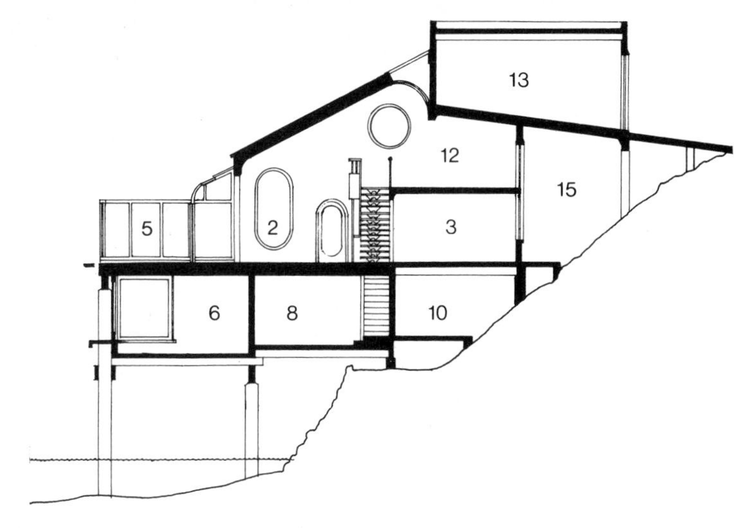

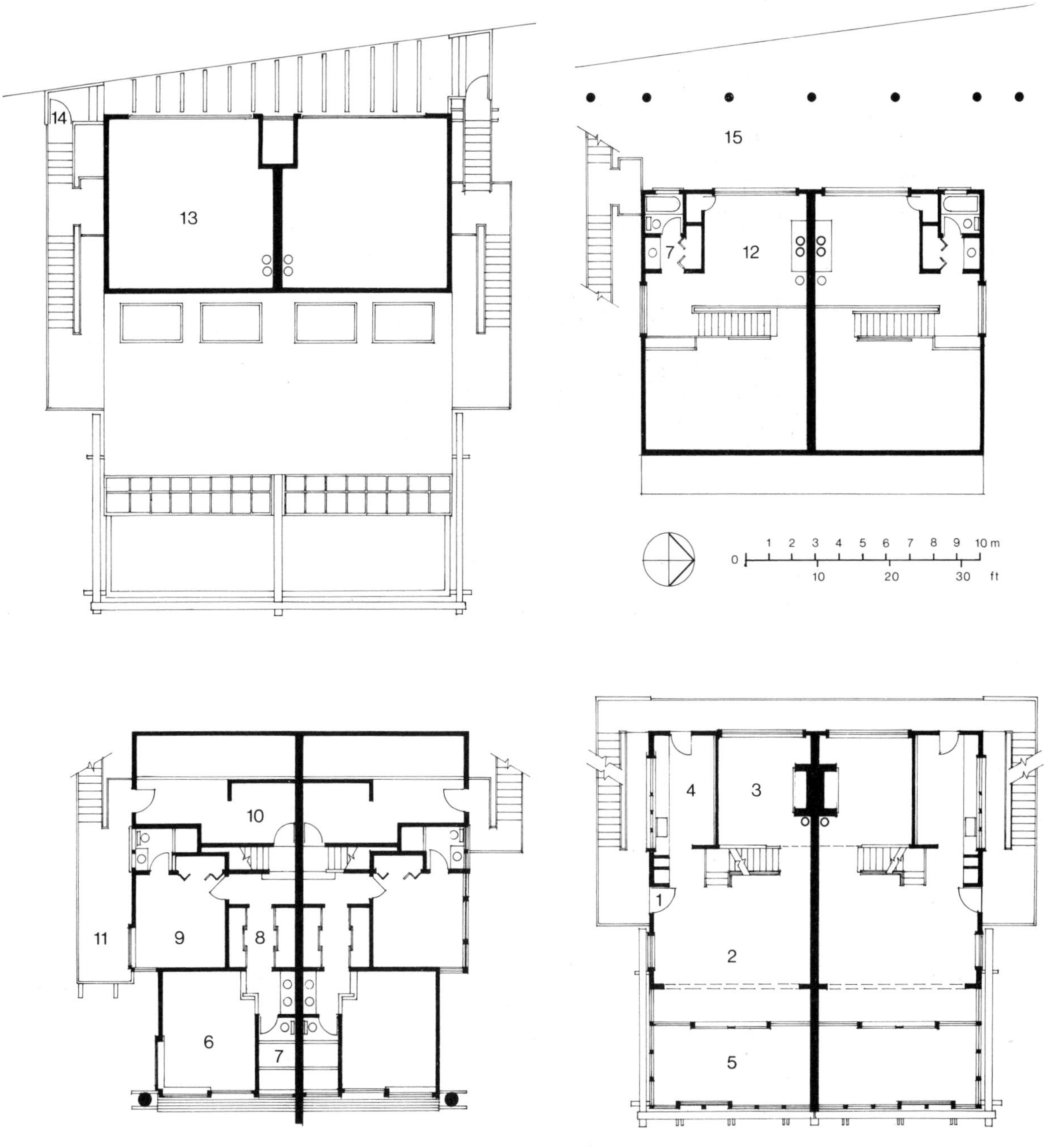

1 2 3 4 5 6 7 8 9 10 m
0 10 20 30 ft

A Duplex House
Tiburon, California, USA
Callister, Payne and Bischoff

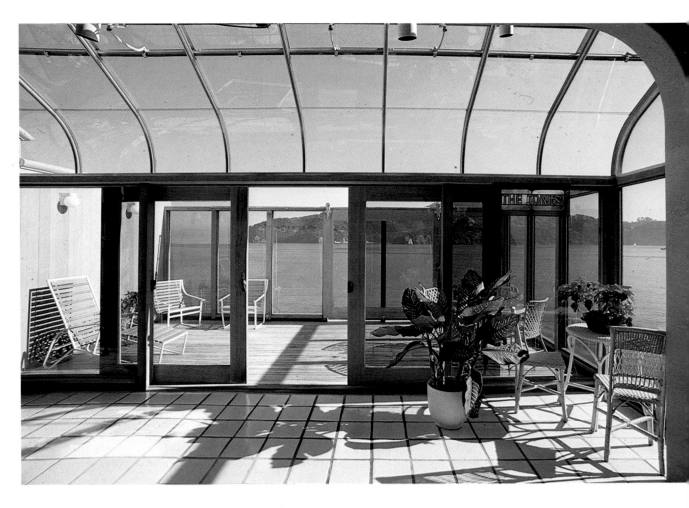

108
A greenhouse forms the seaward wall of the main living area where sliding glass doors open onto the sun deck. Glass screens protect the deck from cool breezes off the sea.

109
The hearth room. The focal point of the secluded lounge is a large circular fireplace, the shape of which is echoed and magnified in the enormous window shared by the gallery above, which looks out onto the cliff face where a fern garden has been created.

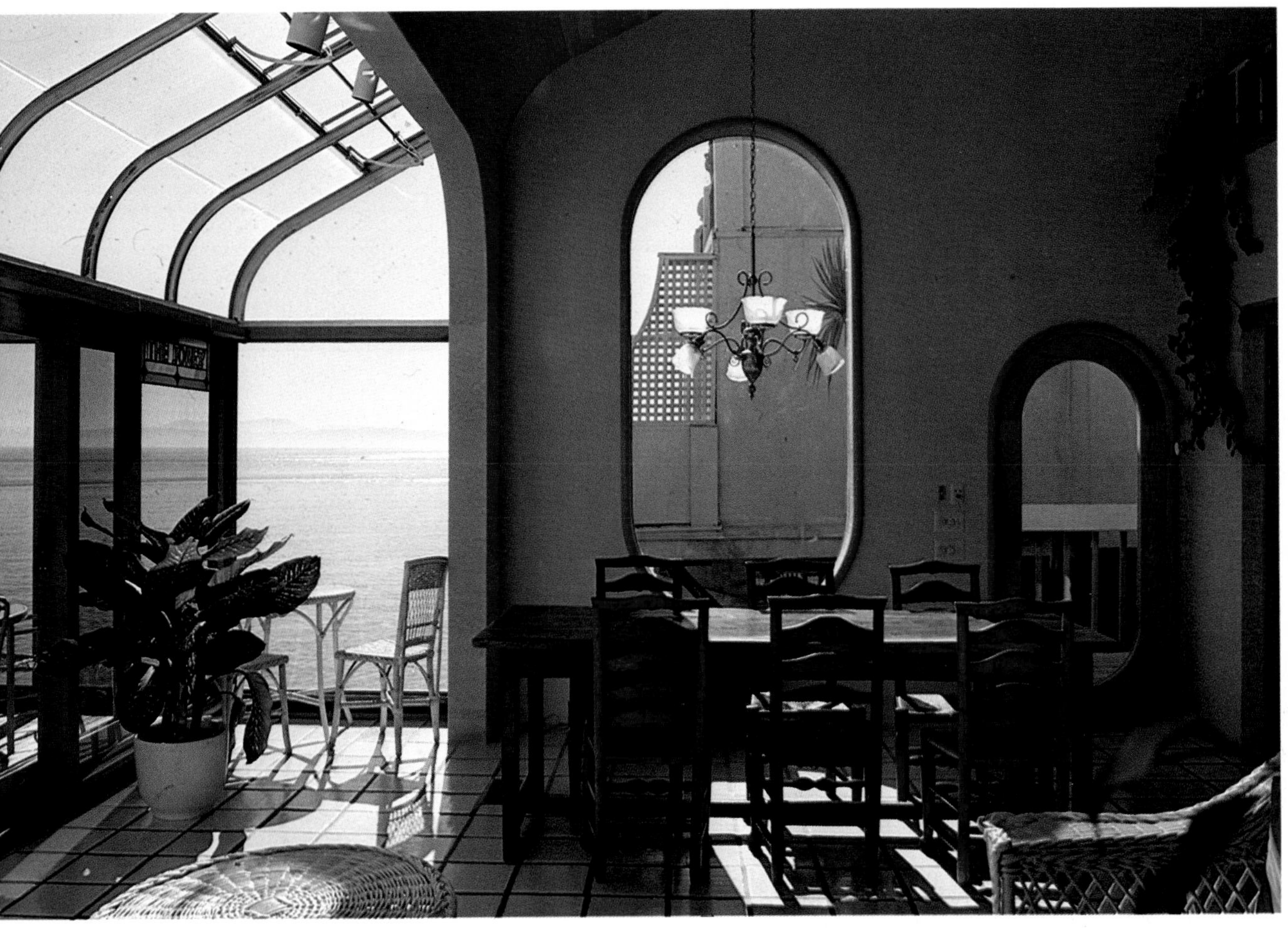

110
The dining room in the solarium. The white Mexican floor tiles throw the brilliant marine light into the centre of the house.

redwood boarded house, one enters directly into the main two-storey living area. Along one side is a greenhouse which opens onto a sun deck protected by glass screens. The floor of the room is tiled with 2.5cm (1in) thick white glazed Mexican tiles on a 2.5cm (1in) mortar bed on the plywood subfloor, creating a finish which reflects the brilliant marine light onto the timber ceiling. The ceiling rises to a curved plexiglass skylight at the rear of the room where a gallery level has been incorporated. With its associated bathroom this area can be used as a spare bedroom. Beneath the gallery are the kitchen and a secluded den with a large circular fireplace.

Both these rear spaces look through halves of an enormous circular window onto a fern garden, which has been created on the face of the cliff itself. The garden borrows light through slots in the driveway apron and is flood-lit at night. Two bedrooms with adjoining bathrooms are situated below the main living deck, 2.4m (8ft) above the high-water mark.

Each unit has a forced air counter flow heating system utilizing a natural gas furnace. Air conditioning was considered to be unnecessary and summer cooling relies on effective cross-ventilation.

A Duplex House
Tiburon, California, USA
Callister, Payne and Bischoff

111
Stairs leading to the mezzanine gallery over the hearth room; the main entrance door is on the left. A nautical quality is evident in the rounded doors and windows and in the simple, elegant structure of the staircase.

112
Looking up to the gallery from the main living area; the kitchen is on the left. The high level of natural illumination is maintained by a skylight which extends the full width of the building at the rear of the solarium. The air return duct, the circular fireplace, the balustrading and the large circular window seen behind continue the nautical theme.

A Duplex House
Tiburon, California, USA
Callister, Payne and Bischoff

The interior spaces of the house have a certain nautical quality enhanced by such details as the boarded ceilings, clean white walls and white tiled floor; the elegant staircase with its hardwood treads supported by wedge-shaped steel plates welded to a tubular steel section; the exposed steel return air duct; and the curved windows and doors, with jambs formed from plywood and frames cut from solid redwood, dowelled and glued together.

The furnishing is of sturdy, comfortable elegance. In the solarium, natural rattan furniture and wooden slatted chairs and tables, painted green, are arranged in groups; while in the back of the house a black leather suite faces a wall entirely lined with book shelves. The dining table and chairs are solid, old farmhouse furniture. Spotlights on tracks provide a brilliant illumination for the whole house, but ceiling and table lamps are also used in the dining and conversation areas for quieter, more intimate moods.

113
View of the gallery on the left and the solarium.

114
Detail of the stairs to the gallery.

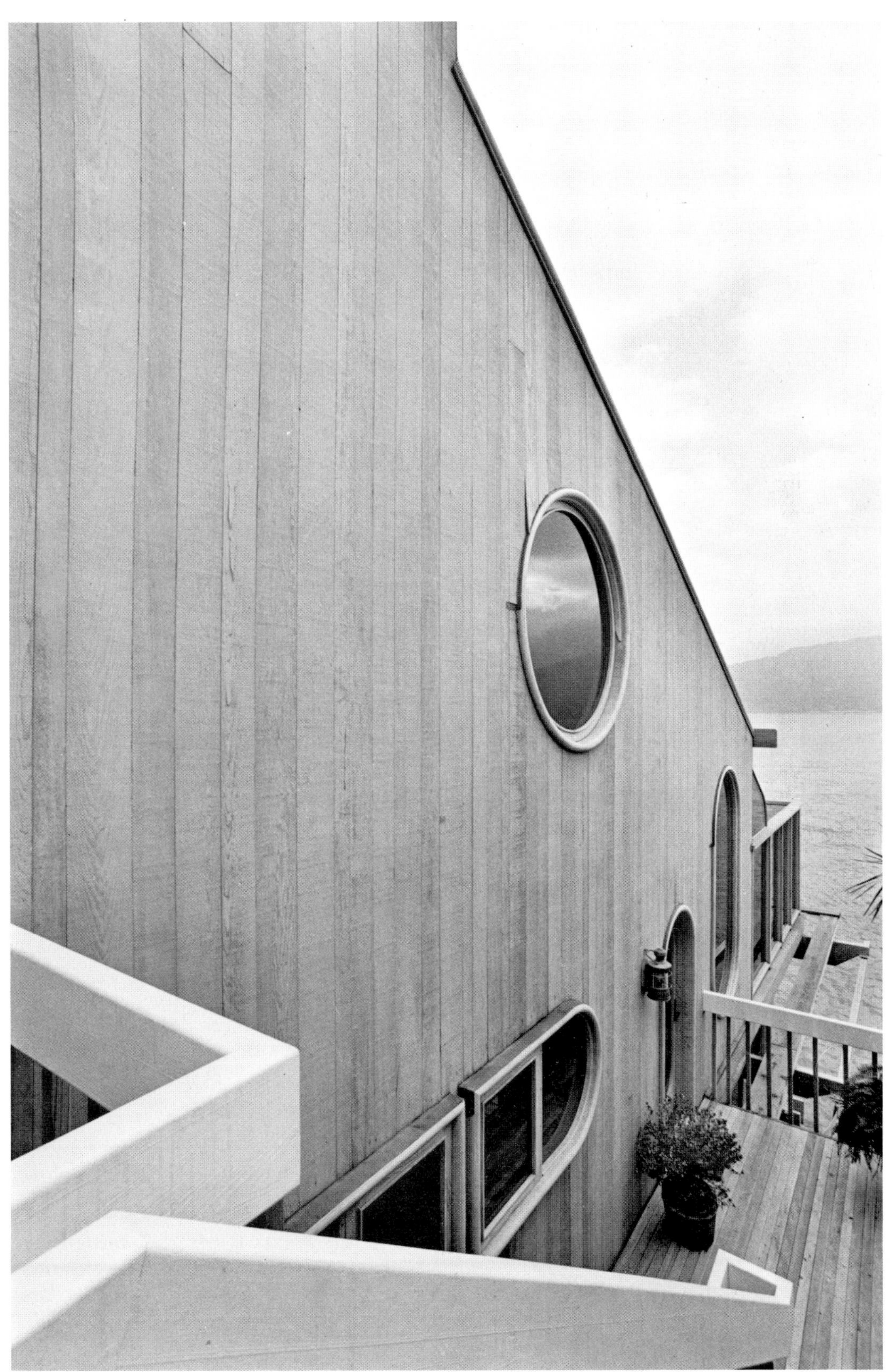

5
ew from street level
wn to the main en-
nce. The curved sur-
unds to the openings set
the redwood cladding
extremely functional in
tecting them from the
n as well as elegant.

The State Correctional Institute Eagle River, Alaska

Architects
Crittenden, Cassetta & Cannon; Hellmuth Obata & Kassabaum

Photography
Stephen Dunham
Kiku Obata
Barbara Martin

Fourteen miles north of Anchorage, on 207 acres of forest near the Chugach mountains at Eagle River, a unique social experiment is taking place. The state of Alaska has built a 7200sq.m (72,000sq.ft) complex to house up to 100 male criminal offenders of all ages and from various backgrounds. It is planned to increase the number of the inmates to 180, with the addition of two more housing blocks.

The purpose of the centre is to gradually rehabilitate prisoners over a period of two years – the final two years of their sentence – until they can once more become ordinary members of society. The architecture reflects this purpose and remains domestic and human, with low-rise, cedar-clad buildings set amongst pleasantly landscaped grounds. The site resembles a small college campus; a dramatic contrast to the majority of penal institutions.

A new inmate is introduced to the centre throug[h] the Special Treatment Unit, which is organised o[n] the lines of a normal gaol with a uniform, large single cells with security doors, a small day room and an outdoor exercise yard patrolled by prison officers. The prisoners are made fully aware of the benefits of normal life in the rest of the centre, but to obtain their release from the Special Treatment

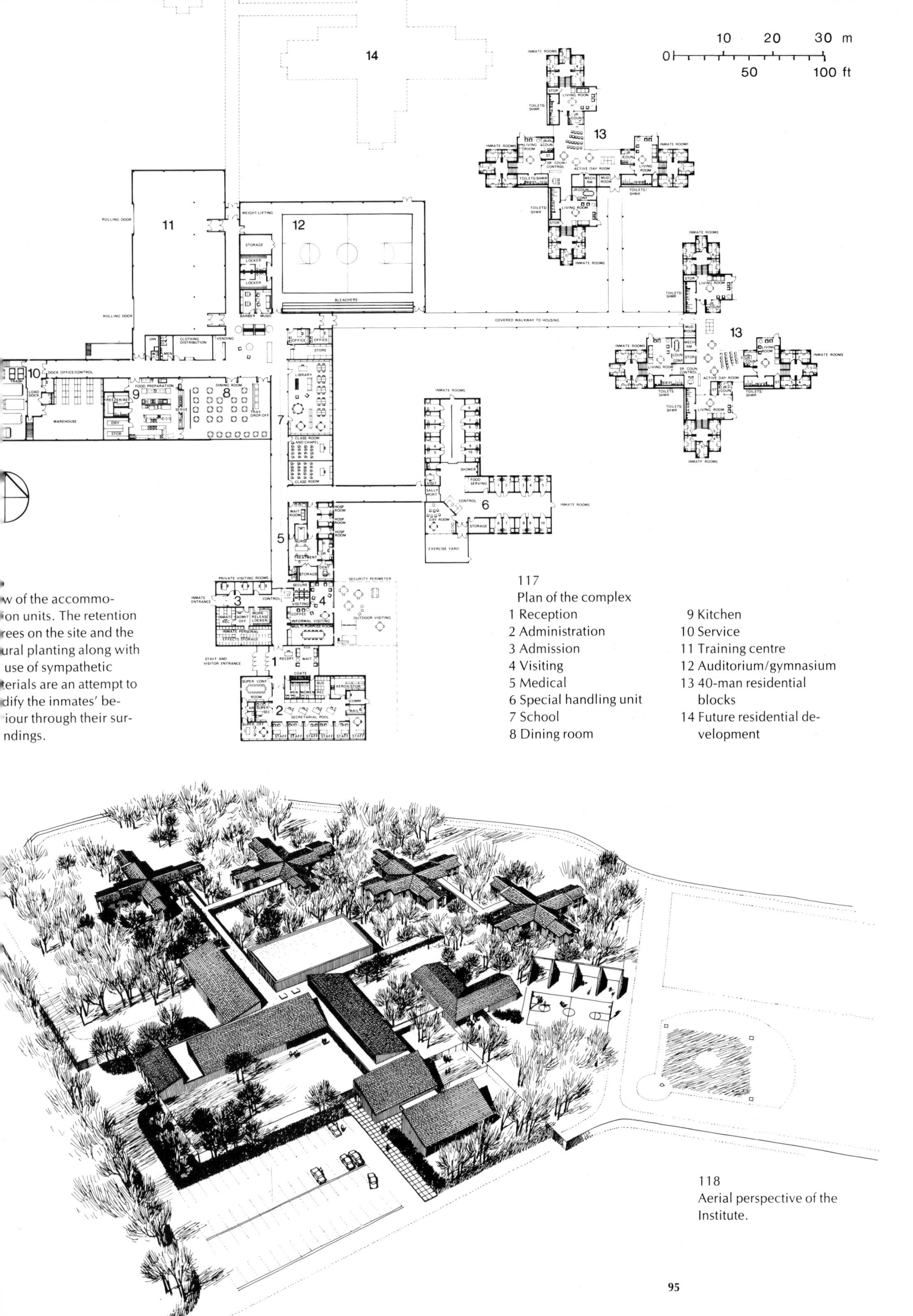

w of the accommo-
ion units. The retention
rees on the site and the
ural planting along with
use of sympathetic
erials are an attempt to
dify the inmates' be-
iour through their sur-
ndings.

117
Plan of the complex

1 Reception
2 Administration
3 Admission
4 Visiting
5 Medical
6 Special handling unit
7 School
8 Dining room
9 Kitchen
10 Service
11 Training centre
12 Auditorium/gymnasium
13 40-man residential blocks
14 Future residential development

118
Aerial perspective of the Institute.

The State Correctional Institute
Eagle River, Alaska
Crittenden, Cassetta & Cannon
Hellmuth Obata & Kassabaum

119
One of the dayrooms at the heart of each housing block.

120
A welder at work in one of the community centre's vocational workshops.

Jnit they must devise their own correctional treatment programme with the help of a personal counsellor. This programme includes all aspects of life at the centre, from daily routine activities to organising study and training schedule, choosing a job and arranging family visits around each individual's timetable. The programme is then formalised into a contract and the inmate is assigned living quarters in one of the two main housing complexes.

Each housing complex has bedrooms for forty men split into four groups. This is expressed in the cruciform plan of the housing blocks formed by four wings with a large central lounge. Each wing has its own smaller day room opening off the lounge. This gives access to the wing counsellor's offices, toilets and showers and ten single bedrooms on two levels. The bedrooms are well furnished, to a similar standard as that found in a college dormitory bedroom. A major part of the rehabilitation programme is a daily group therapy session held in each day room between the wing counsellor and the ten inmates of that wing.

During the day the housing blocks are empty and the community centre – linked by covered walkways to the housing complexes – forms the hub of Eagle River. The community centre has a dining room, barber shop, library, public telephones, gymnasium, classrooms, a medical unit, vocational workshops and administrative offices.

The architecture expresses the relationship of the inmate to society; the individual in his single cell relates to his wing group who relates to the forty men in the housing block through the central lounge, relating in turn to life in the community centre and finally to society in the outside world. Open visiting is allowed either in the main lounge or in an outdoor picnic area with tables and a children's playground. The atmosphere is kept informal: all staff and the inmates wear civilian clothes, the public rooms are furnished with fitted carpets and sturdy timber furniture upholstered in bright colours, windows are large and doors remain unlocked throughout all areas during the day. Obviously, there are security measures: all spaces are monitored by discreet security equipment and there is a 4.3m (14ft) high perimeter fence. However, security is accomplished essentially by the daily work programme, the close relationship between staff and inmates and the layout of the buildings.

121
The inmates' families are received in this outdoor recreation area provided with tables, benches and a children's playground and also in the main lounge seen through the trees on the far right.

The Ishihara Residence Osaka, Japan

Architect
Tadao Ando and Associates

Photography
Kazuyoshi Bando

The street facade of the traditional Japanese town house incorporates open timber screens so that private space and public space interpenetrate: the street becomes an extension of the living space and the internal rooms, semi-public space leading to private apartments. The modern industrial age has made this arrangement no longer necessary or practical, partly because of the smaller nuclear family and partly because of the increased need to protect the individual from noise and pollution.

A site in a closely textured district of Osaka with a mix of housing, shops and light industry presented the architect, Tadao Ando, with the problem of creating some private space in a densely populated area. The owner of a furniture company wanted a house for his wife and their two sons, as well as an office for the company. The architect's brief was to design a building which would effectively exclude its surroundings and which would accommodate several different functions within one small volume. To achieve this the house is planned around three sides of an open court through which the rooms receive most of their light and air and through which the house relates to Nature.

A tall concrete wall encloses the house on all

22
'iew of the house which
ırns a black concrete face
› its densely populated
rban surroundings and
ɔoks inwards to an open
ourtyard.

123
Axonometric of the court-
yard.

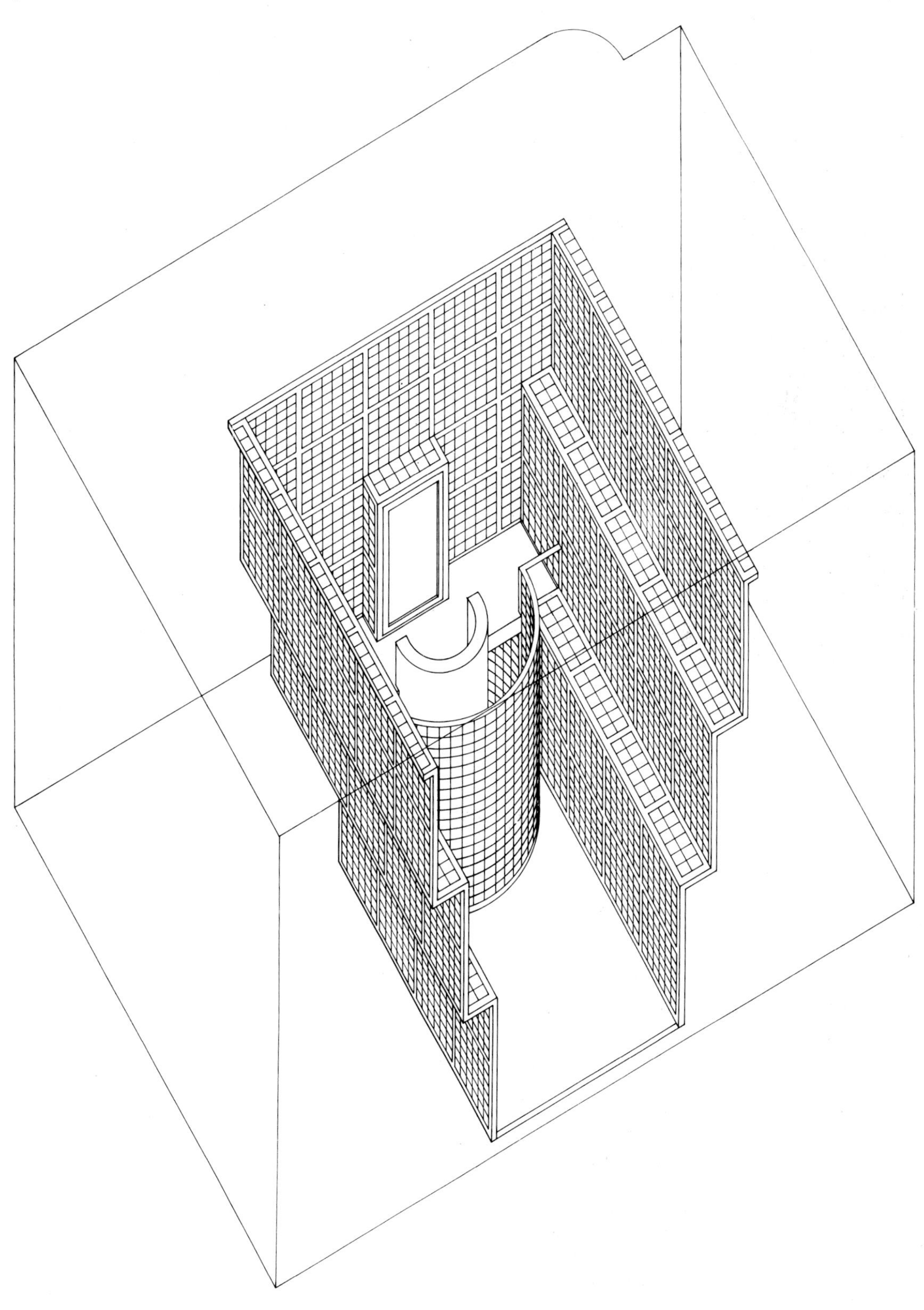

The Ishihara Residence
Osaka, Japan
Tadao Ando and Associates

125
Looking from the office across the courtyard to the Tatami room where traditional screens set behind glass doors protect the participants of the tea ceremony from direct gaze and the distraction of the world outside.

24
'iew from the roof into the ourtyard. Note the pro-ruding door which leads ɔ the living accommo-ation and the curved glass lock screen which en-loses the semi-circular taircase from the main en-ance hall.

sides with only a few small windows and two doors puncturing its smooth face. Set at the corner of two streets is the main entrance door which opens into a large hall paved with stone. The hall is partly open to the elements where a semi-circular stair rises to the first floor terrace in the open court. Light filters into the hall through a curving screen of glass blocks which encloses one side of the stair. On one side of the open court is the entrance to the office, and on the opposite side is the Tatami Room. Both rooms have glass doors opening into the court. The Tatami Room has traditional timber and rice paper screens constructed within the concrete and glass block structure: a room within a room. The lower half of the screens facing onto the court can be slid upwards to permit a view out through the glass doors.

An internal flight of stairs leads from the ground floor to the upper hall, and an adjacent door to the street allows this to be used as a rear entrance to the main apartment. However, the formal entrance to the owner's living accommodation is in the open court, from the terrace at the top of the circular stair; to stress its importance, the actual door protrudes from the glass block facade. The door opens into the upper hall which is a corridor

The Ishihara Residence
Osaka, Japan
Tadao Ando and Associates

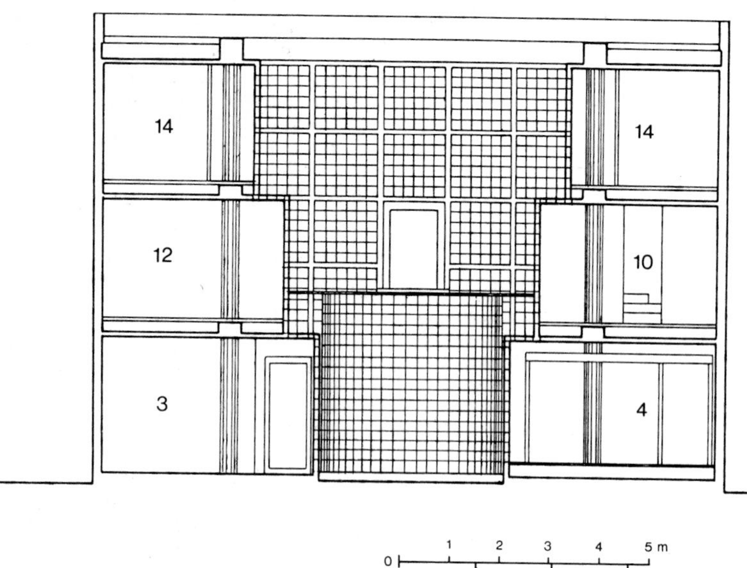

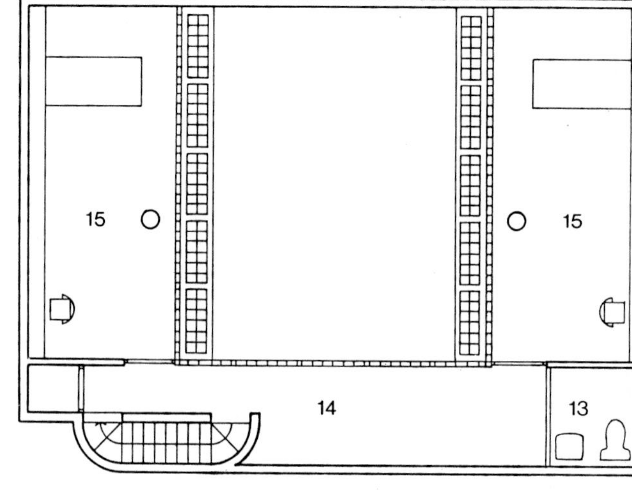

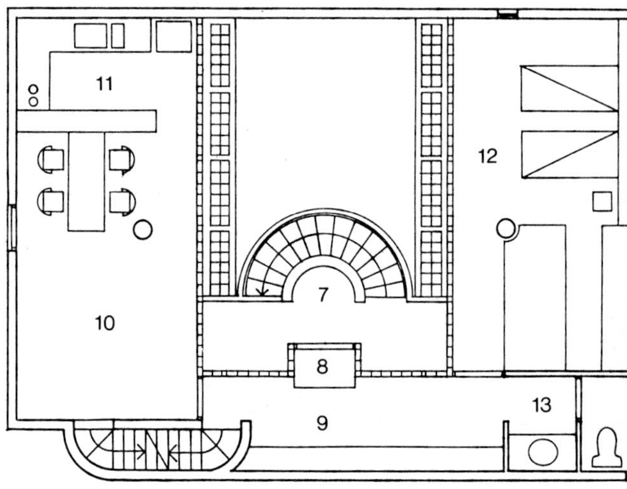

126
Section.

127
Plans of the first, second and third levels.
Key to plans and section
1 Main entrance
2 Entrance hall
3 Office
4 Tatami room
5 Courtyard
6 Bathroom
7 Terrace
8 Entrance to living accommodation
9 Upper hall
10 Living room
11 Kitchen
12 Master bedroom
13 Toilet
14 Sun room
15 Bedroom

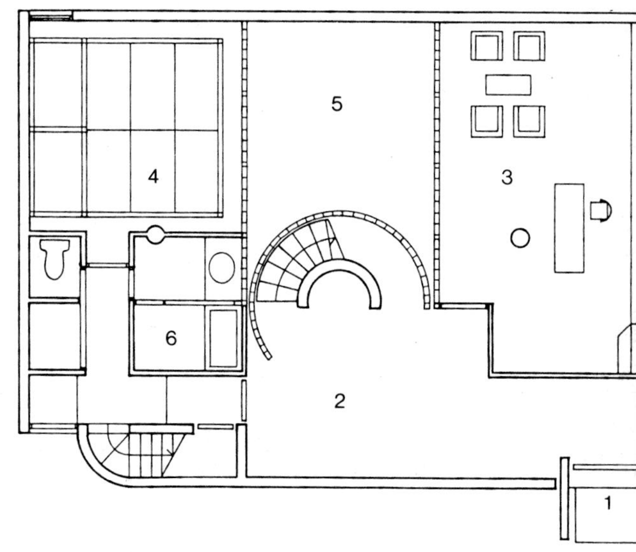

linking the main living and dining area with the owner's bedroom. The two sons' bedrooms, on the second floor, face each other across the court and are reached by a flight of stairs from the living room. The corridor connecting these two rooms is also used as a sun room. By means of the open court with rooms on three sides and the use of two staircases, Tadao Ando has managed to provide a remarkable degree of personal privacy for each inhabitant of the house within a restricted volume.

The main structure of the building is of in-situ reinforced concrete. Three sides of the court are constructed entirely of glass brick panels in a steel framework which steps back at each floor level. All materials used on the interior are left in their natural state: polished timber floors and built-in

128
The square and the circle, traditional Japanese shapes are combined in this view upwards from the courtyard.

129
A glimpse into the courtyard under the paper screens in the Tatami room. By isolating a small part of nature one can more easily appreciate the whole.

The Ishihara Residence
Osaka, Japan
Tadao Ando and Associates

130
The street entrance leads into a hall which is a semi- public space leading to th office and is partially ope to the elements.

131
The semi-circular staircas rising to the formal en- trance to the living accom modation. The paved floo is wet from rainwater en- tering via the stairwell.

132
View of the open plan living room with the dini area and kitchen on the left. The glass block walls to the courtyard fill the in teriors with diffused natu al light.

furniture, exposed concrete showing the impression of the formwork, and the glass blocks. The different patterns of the varying types of formwork on the ceiling, walls and circular columns, the boarded floors and the glass block walls create a rich decorative feeling with the simplest of materials, echoing the traditional Japanese interior.

The design of the house illustrates the ability of the Japanese to incorporate new ideas into their own culture. The Tatami Room surrounded by paper screens and divided by Tatami mats lives happily within the modern structure. The Tea Ceremony is still an important ritual in Japan and many modern homes retain these traditional

The Ishihara Residence
Osaka, Japan
Tadao Ando and Associates

133
The courtyard at night with the curved form of the staircase on the right. The plain glazed panels are opening windows for ventilating the rooms inside.

134
View of the centre of the house at dusk when the glass block walls reverse their function and fill the courtyard with diffused artificial light from the internal rooms.

rooms. The coexistence of opposing ideas is an important part of Japanese philosophy and the Ishihara Residence contains several such ambiguities. The internal court is a recurring device in Japanese architecture, and it can also be seen in Kisho Kurokawa's National Ethnological Museum in Osaka, being neither totally open nor totally enclosed. The stepped form of the open court walls in this particular building makes it an even more undefined space.

During the day the glass block walls filter light into all the rooms of the house, looking remarkably similar to traditional Japanese screens, and at night artificial light turns the glass blocks into illuminated screens enclosing the inner court.

The Citadel Theatre Edmonton, Alberta, Canada

Architects
Diamond, Myers and Wilkin
Design
Barton Myers and R.L. Wilkin

Implementation
Barton Myers Associates and R.L. Wilkin

Photography
John Fulker

The recently completed Citadel Theatre complex stands on a compact site in Edmonton's main civic area. The complex includes three auditoriums designed for a variety of theatrical events. The main theatre is the Shocter Theatre with seating for 685 people, which has an adjustable traditional proscenium arch. By arranging the seats in a wide arc and in a single block, without aisles, the architects have united the audience and brought every seat within 20m (65ft) of the stage. The Rice Theatre is a studio for experimental work and has a flexible seating arrangement for up to 200 people. The third performance space is the Zeidler Hall designed mainly as a cinema for 250 people but also used f[illegible] lectures and poetry readings.

Bisecting the building from north to south is a section of Edmonton pedestrian walkway system, which forms the circulation spine of the new bloc[illegible] All the public functions of the building are linked by this pedestrian mall, which gives direct access to the Zeidler Hall, to the Rice Theatre at a lower level and to the Shocter Theatre upstairs. The rake[illegible] seating of the Shocter auditorium is dramatically expressed in the stepped concrete ceiling of the mall. The new building was constructed over an existing underground car park, and pedestrians ca[illegible]

5
ew of the theatre in its
ic centre setting.

136
Section.

137
Plans at theatre lobby level and mall level.

Key to plans and section
1 Perimeter canopy
2 Pedestrian mall
3 Restaurant
4 Kitchen
5 Entrance to underground car park.
6 Cinema lobby
7 Cinema
8 Meeting rooms
9 Cloakroom
10 Box office
11 Theatre shop
12 Lift
13 Goods lift
14 Studio theatre
15 Upper part of studio theatre lobby
16 Sound and light rooms
17 Theatre lobby
18 Auditorium
19 Stage
20 Carpentry workshop
21 Dressing rooms
22 Rehearsal hall
23 Green room
24 Bar
25 Projection room
26 Fly tower
27 Plant room
28 Cooling tower
29 Lighting catwalk trusses
30 Ramp to workshop
31 Existing underground car park

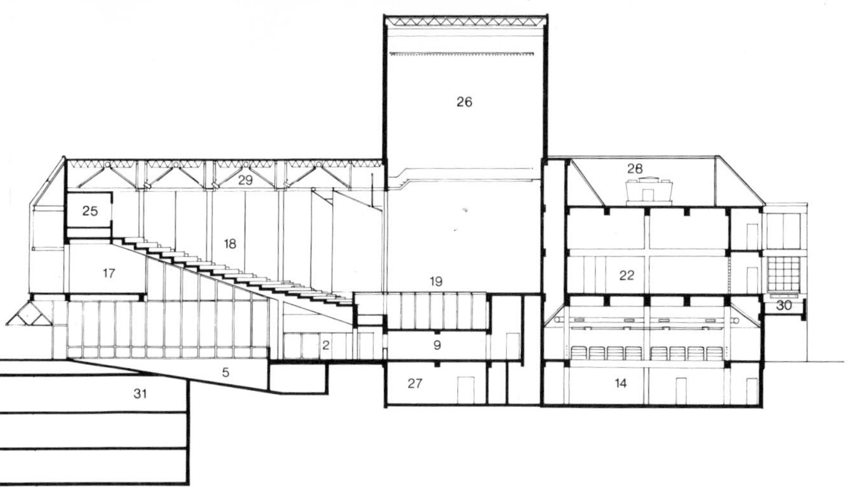

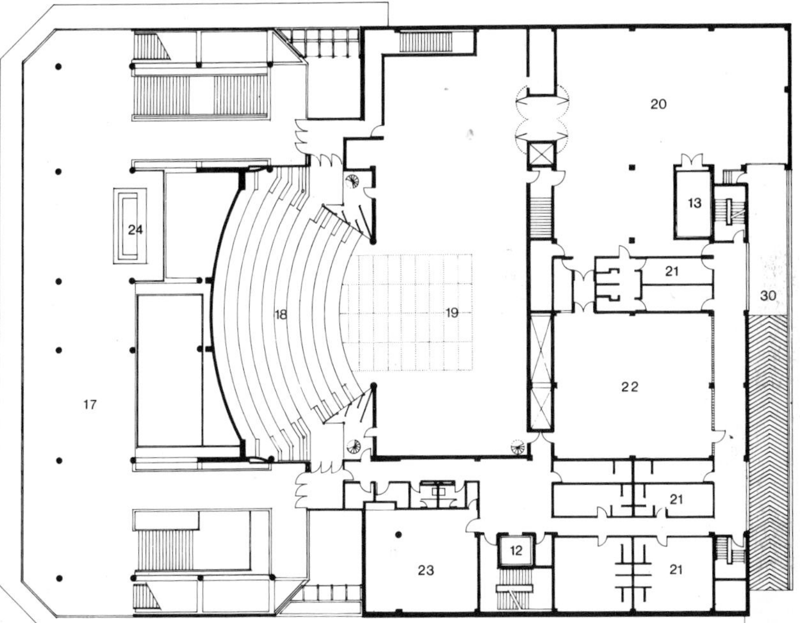

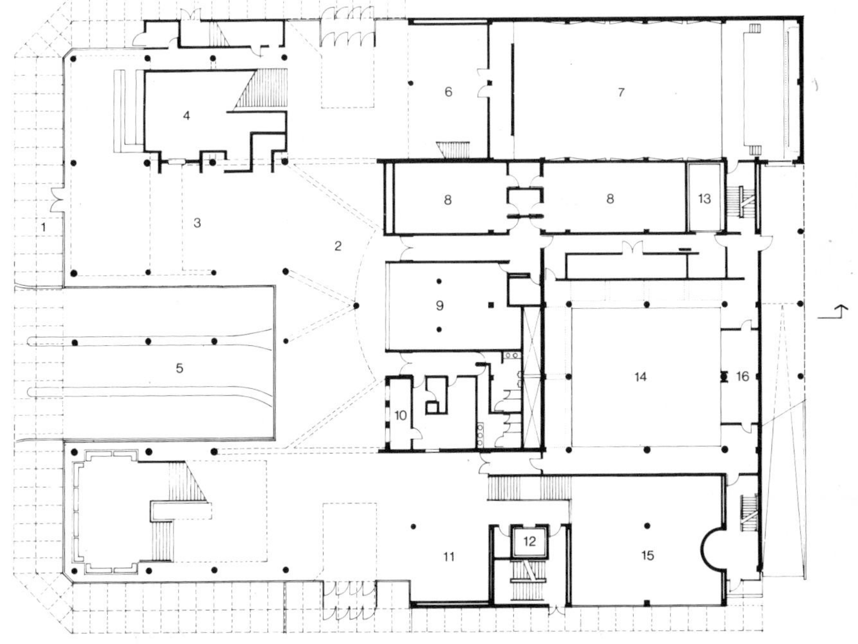

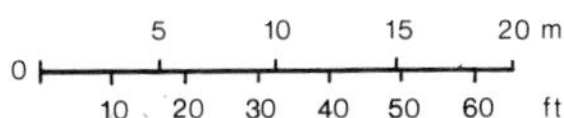

The Citadel Theatre
Edmonton, Alberta, Canada
Diamond, Myers and Wilkin

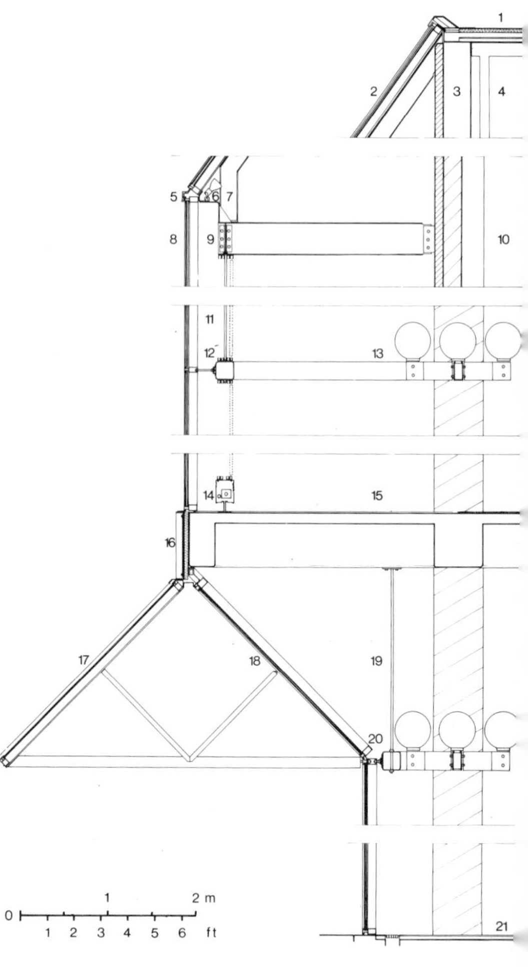

138
Corner detail. The pavement is sheltered by a glass canopy which runs round the building.

look down through windows along the mall onto the access ramps to the garage. Also contained in the central mall are the cloakroom, box office, theatre shop, and the restaurant which in summer can be opened through and onto the pavement. Barton Myers has created an internal street in the traditional sense: a multi-layered, linear space full of activity at all times of day from which open off recreational and living areas. This is in dramatic contrast to the banality of Edmonton's Civic Centre itself, where public buildings such as an art gallery and a library stand as separate entities, unrelated to each other, to the space surrounding them and to the people using them.

The back of house accommodation includes dressing rooms for fifty people, a green room, board room, a large rehearsal room and various workshops. Lorries can negotiate a ramp to the rear of the building up to workshop level from where assembled sets can move through a 6.5m (21ft) high acoustic lock into the wings.

The main structure of the building is a reinforced

39
ection through west
vall
Built-up felt roofing on
50mm (2in) Styrofoam
nsulation on 50mm
2in) concrete slab on
teel decking
Double-glazed skylight
vith aluminium
nullions
Reinforced concrete
ing beams
Roof truss
Heating cables
Artificial lighting
Steelwork to skylight
Double-glazed curtain
vall with aluminium
nullions
Perimeter beam with
racks for insulated
urtain on underside
Sound, projection and
ight rooms
9mm (¾in) diameter
teel suspension rod
20 × 20 (8in × 8in) steel
urtain wall bracing
Globe light fittings
nounted round 56
22in) diameter con-
rete column
Perimeter hot water fin
ube radiation cabinet
obby
Steel spandrel panel
vith Styrofoam insula-
on backing
xterior glass canopy
vith aluminium
nullions
Double-glazed interior
anopy
9mm (¾in) diameter
uspension rod
20 × 20 (8in × 8in) steel
urtain wall bracing
vith 10 × 20 (4in × 8in)
teel brace to concrete
olumn
treet level

40
heatre lobby. The visitor
moves through a complex
eries of spaces before
eaching the auditorium.

concrete frame encased on the west front by an aluminium and glass curtain wall supported by a hollow section steel frame to form the large lobby to the Shocter Theatre. Steel stairs and walkways which give access to the lobby are suspended from large, hollow section steel beams which are also air distribution ducts. Spanning across the main auditorium are twinned trusses constructed from hollow structural steel sections. A continuous metal grid fixed across the base of the trusses forms a network of catwalks for maintaining and adjusting the lighting.

141
The pedestrian mall at night.

142
The theatre bar in the interval. The stepped form of the ceiling is due to the auditorium seating above

L1
L2

The Citadel Theatre
Edmonton, Alberta, Canada
Diamond, Myers and Wilkin

143
Main auditorium. Redwood boarding and red velvet upholstery create a warm festive interior.

144
Detail of the proscenium arch which is composed of adjustable panels.

The Citadel Theatre
Edmonton, Alberta, Canada
Diamond, Myers and Wilkin

145
The theatre lobby at night. Exposed brick and concrete, steel roof decking, brass handrails and light fittings, glass balustrading and globes, and red carpet create a sparkling theatrical interior.

Building materials are left in their natural state throughout the building. This meant that a high level of workmanship had to be maintained with regard to brickwork, structural steel, concrete, steel decking and ductwork, and in the end proves to be a more expensive solution than the more traditional plaster and suspended ceilings method.

On the exterior of the building the main finish is a pressed red brick from Medicine Hat, Alberta, which was formerly part of the Edmonton vernacular. The aluminium curtain walling glazing bars are painted to match and some areas are clad with insulated panels of porcelain enamelled steel. Red brick is also used in the interior, complemented by unglazed red clay floor tiles in the pedestrian mall. All internal steelwork is painted to match the brick, and together with the red carpet and redwood doors continue as closely as possible the monochrome theme. To give the interiors some theatrical sparkle a material common to all traditional theatre interiors has been utilised: brass. This is to be found in the handrails, hardware and light fittings. The theme continues into the main auditorium which has plush red velvet seats and walls and ceiling panelled with redwood. Where the panelling need to absorb sound, the panels are slotted and lined with an acoustic quilt. Some degree of flexibility can be achieved in the acoustics by varying the area of absorbent material behind the ceiling panels.

The building is heated by gas fired hot water boilers which supply fin tube convectors beneath glazed areas and a high volume, low speed ducted ventilation system to the theatres. Although the elevations are extensively glazed, the majority of the glass encloses a comparatively small area, less than twelve per cent of the total building volume, around the solid concrete and brick block of the main auditorium. An insulating quilted curtain is to be provided across the main glazed area in the lobby to reduce energy loss at night and when the theatre is closed. The curtains will be drawn back behind the porcelain enamelled steel panels, on the north and south walls of the lobby.

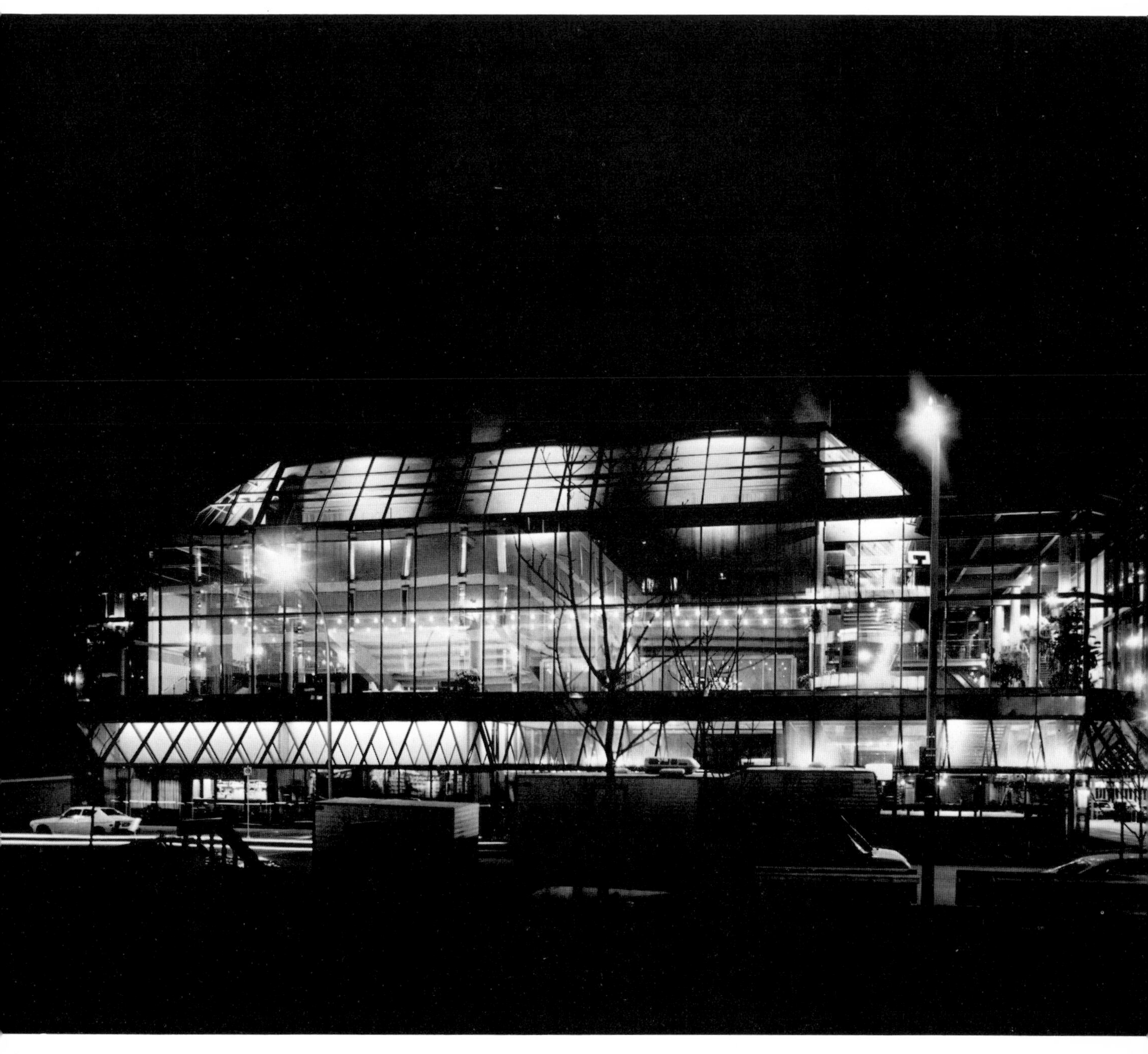

46
'iew of the exterior at
ight.

Finnjet: The Travemünde-Helsinki Passenger Ferry, Finland

Architects
Oy Wärtsilä Ltd Project Team

Interior Designers
Studio Nurmesniemi
Torsten & Vuokko Laakso
Oy Sistem

Photography
Wärtsilä

Following a study of future passenger traffic on the ferry service between Finland and Germany, commissioned by Finnlines Ltd in the late 1960s, it was planned to build one 'super ferry' which would serve the place of three conventional ferries. In 1973, Oy Wärtsilä Ltd were given the order for *Finnjet*.

One of the main requirements for the new ship was speed. Finnlines planned to operate a regular schedule with a journey time of twenty-two hours between Helsinki and Travemünde and two hours' allowance for turn round in port. A speed of thirty knots was needed to maintain this schedule, and this was one of the reasons that gas turbine propulsion was chosen.

Gas turbine engines modified for marine use have been used previously in ships as diverse as container vessels, ice breakers and battleships, but this is the first time that they have been utilized in a passenger ferry. The benefits of this system over the conventional diesel engine system are a smaller size and comparative lightness. If diesel engines had been used, their extra displacement of 3000 tons would have required an output of 90,000hp (66MW), whereas each of the two gas turbines develops 37,500hp (27.6MW) to drive the ship. To

147
The Finnjet underway at sea. The ship has a square practical line expressing her primary function of a short haul ferry.

148
Elevation.

149
Plans of decks numbers 2, 3, 4, 5, and 6.

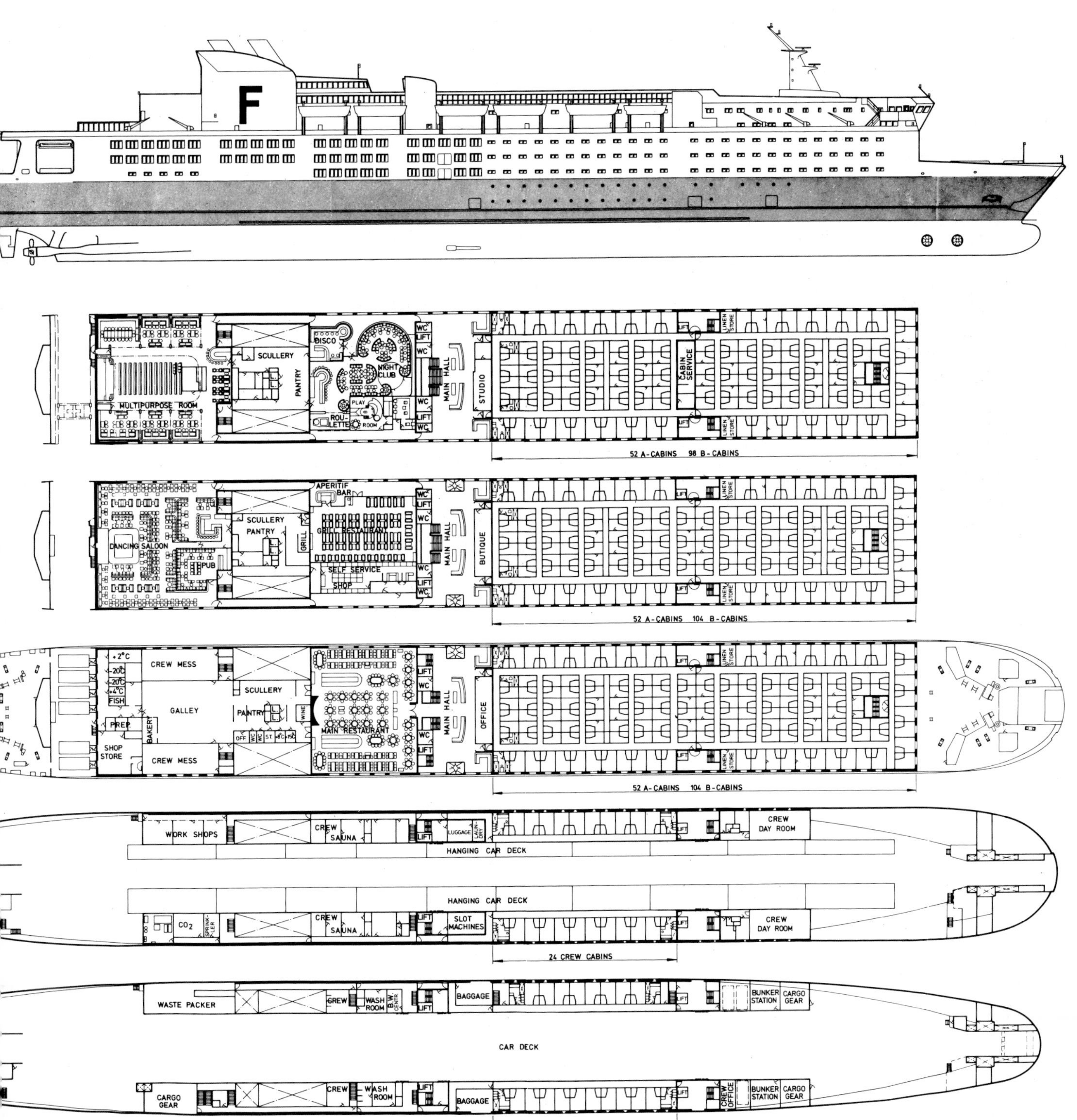

)
central hall on deck 5. the right is a shop and he left stairs and lifts ich connect all decks.

main dining room on k 4 designed by Antti rmesniemi. At each side he room are large self- vice counters.

2
e of the simply fur- hed cabins for four ople. Upper bunks pull wn at night by means of handles visible on the nt wall.

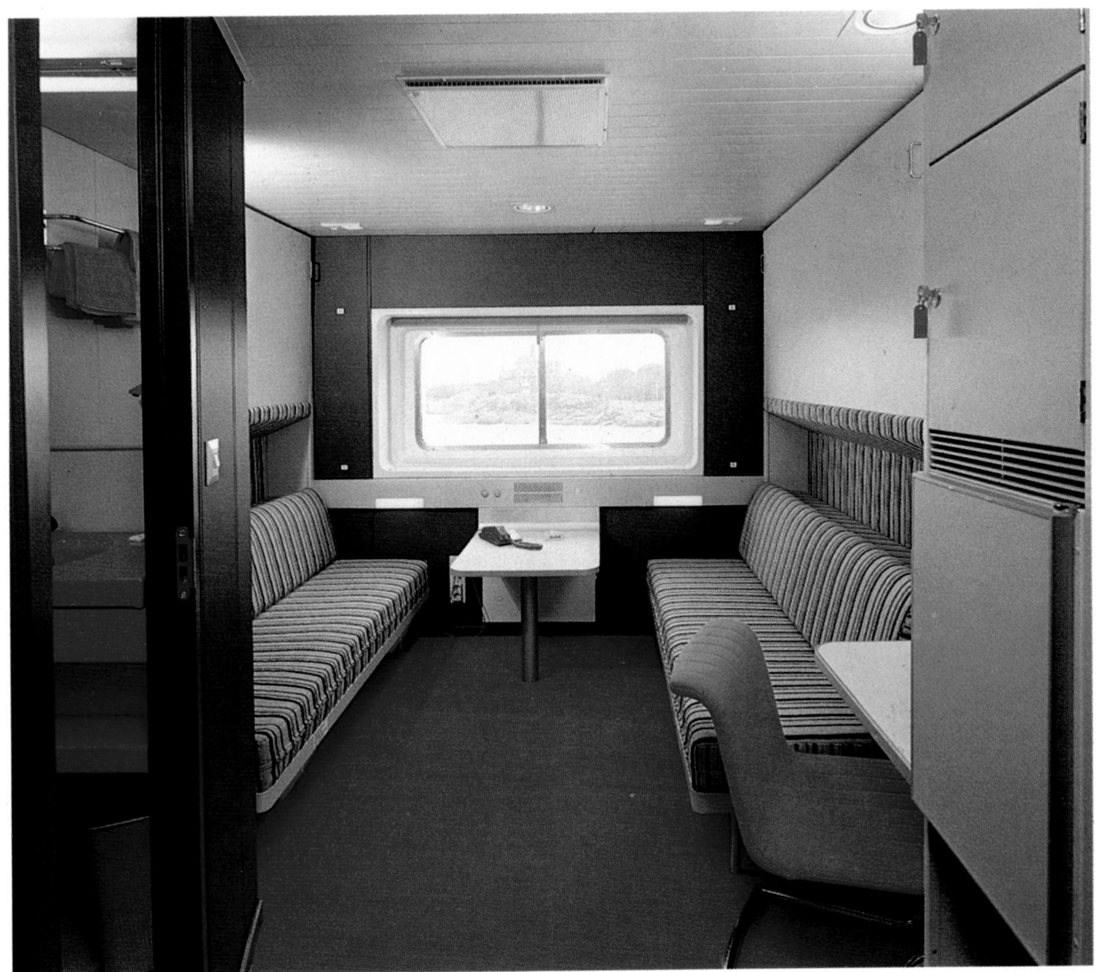

save further space, lifting gear in the engine room enables a turbine to be lifted out onto the car deck so that this area can be used for maintenance. The air intake for the turbines is located aft of the funnels on Deck 10, to reduce the seawater content in the air. The intake ducts are 9sq.m (96.88sq.ft) in section and incorporate a three-stage demister arrangement to ensure that no seawater or dirt reaches the turbines. The ducts also have built-in silencers as do the 3m (9ft 10in) diameter exhaust ducts, which are carried up to the two funnels. Wind tunnel tests were conducted when the funnels were designed, to ensure that fumes did not enter the decks or the air intakes. Electrical power is supplied by five diesel generators, and two low pressure steam boilers provide a heating supply. The air conditioning plant is situated on Deck 7, between the passengers and the officers accommodation, a solution which reduces the length of the vertical air distribution ducts. All the machinery is continually monitored by computer.

To guarantee the running of a tight sailing schedule, all major mechanical systems are duplicated. Each turbine drives a completely independent propulsion plant; if either system fails the ship is still capable of twenty-four knots on one turbine. In addition, all important items such as pumps, filters and separators are doubled within each

system, forming an automatic stand-by system. A third gas generator is kept as a spare.

The design of the hull was a further important consideration in securing the maximum efficiency of the ship. A very slender hull, 200m (656ft 2in) long with a bulbous bow was developed after extensive tests. The port of Helsinki and the majority of the Baltic are under ice for many months of the year, so the hull of *Finnjet* incorporates extra strengthening to meet these conditions. The high degree of spray when travelling at high speed in a wind, as well as the often freezing conditions, have necessitated the closing in of most of the upper decks.

The fast turn round in port has required special planning of all stages of fuelling and supplying the ship. All food and sales goods are packed, ready-sorted into distribution trolleys and brought on-board in containers by the ship special container crane. One of the provision containers carrying beer and soft drinks in bulk is directly connected t the distribution pipe system and pumped direct to the various bars in the ship.

In addition to size and speed characteristics, *Finnjet* can be said to be environmentally safe. Its gas turbines will not pollute the air and noise is kept low. No waste is dumped into the sea; all sol waste is compressed and taken ashore. A new

153
The dancing saloon on deck 5 designed by Vuokko Laakso. The majority of steel columns on the ferry are clad with an aluminium sleeve formed from three curved sections which clip together leaving almost invisible joints.

154
The sky bar on deck 9 which leads out onto the sky deck, the only open area on the ship available to passengers apart from the boat deck promenade.

155
The lighthouse bar situated on deck 10. The bar is reached by means of a spiral stair from the sky bar. Its extensive glazing offers views over the sea in all directions.

156
The children's playroom on deck 6 designed by Oy Sistem and Arto Kukkasniemi. A playful nautical air pervades the room with its 'rigging' to climb on and its own diminutive ship with a brid and wheel.

157
The swimming pool on deck 1 designed by Oy Sistem and Yrjö Wegelius. Adjacent to the main pool are a small circular cold plunge pool (centre) and solarium (right).

158
The sauna on deck 1 designed by Oy Sistem and Yrjö Wegelius.

sewage system has been developed, based on the use of an air vacuum as the transportation medium, instead of the usual water medium. Each flushing action utilises only 1.21lt (2pts) of water compared with 10–15lt (2–3 gallons) used in a conventional system. The sewage is then treated biologically and chemically and the small amount of remaining sludge is disposed of ashore.

Access to the car deck on Decks 2 and 3 is via a door in the transom stern. The deck itself is flexible to cater for a varying proportion of lorries to cars by raising or lowering mezzanine floors. *Finnjet* is also fitted with a bow visor to allow drive-through operations.

Access to the ship for passengers on foot is at two levels on Decks 4 and 5, just aft of mid-ships, into a hall containing the main staircase and lifts to all levels. A colour coding system is designed to facilitate circulation: the traditional colours of red to port and green to starboard are used and the theme is carried through to items such as boarding tickets and cabin key tags. A simple system of symbols has been adopted to indicate the location of the public areas.

The unusual planning of the passenger accommodation is another innovatory concept in this ship. All 1532 passengers are housed in cabins for two or four persons, and the majority of these are placed in the forward section of the superstructure on Decks 4, 5 and 6. This ensures that noise and vibration in the cabins are kept to a minimum, as the machinery is located as far aft as possible. The

Finnjet: The Travemünde-Helsinki Passenger Ferry
Oy Wärtsilä

159
The officers' dayroom. The high quality furnishings of the passenger accommodation are maintained throughout the crew's quarters.

vertical arrangement of the cabins simplifies the ducting of services. Each cabin has two sofa-beds, WC and shower, a refrigerator, a telephone and radio, adjustable air conditioning and a facility for television. The two person cabins are 8sq.m (86.11sq.ft) in area, the four person cabins are 12sq.m (129.17sq.ft). In addition there is some low-cost accommodation on Deck 1, below the ca deck.

The main public spaces, situated aft, include a conference centre for up to 377 people. This area i planned with a central 125 seat congress room, which also serves as a cinema. Each seat is fitted with audio facilties for translation. To either side o this space are areas which can be divided up by sound-proof folding partitions for smaller meetings or be used as part of the central space. Restaurants lounges, bars and a sauna complete the facilities offered by this highly sophisticated ship.

0
as turbine engine
ir inlet
ow pressure compressor
igh pressure com-
essor
ombustion chambers
urbines
ower turbine
xhaust outlet
ower take-off

1
as turbine machinery
as turbine
ir inlet chamber
ir filters
ypass channel
ir vent and sound
ampers
xhaust vent and sound
ampers
eduction gear
isengaging couplings
ariable pitch propeller
itch control device

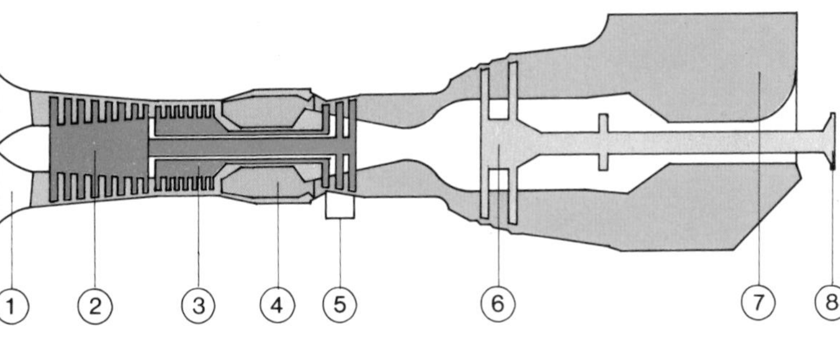

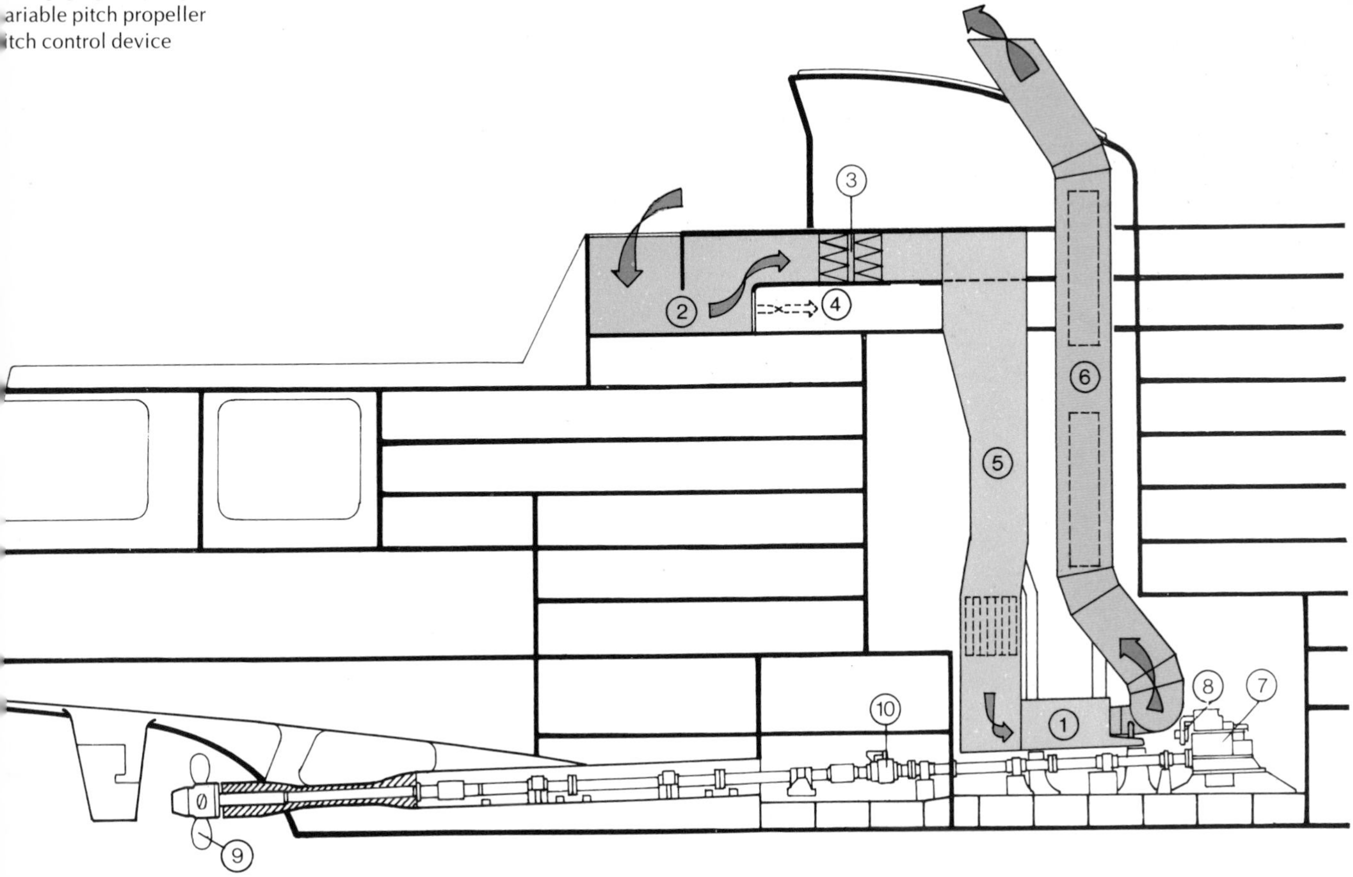

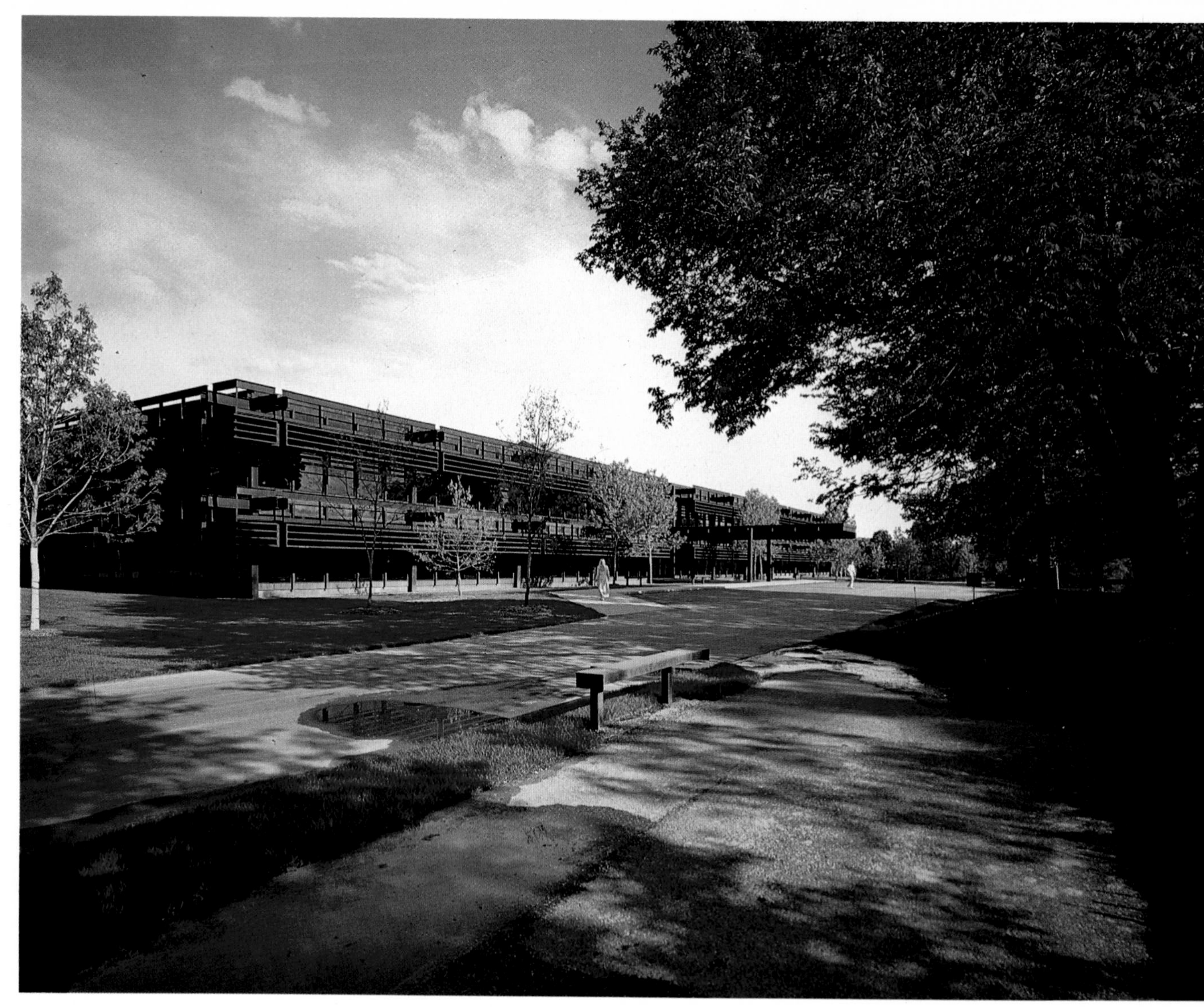

The West Office Building for Deere & Co
Moline, Illinois, USA

Architects
Kevin Roche,
John Dinkeloo
and Associates

Photography
Alexandre Georges

In the 1950s, both Kevin Roche and John Dinkeloo were closely involved with Eero Saarinen in the design of the Administrative Centre for Deere and Company, which was completed in 1964, three years after Saarinen's death. Saarinen ran his office on very liberal lines: he was prepared to delegate considerable responsibility, even to an active participation in the design process. It was therefore a great challenge to Kevin Roche and John Dinkeloo when they were asked to extend the Administrative Centre. Their brief was to add 20,000sq.m (200,000sq.ft) of office space for 900 employees to the original 30,000sq.m (300,000sq.ft).

Saarinen's original buildings comprise the main office building and, to the east, the Product Display building and the Auditorium. These two buildings are connected by an enclosed pedestrian bridge which leaves the main building at third floor level. Roche and Dinkeloo decided to position the new block to the west of the main building and connect it to the existing building by a similar footbridge, on the same axis and at the same level as the original bridge. It is not surprising that the new West Office building is in complete harmony with its neighbour. This is partly because they both utilise Corten steel, a material which eventually builds up a

162
The new office block seen from the west. This is the vehicular access and a porte-cochere is provided seen on the right.

163
Site plan
1 West office building
2 Main building

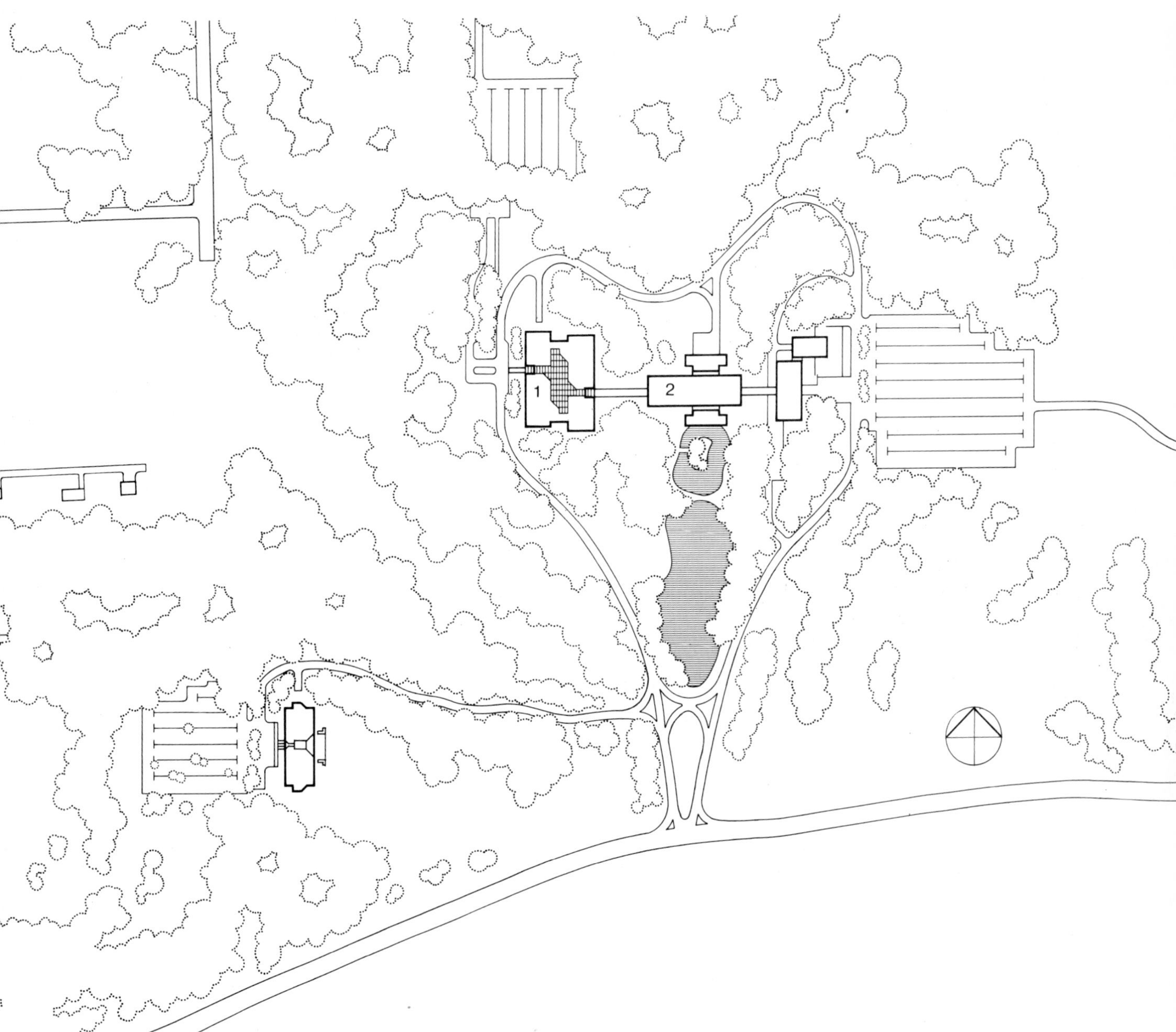

rust-coloured, corrosion-resistant outer layer.

The formal axis set by the existing buildings penetrates the new building and is then broken by a strong diagonal. It is here, in the heart of the new office, that one finds a remarkable contrast with the 1964 building. The rigid grid of the structure is prised apart to create a large indoor garden, approximately 1100sq.m (11,000sq.ft) in area, which extends upwards to the full three storeys of the building to finish in an arched roof, fully glazed with solar glass. The garden brings life and interest to the adjoining open plan office areas and, in one corner, the cafeteria flows out into the atrium.

Across the centre of the garden, at first floor level, is a diagonal bridge which carries the main pedestrian route over the garden before terminating in the main entrance and reception area for the West Office building. The architects took particular care over designing the planting layout of the garden. Trees such as weeping figs, coffee and southern yews, together with smaller shrubs and plants, form the permanent planting. The relatively low level of light in the atrium meant that the trees had to be gradually conditioned to their new environment before being finally introduced into the indoor garden.

The Citicorp Centre
New York, USA

Architects
Hugh Stubbins and Associates Inc

Photography
George Cserna, Cervin Robinson

Among Manhattan's first skyscrapers and the more recent anonymous blocks clad in black steel and tinted glass, stands a sleek and gleaming newcomer: the Citicorp Centre. This project is an early example of New York's 'incentive zoning' policy, whereby the provision of public space at pavement level is traded for an increase in the permitted development of office floor area. The Centre comprises a 59-storey office tower, a seven-storey podium block, with a central atrium and three-storey shopping mall, St Peter's Lutheran Church, and a sunken plaza which gives direct access to the city subway.

To open up the space at ground level the tower i raised up on four piers, 34.7m (114ft) above street level. This allows the church, on its corner site, to appear independent from the mass of the bulding.

The large amount of space for public amenities on the lower levels has been made possible by the brilliant structural design of the tower. The four, 7.3m (24ft) square piers are not, as one would expect, at the corners of the square tower but in th middle of each elevation. Massive structural steel chevron bracing supports the floors off the piers in a series of six 8-storey high triangles. These feed th wind load and half the mass of the tower into four

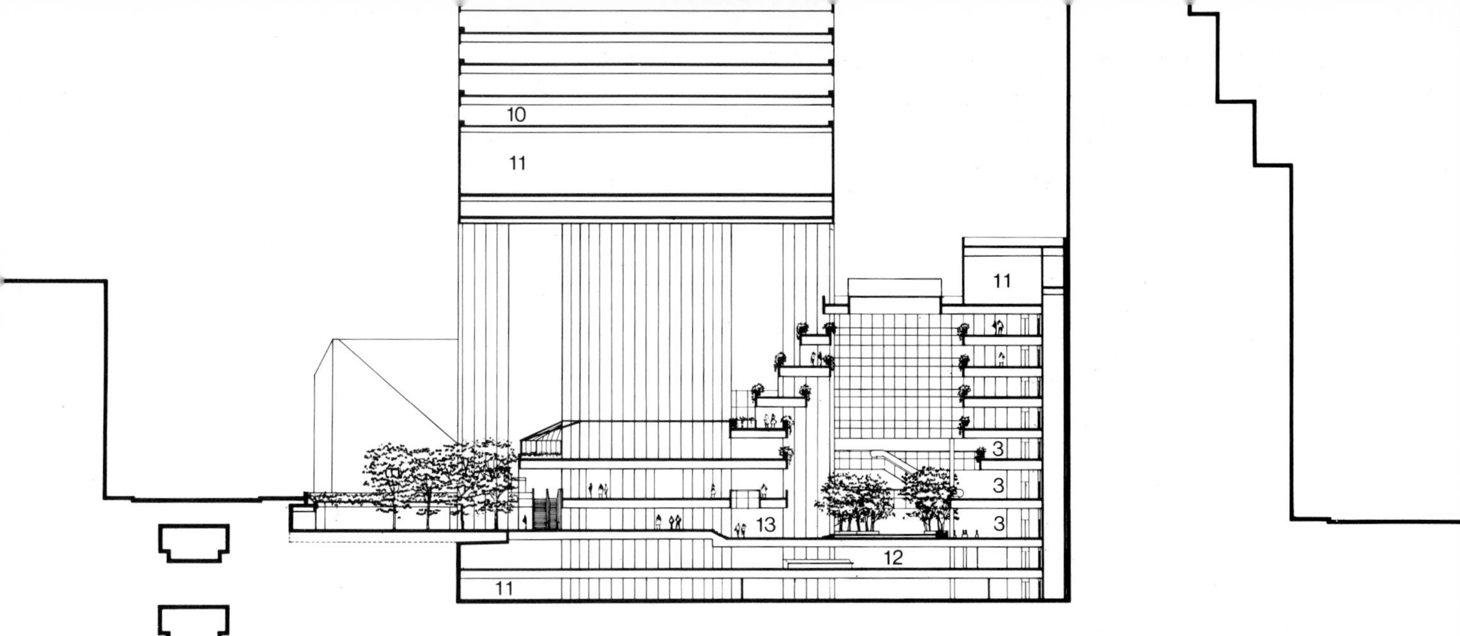

72
:. Peter's Lutheran Church
'ouches below the north-
est corner of the tower.
o further emphasize its
ndependence from the
ommercial values which
e tower represents, the
hurch is clad in granite in
arked contrast to the
ass and aluminium of the
wer.

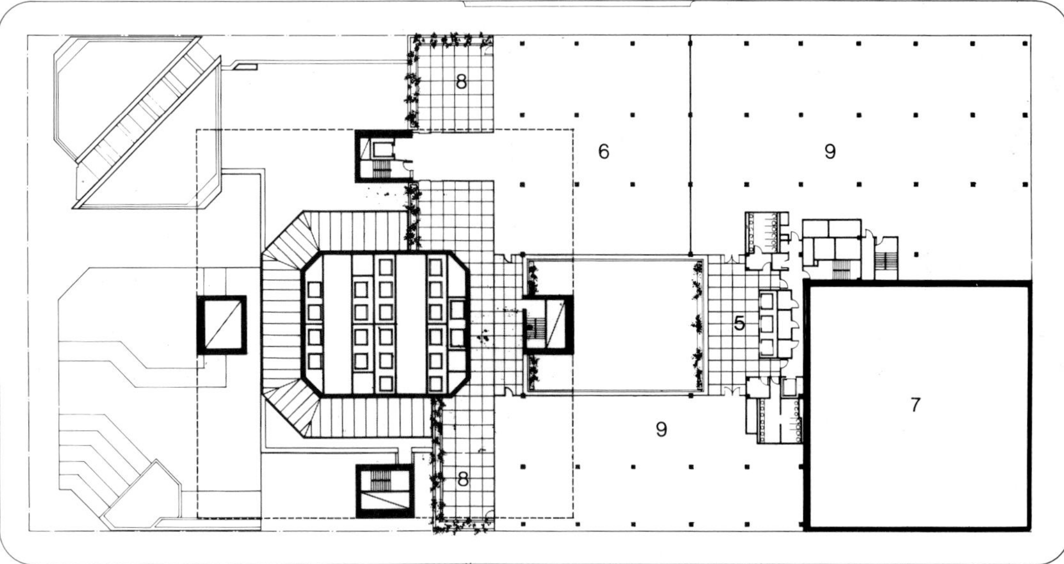

73
ection of lower part of
entre.

74
ans of street level and
ird level.
ey to plans and section
tairs from pavement
own to main con-
ourse
rcade
hops
ervice bay
ifts
hurch
xisting building
errace
xecutive offices
ffices
lechanical
estaurant
lain concourse

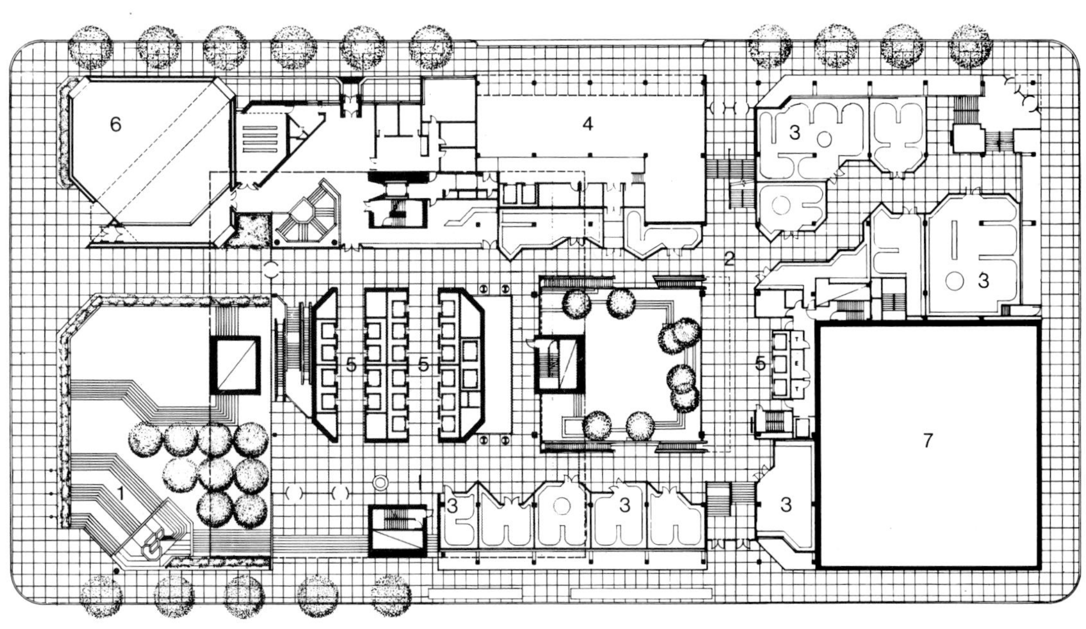

The Citicorp Centre
New York, USA
Hugh Stubbins and Associates

175
Section through the tower showing the principal structure.

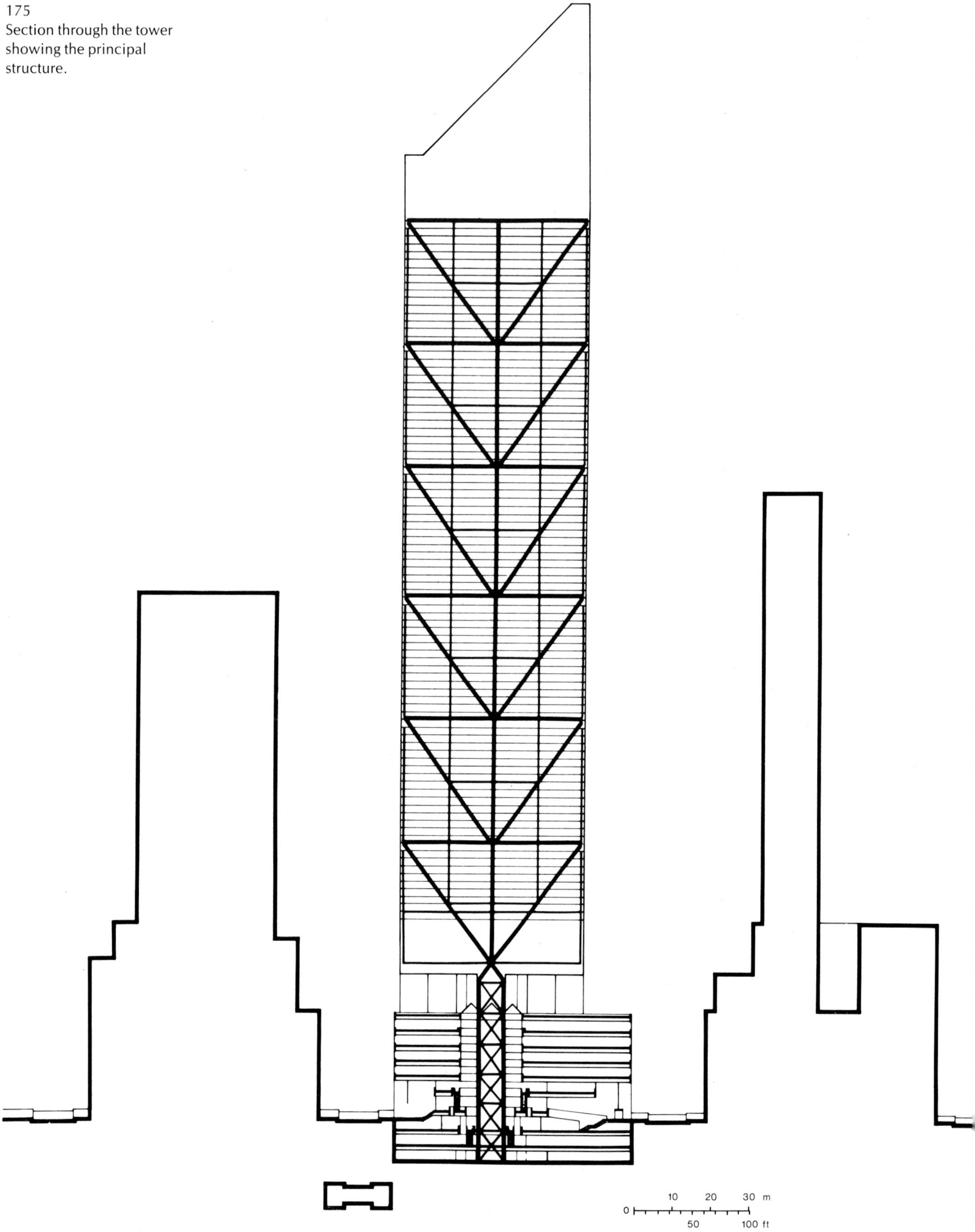

10 20 30 m
0
50 100 ft

.5m (5ft) wide mast columns which connect to the iers. The remaining half of the mass is carried by ie central service core. Foundations to the tower o down 15m (50ft) to solid bedrock. The piers iemselves could have been designed to appear iuch thinner, but were expanded to allow for uctwork and stairs. Floors are of steel decking /ith a concrete screed. It is to be regretted that lugh Stubbins chose not to express the diagonal racing on the exterior of the tower: hiding the iassive steel cross members behind the facade iakes them appear more intrusive in the context of iterior spaces. The great benefit of this structural rrangement, apart from being extremely economi-al in its use of structural steel, is that it creates ompletely unobstructed interior space. Each floor i the tower has an area of 2270sq.m (24,400sq.ft) nd is served by a square central core containing levators, lavatories, vertical ducts, store rooms nd fire escape stairs. Around the core is uninter-upted office space 14m (45ft) deep.

One of the most revolutionary features of the ew tower is the tuned mass damper, which has een developed to increase the comfort of occup-nts of high-rise buildings by reducing the swaying iotion caused by high winds. At the Citicorp entre the damper consists of a 400 ton block of oncrete, which is equivalent to half of one per ent of the mass of the building, located at the top f the tower within the slanting crown. The block is iounted on oil bearings and is connected to the teel frame of the tower by a series of pneumatic istons. When the building moves, the block re-iains momentarily stationary then sways in the pposite direction. The pistons can be tuned to the atural frequency of the building by bleeding or dding nitrogen to the pneumatic pistons. By this ieans the acceleration of the tower, due to iotion, has been reduced by approximately 40 per ent.

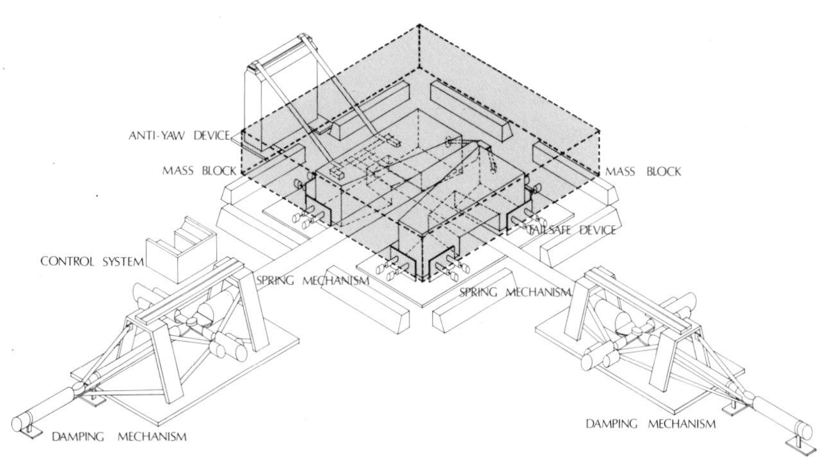

176
View of the tuned mass damper.

177
Diagram of the tuned mass damper mechanism.

The Citicorp Centre
New York, USA
Hugh Stubbins and Associates

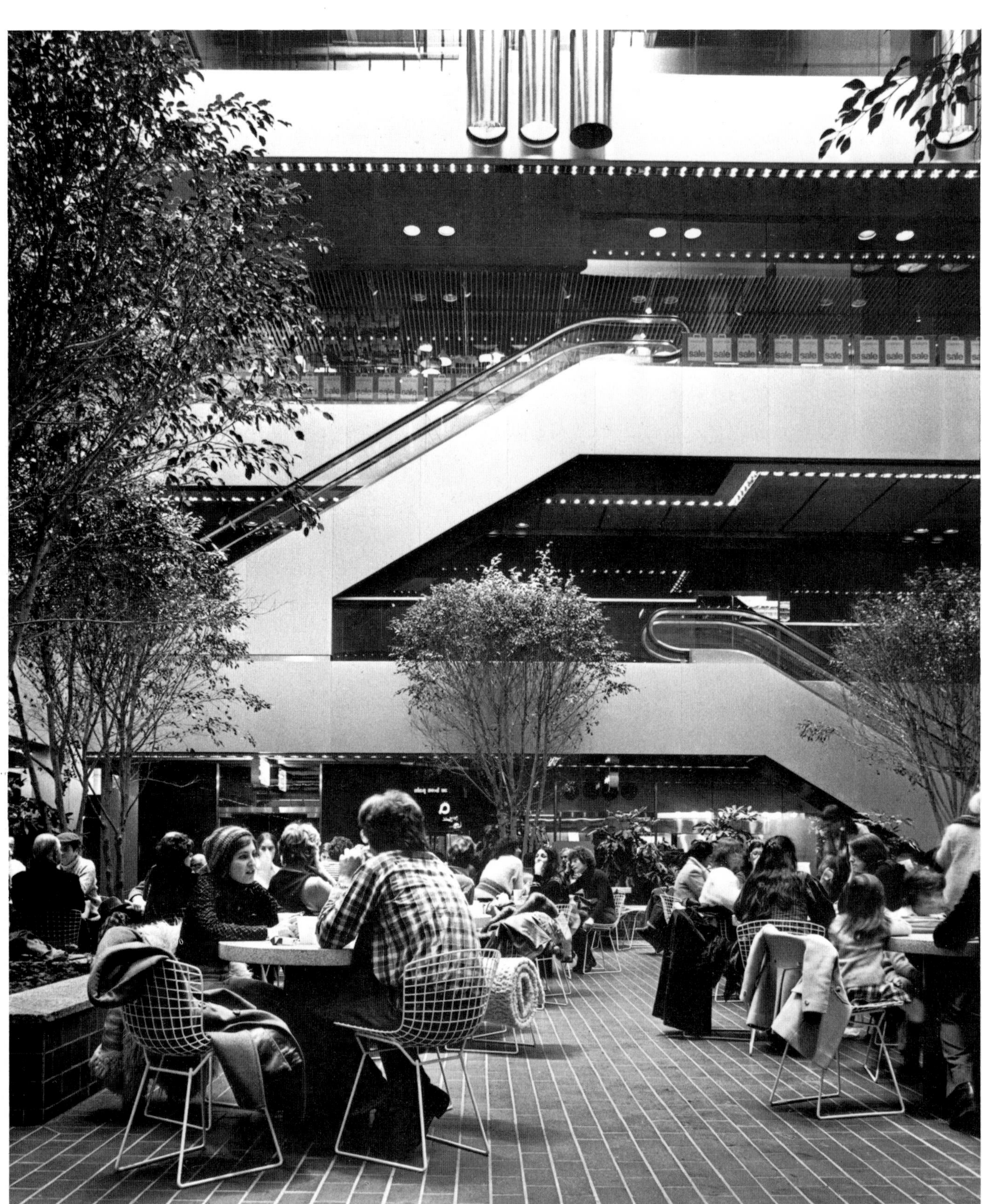

Hugh Stubbins, architect of the development, es the earlier skyscrapers as expressions of the achine cult, of relentless commerce, and he has ttempted a solution which relates more to the dividual.

Under the tower itself is a seven storey low-rise lock, with a skylit atrium which is New York's first r conditioned covered pedestrian space. The ain concourse, set 4.26m (14ft) below street level nd directly connected to the city subway, is a 36sq.m (9000sq.ft) sunken plaza with a land- caped courtyard containing nine 7.6m (25ft) tall ees. Shops and restaurants open off this space on iree levels. In part because many of the buildings orn down to make way for the Centre housed estaurants of several nationalities and price range, was decided that the new mall should be devoted ainly to food. There are now Hungarian, Swiss nd Greek restaurants among others, a patisserie nd boulangerie and a bookshop specializing in ookery books. Wide flights of steps cascade down om the corner of Lexington Avenue and East 53rd treet to the concourse. A large water sculpture arks this main entrance and helps neutralise the affic noise. Brick pavers are continued from the avement down the steps and used throughout the hopping mall to unite the interior spaces with the xterior. Under the trees are chairs and tables at vhich anyone may sit to eat their own food. etween East 53rd and 54th Streets, a shopping rcade runs through the atrium at street level. All nese features contribute to the resounding success f this space, which is crowded at all times of day.

178
The atrium. The central space is kept constantly alive by making it the hub of a busy shopping precinct specializing in food.

179
Looking down into the atrium from the pedestrian mall at street level. Materials used on the exterior of the building continue inside: terra-cotta brick pavers on the pavements and plaza extend into the shopping areas and the walls around the atrium are clad in aluminium panels similar to those outside.

180
The sanctuary of St. Peter's Church seen from the balcony. All church furnishings and fixtures were designed by Massimo and Lella Vignelli. The colourful geometric needlepoint cushions are being executed to their design by members of the congregation.

181
The altar, seen here in its traditional position, can be placed anywhere and the movable oak pews rearranged accordingly.

Another very important humanizing factor on this particular site was the existence of St Peter's Lutheran Church, which has stood at the corner of Lexington Avenue and East 54th Street since 1902. St Peter's is one of the most successful urban churches in America mainly due to the Reverend Ralph Peterson who organizes jazz concerts, and even jazz masses in the church. Duke Ellington used to give an annual concert there, and nowadays there are frequent late afternoon jazz performances. In 1969 the congregation voted to sell the property to the First National City Bank on condition that a new church would be built on the same site. Reverend Peterson also insisted that the new development should be a place where ordinary citizens could shop, eat and relax as well as worship.

The interior of the church relates directly to the outside: the sanctuary floor is one storey below pavement level and a large window allows pedestrians on Lexington Avenue to look down into the magnificent interior, and to be attracted inside the church. Because of the varied functions held in the church, the seating has been designed to be totally flexible. Around the perimeter of the sanctuary is a series of large oak-faced steps. The top sections of these steps are hinged and can be opened, revealing upholstered cushions, to form the backs of additional pews. The central pews with fold-down kneelers, the altar and pulpit are all movable, so that the floor can be cleared for performances requiring a completely free space. A sophisticated lighting grid has been incorporated just below the skylight.

The Citicorp Centre
New York, USA
Hugh Stubbins and Associates

Hugh Stubbins and Associates have, in the past, advised their clients on the commissioning and collecting of works of art. For this particular project, they were responsible for Louise Nevelson being awarded a major commission for the Chapel of the Good Shepherd which adjoins the main church. She has designed a series of wooden relief panels for the walls on the themes of the Apostles, the Resurrection, the Holy Trinity and the Cross of the Good Shepherd. All the scriptures are painted white as is the rest of the room, apart form the background and horizontal bar of the crucifix which are covered in gold leaf, providing the only colour in the room and focusing attention on the simple altar. After the turmoil of the street of central New York only yards away, the cool contemplative interior is a welcome relief to the city dweller seeking a moment for meditation and prayer.

182
The Chapel of the Good Shepherd looking towards the altar.

183
The Cross of the Good Shepherd provides the focal point of the simple white interior.

The Citicorp Centre
New York, USA
Hugh Stubbins and Associates

At 279m (914ft), Citicorp is the seventh tallest building in New York and the tallest bank building in the world. On its top it has a 49m (160ft) high distinctive sloping crown. In a preliminary scheme this was to house 100 apartments, each with an enclosed balcony facing south, but this was not granted a zoning variation. In a later scheme the feasibility of installing solar collectors on the sloping face was examined but, at the present state of technology, was found to be economically unjustifiable. It remains, however, a future possibility. The form was therefore retained and now contains cooling towers and mechanical equipment. The structural steel frame is clad with a curtain wall which is 56 per cent aluminium backed by 50mm (2in) Thermofibre insulation and 44 per cent double-glazed insulated reflective glass. The unusually low ratio of glass area to aluminium area, to reflect direct sunlight, keeps the building cool in summer and warm in winter. Glass and aluminium spandrels are on the same plane on the exterior face to allow the automatic washing machinery to keep the building shining clean.

Citicorp Centre has been designed to use considerably less energy than similar buildings of more conventional construction and savings have been conservatively estimated at 42 per cent. Apart from the curtain wall there are several other energy conserving features. Heat generated by light, people and office equipment is recycled and provides enough heat for the entire building until the outside temperature falls below freezing. An energy storage system was considered but was found to be too expensive in terms of the rental space it would have displaced in Manhattan. A high-efficiency, low-brightness, single tube fluorescent light fitting has been designed for use throughout the building to reduce the consumption of electricity while maintaining the high lighting levels required by the modern office user.

All mechanical operations, including air conditioning, the sprinkler system and the elevators, are controlled by a central computer whose advanced technology can help save energy by making the various systems more efficient. Citibank has capitalized on the efficient plant of their new building by connecting it to their existing headquarters building across Lexington Avenue. At peak loads the plant only serves the new building, but for 80 per cent of the time it can supply the demands of both. To save space, as well as reduce energy consumption, Citicorp has twenty double-deck elevators, serving odd floors from street level and even floors from concourse level.

184
St. Peter's Church on the corner of Lexington Avenue and 54th Street. The street level entrance is on the right. The church can also be entered from the concourse level one storey below at the same level as the sanctuary floor.

185
The tower in its Manhattan setting: its facade treatment contrasting with the less energy-conscious design of a neighbouring block.

Elements of Architecture: Light
Pieter de Bruyne

Licht und Finsternis führen einen bestandingen Streit miteinander.
J.W. Goethe

Light is so fundamental that it has come to symbolise life itself just as its opposite, darkness, symbolises death.

We are influenced by the gradations in light which, almost unperceived, alter our moods. The sharpest contrasts in light and shade are associated with joy and sorrow: we associate bright, glittering light with festivities and freedom, but in times of sorrowful happenings we seek darkness. Between these extreme situations infinite gradations occur, sometimes brutally, sometimes imperceptibly altering out inner tranquillity.

Despite its immaterial and intangible nature, light is inseparable from the notion of architecture. For, beside structural and functional properties, architecture can call forth an aesthetic response, create an atmosphere and generate emotions through the use of light as one of its fundamental elements.

Metaphysical and philosophical as well as symbolic and scientific interpretations of light regularly appear in architecture and frequently have a great impact. From the very beginning of architecture, temples, churches, palaces and other important buildings have, in their massive strength, demonstrated at least one and often a combination of these interpretations. In man's domestic dwellings too, light provides vigorous and inspiring architectural forces. There too light acts upon the state of mind in such a way that it transcends its merely functional role.

The intensity of light can be accurately measured nowadays, and light coefficient tables already have a history behind them. The subtle properties of light we wish to deal with here are, however, far more difficult to measure, yet we cannot do without them in living architecture.

We may tend to think that modern technology has succeeded in superseding darkness. Large glass windows provide the interior with almost unlimited floods of light and, at night, artificial light can simulate a midday atmosphere. Yet, this range of technical aids seems unable to satisfy a number of specific human needs. Builders often revert to small windows and sparse light. Restaurants frequently have candlelight. Does this not point to the fact that the architect cannot supply all requirements with mathematical indexes alone? Yet, what is the origin of these forces of attraction and repulsion between light and darkness, both within and without the architectural space?

Paradoxically, the history of architecture begins with defining darkness. The first human being ventured, torch in hand, into the naturally formed 'interior': the cave. He was surrounded by mysterious darkness; only the glow of his torch allowed him to perceive forms. The enclosing space contrasted with the infinite 'outer' space, where light alternated naturally with darkness. The discovered space became man's shelter and the place where he expressed his fearsome experiences.

In the first buildings, man *intentionally* created dark spaces where he could express these experiences, as is proven by archaeological discoveries. In the neolithic settlement of Catal Hujuk (Anatolia) for example, the paintings in the houses were very much like those in the caves. In these dwellings, the infiltration of light was kept to a minimum; it penetrated the space through a small opening in the ceiling which, at the same time, served as an entrance. The same technique was used in ceremonial spaces. In megalithic buildings (for example, in Malta) and in the first temples, the interior was totally dark. The contrast between natural light and artificial darkness was the actual base on which a plurality of interpretations grew. Eventually the tendency prevailed to use dark spaces as a medium for expressing psychological, symbolic, metaphysical and philosophical interpretations.

It goes without saying that there is no conclusive evidence that these interpretations of light could be found as archetypes, separately or in combination, at the very origin of history. Nor can we easily draw the line between these interpretations and the builder's merely functional intentions.

In religious buildings the association between the architectural solutions of light and the metaphysical aspirations can be more clearly determined than in secular dwellings. Yet it may be assumed, despite a few exceptions in modern architecture, that our appreciation of any light situation is not influenced by the purely functional properties of light alone. The triumph of the 'luminous wall' over the solid stone wall meant not just the provision of more light, but a psychological victory over reticence and darkness. Thus, the intensity of light achieved in secular buildings may be said to have psychological value in so far as it is in direct ratio to an 'open', as opposed to a 'closed' way of life.

A particular light atmosphere dominates a whole environment in which forms, people and objects are interrelated, while each obtains an independent reality. Therefore, the light atmosphere that has been created inside a building is related to the natural light atmosphere in a village, a town, or a region where it is determined in turn by the condition of the soil (vegetation or desert), natural

186
Detail of gallery surrounding the cortile of Palazzo Ducale, Urbino, Italy, 1444–82, by Luciano Laurana.
The transition between outside and inside has been softened by an intermediate zone, while the contrast of light and shade emphasizes the rhythm of columns and arches.

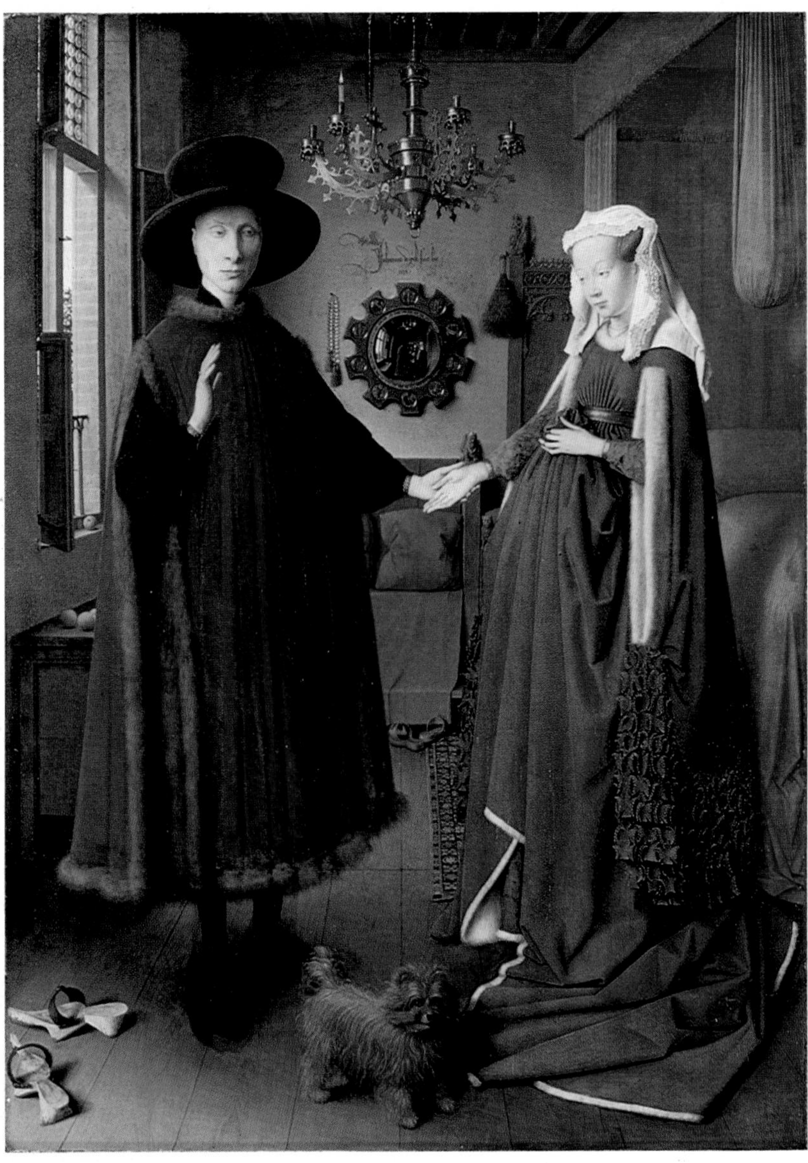

187
The Marriage of Giovanni Arnolfini and Jeanne Cenami, 1434, by Jan van Eyck, National Gallery, London.

Natural light enters this interior through a window unencumbered by curtains. The direct effect on the different colours and textures of the materials, the reflections on the figure of the bride, on the chandelier (on which burns a single candle) and on the round mirror in the background, are striking examples of 'Gothic' light.

materials (wood or stone), coloured or monochrome buildings, and the people (naked or clad). But the light atmosphere inside a building also depends on other determining factors such as the light system, the materials used, and ultimately on the style of living. The light atmosphere is a clear indication of the attitude to life of the people who created the building. The painter aptly synthesises this all-embracing and enveloping light in his work. We find examples of natural light atmosphere in the landscapes of van Ruysdael, van Gogh or Cezanne. The interiors of van Eyck, Vermeer or van Gogh provide us with examples of contrived light atmosphere. In paintings the sensory light becomes transcendental light. For example, in van Eyck's work: 'Het Echtpaar Arnolfini', the blissful intimacy between man and woman harmonises perfectly with the sunwarmed, sunlit interior. This painting is an example of the 'Gothic light' in the middle-class house and is very much like the 'Gothic' light we can still admire in the cathedrals built in that time.

In his work *The Philosophy of Interior Decoration* (Longanesi & C. Milano, 1964) Mario Praz analyses the western way of life in a series of illustrations of paintings. Image after image demonstrates the multiple significance of light limited by time and function. Here the value of painted illustrations is twofold, giving us a personal, emotional interpretation of light atmospheres and providing us with a survey of the various light systems.

The determining elements utilised in creating a light atmosphere in building cannot be fully analysed here. By way of illustration, however, we may give a few of the many striking achievements in this field.

A clear distinction should be made between the determining factors that deal respectively with the outside or inside of a building, bearing in mind that outside and inside are always related, whether they are in sympathy with or contrast to each other. We find an example of the latter in the pyramids: the outside catches the light and reflects it over an immense surface, thus identifying the building as an indistructible 'light beacon' and an undeniable witness to man's energetic presence on the surface of the earth; the inner corridor and tomb are wrapped in total darkness and, enclosed as they are within a solid mass of stone, become integrated into the earth itself. The whole demonstrates the utmost contrast, both formally and symbolically, between light and darkness.

The play of light and darkness is not restricted to the internal-external relation. The use of the contrasting properties of light (surface) or dark (relief or aperture) parts on the outside of the building becomes fundamental and inspiring after the rhyth-

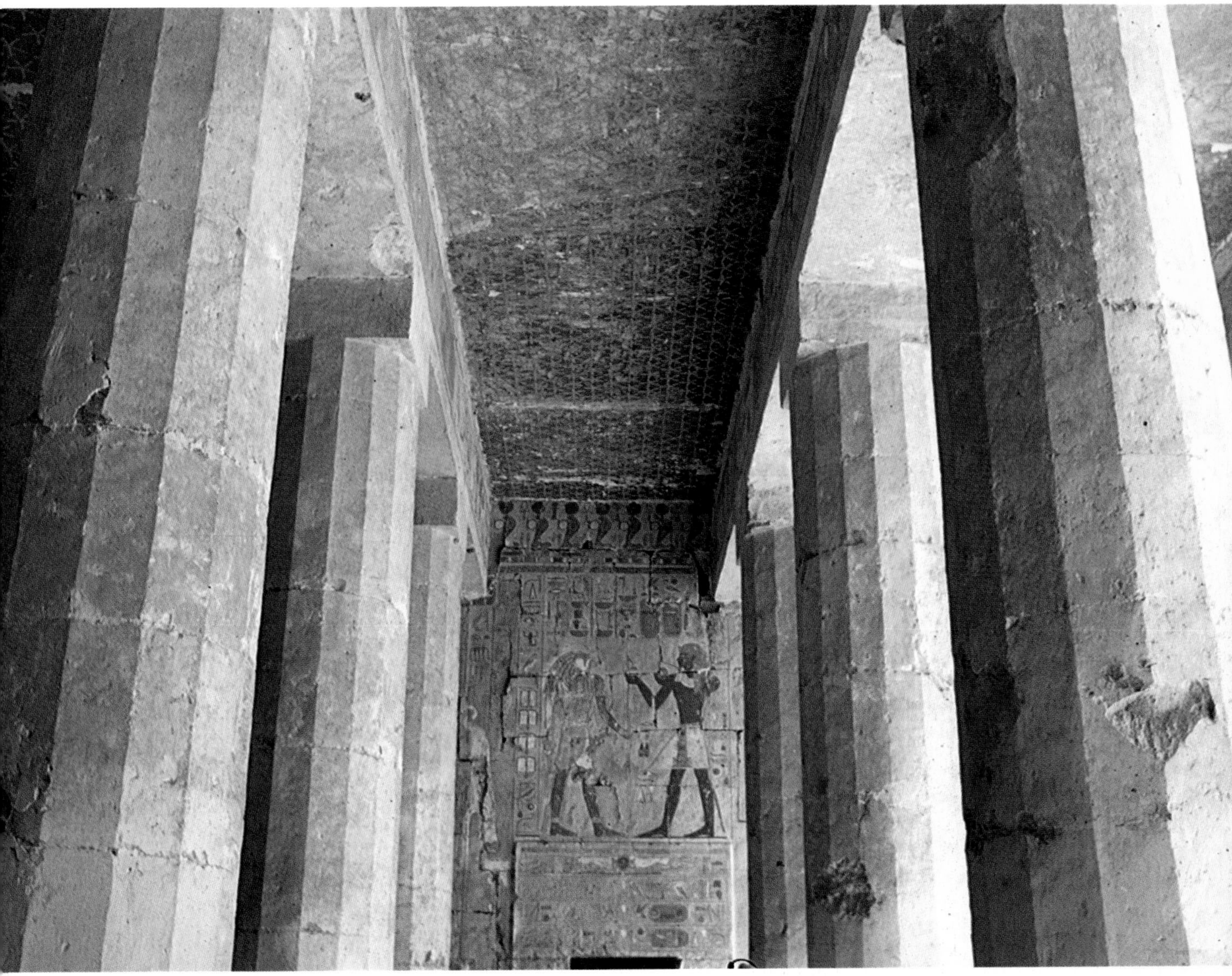

88
etail of colonnade of the
econd terrace, Temple of
Queen Hatshepsut, Dair-
-Bahri, Thebes, Egypt,
520 BC.

Light creates a rhythm of longitudinal planes on the poligonal columns, and these delicately shade light round their form, from brightness to darkness.

ical quality of the walls of King Zoser at Sakkara nd the terraced temple of Queen Hatshepsut. The ontrast between light and dark parts creates posi- ve and negative forms, while the rhythmically onstructed parts of the building (columns) use to a aximum one property of natural light: the effect f shadows.

Shadow-entities optically divert planes and vol- mes and divide space in ever-moving parts, while maintaining a harmonious relationship with the architectural elements. Open or covered planes or elements may be placed in sharp contrast and as a result they are neatly, graphically outlined. Alternatively, they may blend together to achieve a plastic whole. In the entrance hall of Queen Hatshepsut's terraced temple there is an ever-varied intensity of natural light, created by the polygonal structure of its columns.

189
Residence of the Middelheim-park, Antwerp, Belgium.
Light falling across the simple white facade produces a delicately modulated effect.

190
Detail of the Basilica, Vicenza, Italy, 1549, by Andrea Palladio.
The use of one material a fine hard white stone, and the simplicity of the architectural decoration create a contrast of extremes of light and darkness, revealing the fine proportions of the facade

The delicate composition of the architectural elements in the Residence of the Middelheimpark, in Antwerp, creates an intensely poetical effect: a single tone, white, brings about a wide range of greys and creates optically intriguing effects.

The negative forms on the facade of the Basilica at Vicenza, by Andrea Palladio, seem to be drilled clear through – an effect which is particularly striking in the lunettes. Details become subordinate to the whole and openings and arched forms are accentuated.

In the Greek temple, where the architectural accent is mainly on the outside, every nuance of contrast and rhythm is accentuated. There is extreme contrast between the overwhelmingly lit exterior, the colonnade, and the shadowy interior, hermetically sealed for the uninitiated, the cella. Rhythm and contrast exist too between the columns themselves and in their chiselled fluting. An intermediate zone between the interior and the exterior is formed by a transitional space, the peristasis, where the shadows of the columns are projected onto the walls of the cella. This passage between the interior and the exterior acquires an independent atmosphere which is characteristic also of later buildings, for example religious houses and galleries.

The intermediate zone 'catches' the light in an

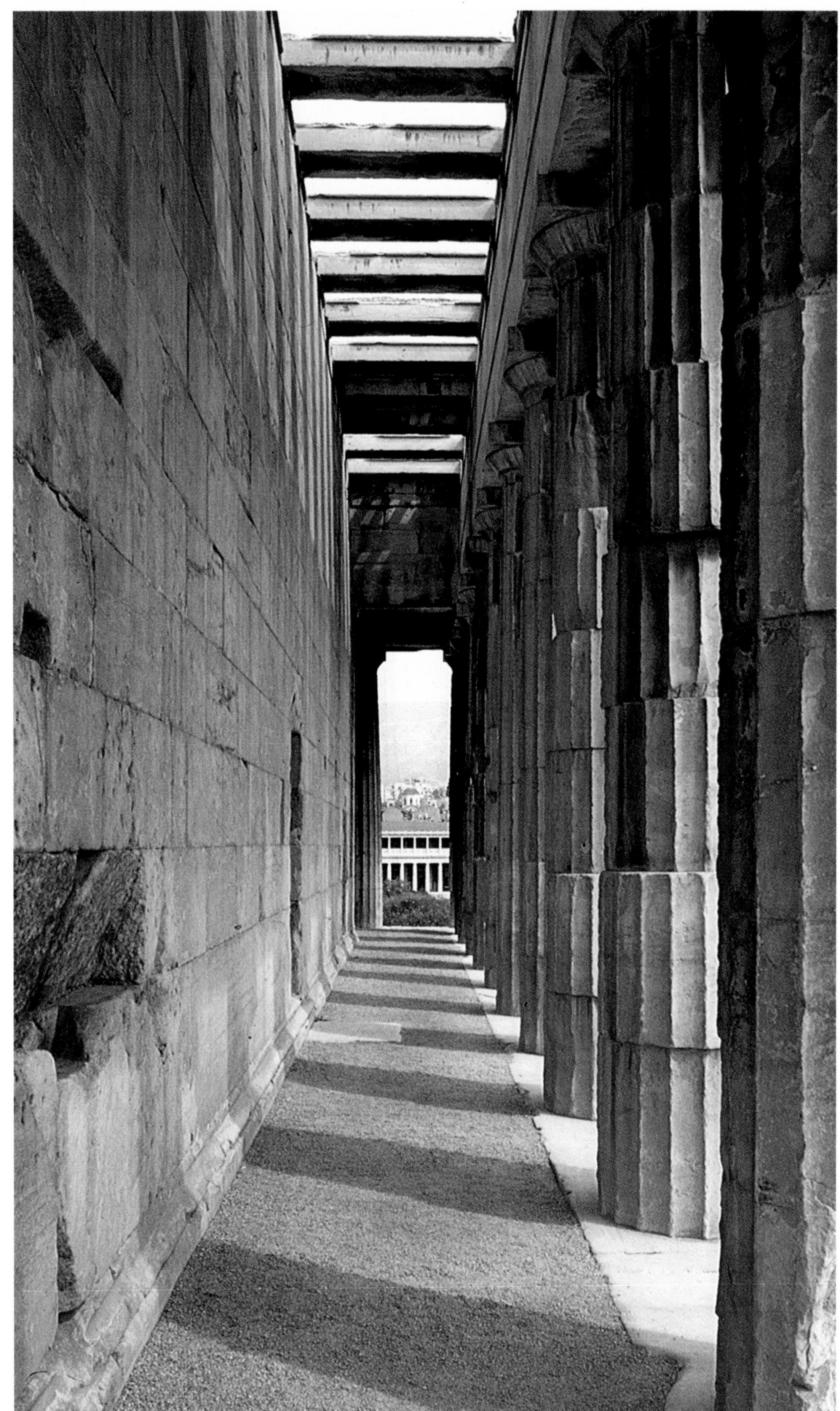

91
)etail of peristasi, These-
on, Athens, Greece, 447–
432 BC.

An intermediate zone
)etween the outer temple,
xposed to natural ele-
nents, and the dark, mys-
erious cella. Deeply fluted
columns cast rhythmic
hadows across the peris-
asi and onto the walls of
he inner temple.

192
Galleria degli Antichi, Sabbioneta, Italy, 1584.
A vaulted arcade forms an ambiguous space, neither enclosed nor open, where light and shadow produce fascinating patterns.

193
Double row of 'torii', Inari shrine, Kyoto, Japan.
Brightly coloured structures form a tunnel of light through the woods surrounding the shrine.

94
'avilion in the garden of he Musée de l'Ecole de Nancy, France, by Eugène 'allin.
The glass roof shades a errace on the top of the building, mediating be-ween the solid form below and the open sky above.

195
Detail of the facade, Casa Milá, Barcelona, Spain, 1905–10 by Antoni Gaudi.
The ever-moving shadows of the surround-ing trees intermingle with he metalwork of the bal-conies on the plastic, or-ganic form of the building. The rough texture of the surface softens the large areas of light and shade.

exceptionally intimate way, divorced as it is from direct exposure to natural or reflected light. The shadows act, in perspective, like the steps of a staircase inviting the spectator to explore the temple or gallery.

Other elements too are used to link natural light and space. The 'torii' of the Inari shrine in Kyoto, placed as they are at regular intervals, allow the light to penetrate playfully from above and from both sides. In combination with the colour shades a 'light tunnel' is formed, similar to that which one might see in a pergola.

In the pavilion in the garden of the Musée de l'Ecole de Nancy, a sand-blasted glass roof medi-ates between light and the building. The glass entity relates to the wide sky, but the matt material gives it independence, thus creating in the space beneath an atmosphere adaptable to climatic changes. The shadows of plants and trees become part of the massive, organic substructure, thus integrating form and light. A similar visual link between building and nature can be seen on the facade of Antoni Gaudi's Casa Milá, in Barcelona. The ideal interrelation of building and surroundings

196
Detail, Casa de las Conchas, Salamanca, Spain, 1512–14.

The architect has enriched an otherwise fortress-like building, with small windows, by decorating the wall with shells which at a certain time of day appear to be independent of the structure. The elaborate decoration around the windows makes them appear larger, stressing their importance and providing a transition between the brightly-lit wall and the dark opening.

and the effect of penetrating light touch our aesthetic senses when we enter the Campo Monumentale in Pisa, walk in the Piazza San Marco in Venice or stroll around a parish church which is flanked by trees.

The surface of a building itself may reveal the architect's intent, both by its texture and by any elements added to it. In the Casa de las Conchas in Salamanca (sixteenth century) shells occupy the surface. Floodlight, however, seems to cut them off the wall, an illusion strengthened by their cast shadows.

The interplay of light and darkness, of volume and shadow, is also to be found between several buildings. A narrow gap, such as narrow streets, staircases or arches, accentuates the illuminated area which thus appears to be a surface cut out of the infinite light source. The distance between the tower and the church of San Biagio at Montepulciano, by Antonio da Sangallo il Vecchio, allows a blade of natural light to penetrate. The 'freeing' of the tower creates an 'imprisoned' light zone between both constructions, composing a fascinating whole. The very concentration of light raises the tension between both massive volumes.

Roman architects applied this technique with maximum expressive force. In the Pantheon, for example, the space is integrated with the cosmos while the interior is given a pronounced independence from the outside solid mass. Here, the various interpretations of light mentioned earlier are concentrated in one place. The very interaction of space-mass and the natural effects of light enhance symbolic values.

'97
'he Church of San Biagio,
'lontepulciano, Italy,
518–29, by Antonio da
angallo il Vecchio.
A narrow gap between
ıe church and the free-
:anding bell tower on the
/est elevation emphasizes
ıe separate functions of
ıe two elements and
reates a unifying tension
ı the composition.

98
)etail of cortile, Palazzo
'ecchio, Florence, Italy,
470, by Michelozzo
'lichelozzi.
The upper edge of the
ourtyard frames a section
of the sky, which thus ap-
ɔears to be cut out. The
ɔpening illuminates the
valls with varying intensity
of light.

199
Santa Maria della Consolazione, Todi, Italy, 1508–1604, by Cola da Caprarola.

The Greek-cross plan popular during the Italian Renaissance, with a large central dome and windows spaced at regular intervals, allows the interior to be lit with an even natural light and the architectural volume to be appreciated in its entirety.

200
Suleymaniye Canii, Constantinople, Turkey, 1550–7, by Sinān.

Based on the great Byzantine Church of S. Sophia, built 1000 years earlier, this Islamic Mosque has a remarkable resemblance to the Renaissance church interior. The structure is more massive than the Italian building, but this is disguised by the skilful construction of the windows.

201
Church of San Lorenzo, Turin, Italy, 1688– by Guarino Guarini.

Light becomes interwoven with architecture, illuminating the symbolic geometry of the heavenly dome which appears to be detached from the solid, earth-bound structure below.

202
The Parish Church, Villa Pasquali, by Antonio Bibbiena.

Coming from a family of theatre architects, Bibbiena uses light in a truly theatrical manner to create illusion of light and space.

The Roman 'Domus' enclosed in its atrium and peristyle a cut-out piece of heaven from where the zenithal light came in. The enclosed 'living cocoon' is enlarged internally by perspective interplay, while the light streams unimpeded through the opening, destined for the inhabitants alone. Later examples of this pronounced accentuation of symbolic values are to be found in Guarino Guarini's architectural work.

In architecture, both natural properties and interpretations of light are linked to the expressions that are characteristic of people or time. The architectural style is in a way complemented by a light style.

The Egyptians preferred a sparingly lit space. The tombs within the pyramids were dark and the ceremonial buildings were dimly lit through light grooves near the ceiling, as in the temple in the valley of Chephren or the celebration hall of Thoutmosis III at Karnak. From a well-chosen angle the light was often projected onto the image of a god. The same method of illumination was followed in the inner space of secular buildings, as in the working-class houses of Dair-el-Bahri.

It was not until the Gothic period that the aspiration of drawing up transparent walls was realised. The 'lateral' light facilitates a direct contact between the interior and the exterior of a building, and the architect has more possibility to create the optimum light atmosphere. In the Gothic cathedral, the walls radiate an autonomous colour. Light is tied to intense, vivid hues and helps the architectural space to take shape. Natural light is exalted to 'supernatural' light. It penetrates the space in an endless series of directed beams and facets.

As opposed to the Gothic cathedral, the Renaissance temple is full of 'natural' light. The light sources are spread out regularly, with precise speculative intention. All the architectural elements are illuminated with equal intensity. The space as a whole prevails, not the separate accentuation.

The Islamic Mosque shows a remarkable resemblance to this Renaissance conception of light, as we may observe in Sinam's Suleymaniye Canii in Istanbul. Here the even intensity and the nature of the light are enhanced by the delicate use of colours which has the effect of turning the inner space into a homogeneous colour entity.

In the Baroque church, the passage of light is woven into the architectural concept to become an illusive and symbolic element. In the church of San Lorenzo in Turin, by Guarino Guarini, the play of light emphasises the bold construction of the dome and creates illusionary visual effects. The upper part of the building becomes a 'vision of light', the

203
Notre Dame du Haut, Ronchamp, France, 1950–5, by Le Corbusier.

Deep set, splay-jambed windows send shafts of coloured light into the gloomy interior, producing an archaic effect to express the religious symbolism of the building.

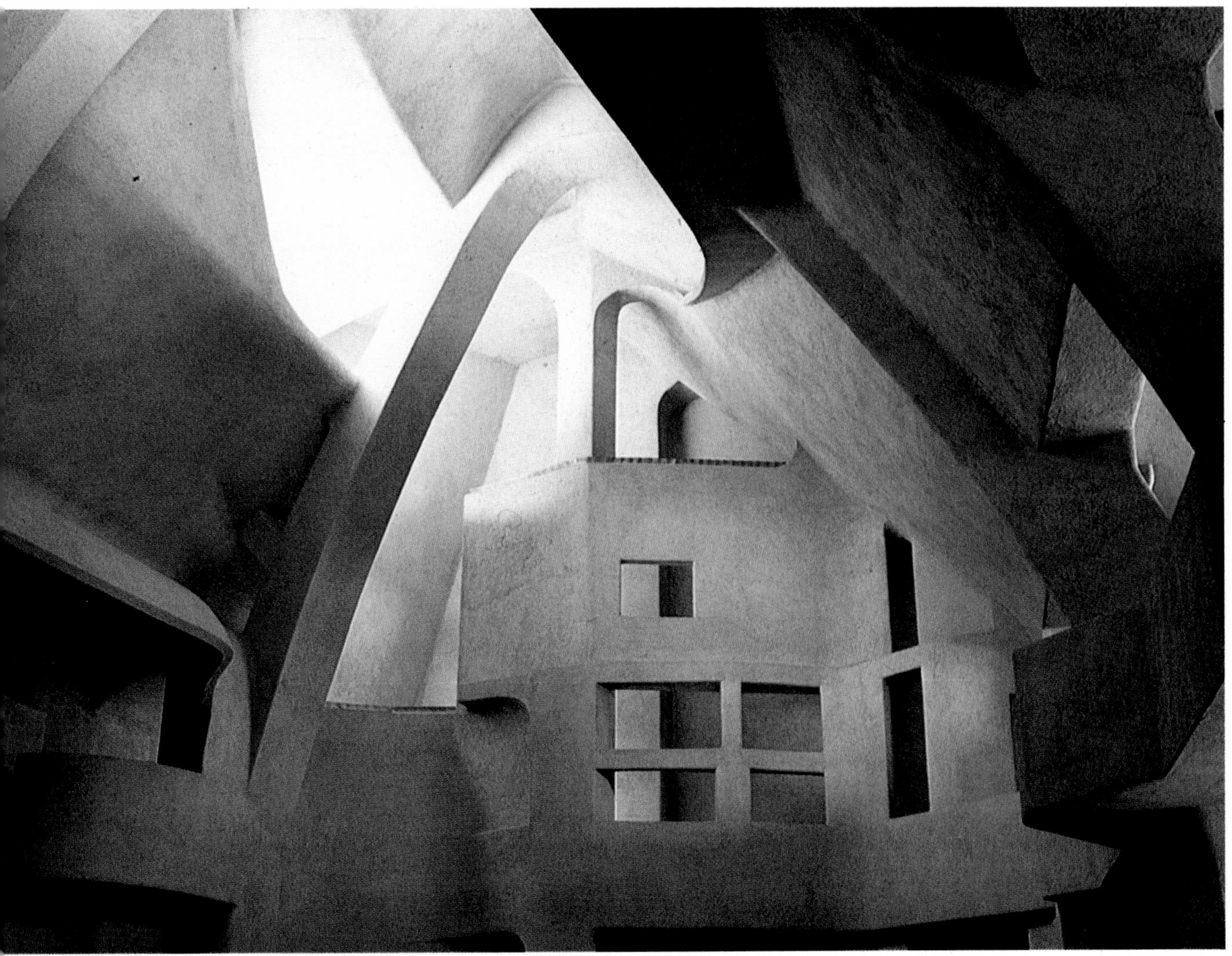

204
Church of Borgomaggiore, San Marino, 1961, by Giovanni Michelucci.
The perpetual struggle between light and darkness is here dramatically realized in three dimensions.

perforation and the concealed light spaces seem to detach the lantern from the dome.

In the Parish Church at Villa Pasquali, by Antonio Bibbiena, both the double dome and its perforation create a theatrical effect. The massive structure acquires the fragility of lace, and, as in a vision, light pours through its meshes. The colour of the outer wall, a light blue, intensifies the illusion and enhances the reflections.

In addition to these historical examples there are realisations of more recent origin which indicate how light can determine the character of the building and realise special intentions. In the chapel at Ronchamps, Le Corbusier obtains an archaic character by placing irregular niches in the massive walls; a massiveness that is openly exposed, for the wall is fenestrated on the outside. Light beams are literally guided and directed by the oblique niches.

In the church of Borgomaggiore at San Marino, by Giovanni Michelucci, form and light create a dramatic effect in the irregular structure of the interior. The sources of light are indirect and create sharp contrasts in the perforated structure. The violent opposition of bright planes and dark openings results in an overwhelming atmosphere. Here light saves us from the appalling darkness. The struggle betwen light and darkness has been elaborated into an architectural poem about life and death.

Coloured glass reduces the intensity of light and creates a specific light atmosphere in accordance with the colour pattern, as in coloured windows. Its effect influences our psychological attitude towards the space and it may lead to symbolic associations. In the San Francisco Cathedral, by McSweeney, Ryan and Lee assisted by Pier Luigi Nervi, the architectural volume is split up in the symbolic form of the cross and light penetrates through narrow apertures filled with coloured glass. In this building, the most advanced technical, mathematical and geometric realisations are in perfect harmony with light and colour. In Paolo Soleri's studio in Phoenix, the light atmosphere is determined by the coloured dome. Natural and coloured lights are in sharp contrast to each other. Red colour tones create an illusion of unreality, for 'red' has been used instead of the more familiar 'blue', the symbol of the heavenly colour.

Coloured light may create an autonomous element inside a space filled with natural light. In one of my furniture designs that consists of a frame filled with blue glass I enclosed, as it were, an amount of blue light within the volume of the structure. I did the same in a room: natural light penetrates the space through blue windows and becomes an autonomous and intense blue mass. Listening to music in this space is a deeper and more intense experience: beside the psychological factors of calm and reflection, the unreal atmosphere is associated with the infinite. In a bathroom

205
Detail of dome, San Francisco Cathedral, California, USA, by McSweeny, Ryan and Lee assisted by Pier Luigi Nervi.

Nervi's brilliant structure of concrete is in complete harmony with the coloured light which divides it in the form of a cross.

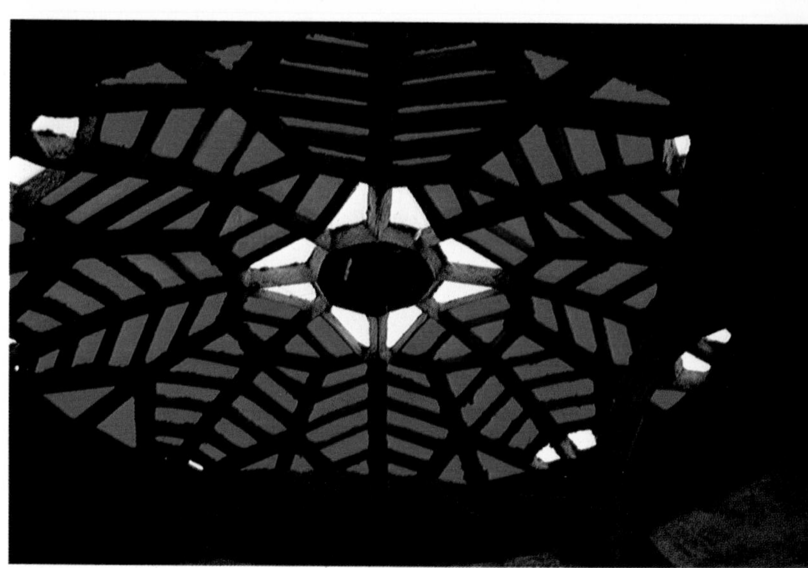

206
Detail of ceiling in the entrance hall, Studio of Paolo Soleri, Phoenix, Arizona, USA.

Red glass is used in contrast to the natural desert light to create an illusion of unreality.

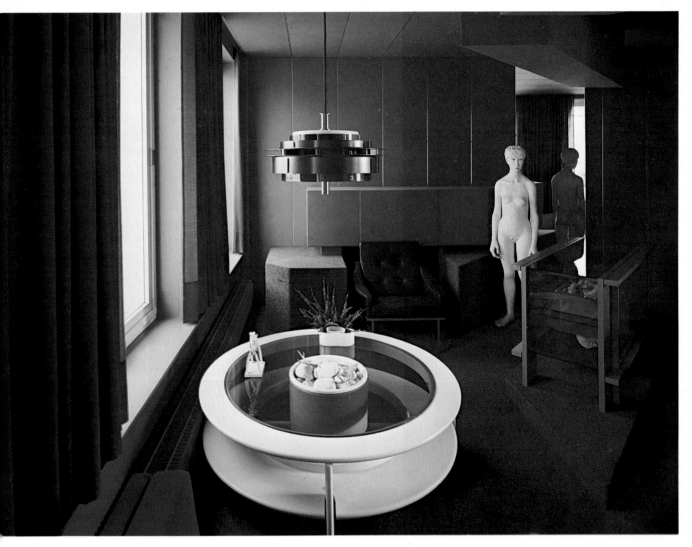

207
Private studio of the architect, Aalst, Belgium, 1974, by Pieter de Bruyne.

Light filters through blue glass to create a calm, meditative interior where all elements appear to be united.

208
Furniture design by Pieter de Bruyne, 1972.

The frame is filled with blue glass, to enclose a distinct volume of blue light.

I realised the opposite. There the delicate colour tones, the reflections of light provided by glossy materials such as mirrors and ceramic walls, create a surrounding suggestive of water and nature. The materials, united by light, acquire not only a symbolic character, they also enhance the natural atmosphere. As a consequence, the bathroom is used more intensively. Our homes could become spaces where a succession of light and colour-tones surprise us agreeably and dispel the monotonous light. The interior would radiate calm, intimacy and poetry.

By contrast, light entering through a window which is considered as a plane cut out of the light source can dramatically intensify the character of an interior space. One of Paolo Soleri's windows in Arcosanti looks like the frame of a majestic landscape. Beyond the large window is a second screen of precise geometric dimensions: an unusually large circle. Horizontal and vertical lines divide the window into small frames, each of which cuts a large plane out of the landscape beyond, where atmospheric conditions keep evoking new visions. The beholder is deeply impressed by the varying facets of natural light, from the diffused light at sunrise till the red afterglow at sunset. He is inevitably influenced by light and colour and the atmosphere determines his attitude towards nature.

A glass roof illuminates the corridors within the Lewis Medical Building in San Diego, by Simpson and Gerber, and at the same time splits up the architectural volume. The result is a neat ensemble of coloured structures, natural light and some white planes. Subdued light and the specific choice of the fragile streak of light enhances the suspense. The view has been diverted from the heavy traffic alongside the building to the serene heaven. The atmospheric conditions are more intensely experienced and working inside the building becomes more agreeable.

In the villa Savoye in Poissy, by Le Corbusier, the inner wall receives along its entire length a lateral

209
Bathroom, by Pieter de Bruyne, Aalst, Belgium, 1975.

The highly reflective materials suggest the presence of water and nature.

210
Detail of skylight, Lewis Medical Building, San Diego, California, USA, by Simpson and Gerber.

Light sharply divides the architectural volume bringing a calm, ordered atmosphere to the busy corridors below.

211
Window at Arcosanti, Arizona, USA, by Paolo Soleri.

A large circle behind the window frames and delineates the landscape beyond.

212
Dining room, Villa Savoye, Poissy, France, 1928–31 by Le Corbusier.
Continuous bands of horizontal windows flood the uncompromising interior with light and emphasize the open plan of the interior space.

213
Living room, the home of the architect, Los Angeles, California, USA, 1933, by Richard Neutra.
The separation of inside and outside has almost disappeared in an attempt to achieve harmony with nature.

214
Detail of passage leading to the Council Chamber, Town Hall, Säynätsalo, Finland, 1949, by Alvar Aalto.
An intimate atmosphere is created by the use of natural materials and by the subdued light from the high level windows reflecting off the warm timber ceiling.

illumination. Horizontal light enhances the concept of 'free plan' on which the building is based, and pervades the whole space according to its gradation which, in turn, depends on the high or low position of the sun. The wall in architect Neutra's own house in Los Angeles is as transparent as possible. The inside almost forms one whole with the outside, also in terms of light. In both solutions (Le Corbusier's and Neutra's) the choice of the light scheme corresponds to the 'open' character of the space. Atmospheres of light and colour are in close harmony with nature.

The opposite of these 'open' light solutions are those solutions which create an intimate atmosphere by their 'close' construction. In the corridor of the town-hall of Säynätsalo, by Alvar Aalto, the windows are built near the ceiling, between the rafters. The space is a closed, warm one, because of the reflection of the light onto the wooden ceiling. Alvar Aalto often used such window constructions: they offer the spectator a view onto surrounding tree tops and catch the reflections of the leaves.

It is obvious that between these extremes, 'open' and 'closed', lies a wide range of possibilities. All of them have a distinct influence on the inhabitant, both through form and psychological intent. There is no doubt whatever that we should attempt to reach a better understanding of the possibilities and significance of light in architectural composition. Properties such as intensity, atmosphere and character of light should be studied and evaluated in every architectural structure. As a result, purely formal construction of windows, such as we see in prefabricated houses for example, would prove to be unjustified when we consider the impact of adequate light diffusion and the significance of light. Any architectural structure that has been built at a given place can become an autonomous entity through the skilful deployment of light.

The examples mentioned earlier illustrate many of the possibilities in the use of light. The poetic, calm and intimate character of the house requires particular consideration and should be subject to closer study. Good architecture is only possible when we are willing to experience all the properties of light. It requires a feeling for subtle light-gradations which is probably not consciously present yet, although it might be stimulated by successful architectural realisations. In this process, psychological as well as purely technical requirements should be taken into account.

In the search for an harmonious surrounding, light and its modulating properties in architecture may become a contributing factor to the creation of a more complete and agreeable atmosphere in life.

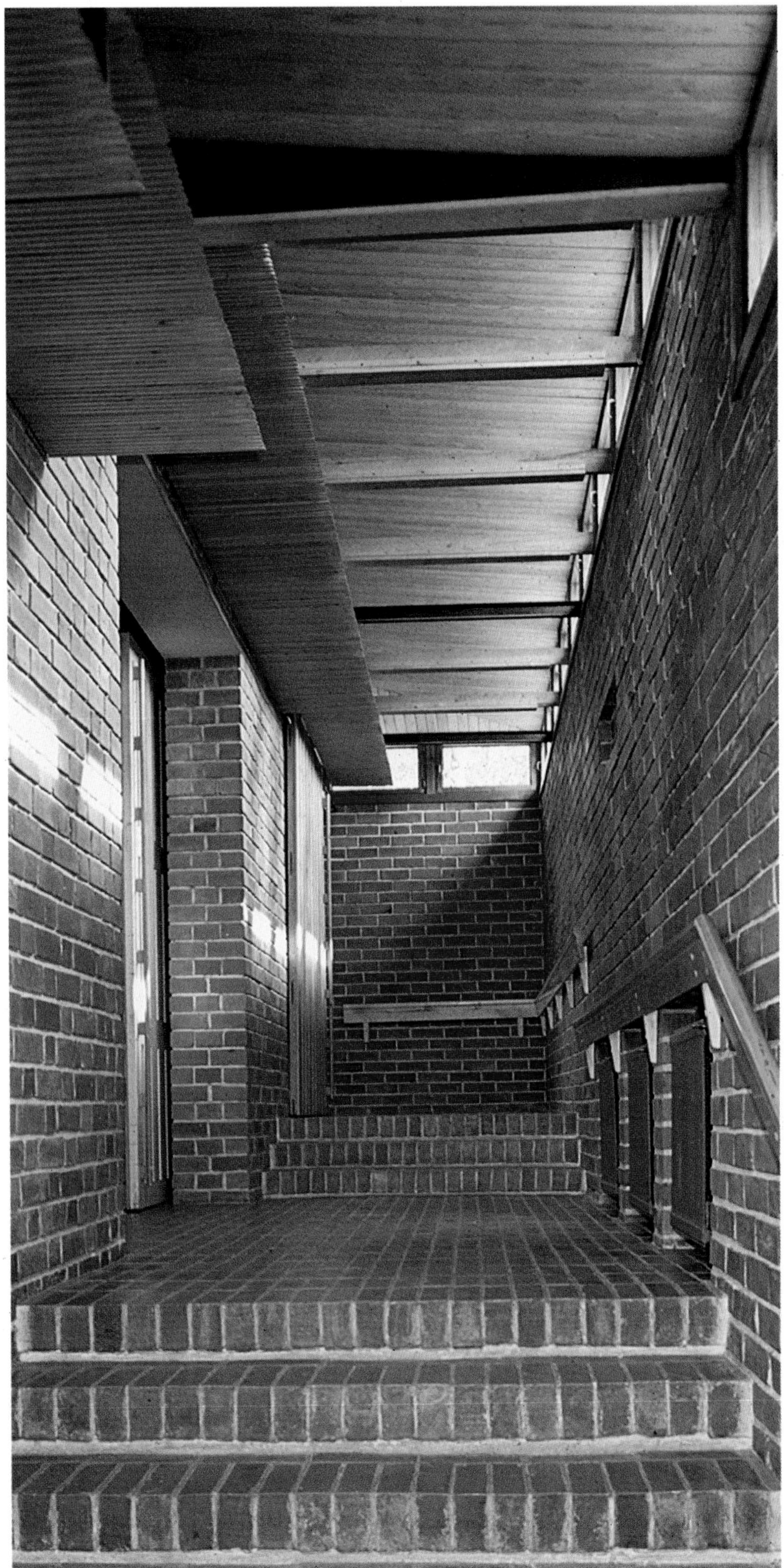

Trends in Furnishing and in the Decorative Arts

215
Folding chair: ash frame with canvas seat. Designed by Steen Østergaard and made by Niels Roth Andersen, Denmark

216
Chair: laminated ash or beech frame with leather seat and back. Designed by Hans J. Wegner for an organic furniture competition in 1948 and produced in 1979 by Johannes Hansen, Denmark

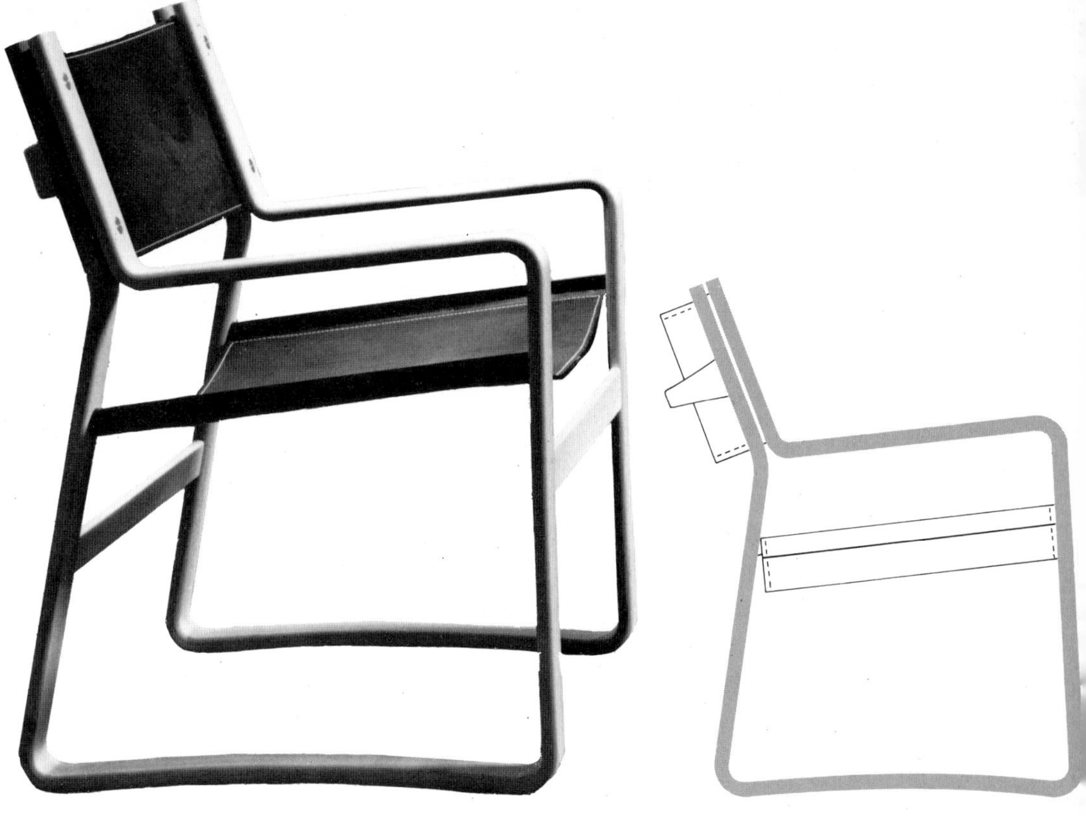

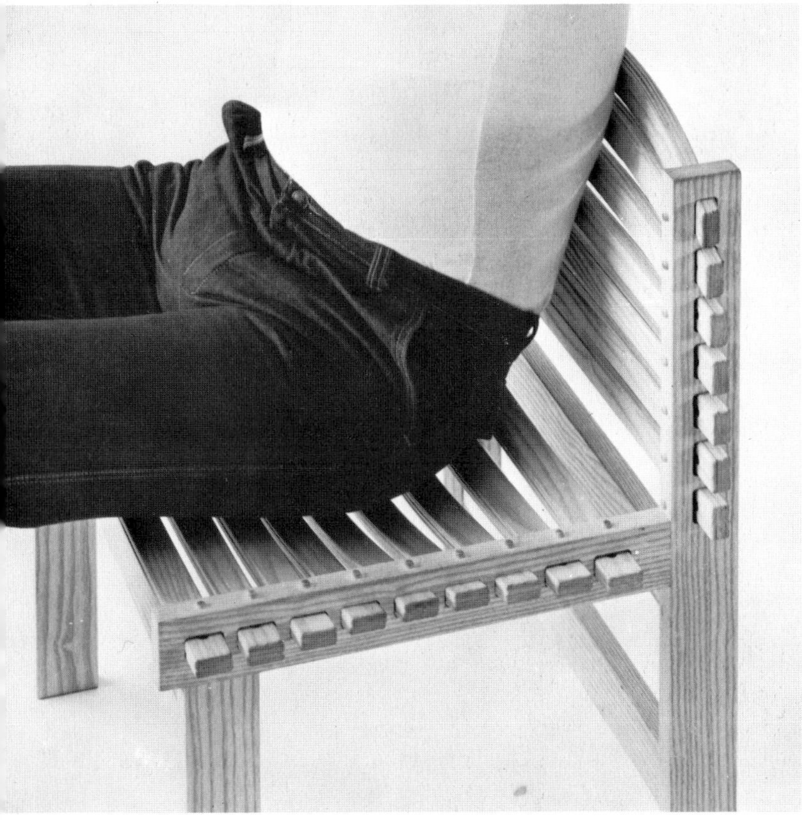

217
Bench: the semi-circular shape allows the bench to be formed from only the back sections on which it stands interlocking with the sections forming the cantilevered seat. Natural mahogany.
Designed by Per Borre and made by Wørts Møbel-snedkeri, Denmark

218, 219
Chair: hardwood dowels expressed in the frame of the chair pass through oblong holes in the ends of the wooden slats which form the seat and back of the chair. The slats are solid ash thinly sliced and left unglued: the natural spring in the wood allows them to adapt to the shape of the human body.
Designed by Gunnar Aagaard Anderson and made by Søren Horn, Denmark

220
Avec chair: a demountable frame fitted with studs can be assembled in a few minutes. The canvas cover is attached to the frame by means of buttons, and cushions are filled with polyether wadding. The chair is also available packed in a special canvas sack.
Natural birch frame, black or natural canvas cover.
77cm × 84cm × 43cm
(20¼″ × 33″ × 17″)
Designed by Eero Aarnio for Asko-Upo, Finland

221, 222
Body chair, 1979: adjusts to six upright and to four reclining positions. Used as an easy chair it can rock forwards. The lumbar support can slide upwards or downwards to suit the individual. Natural ash, with black lacquered metal parts.
Designed by Jim Warren for Pearl Dot Furniture Workshops, England

225, 226
Table, Cogne 1976: the essentially geometrical shape of the piece, based on sections of a cube, is broken by the use of colour and by the reflections on the lacquer finish, symbolizing the subtle variations of natural elements.
50cm × 135cm × 135cm (19¾″ × 53⅛″ × 53⅛″)

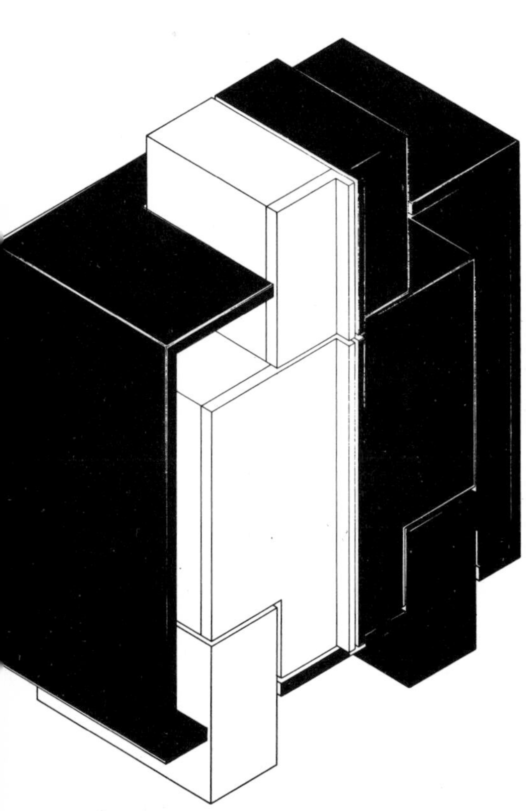

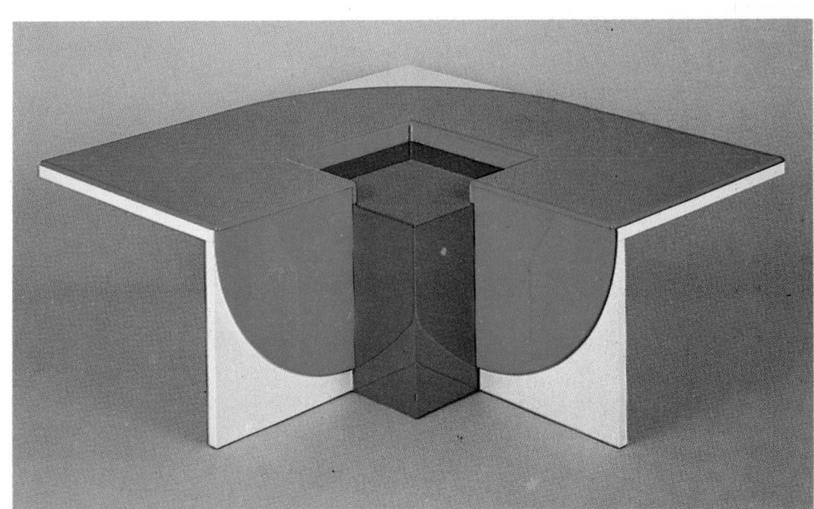

223, 224
Container, 1978: the volume is symmetrically divided into a black and white, highly polished section and encased in a matt black 'container'. The container is divided by the supports in the upper part of the piece.
Black and white lacquer, 134cm × 100cm × 50cm (52¾″ × 39⅜″ × 19¹¹⁄₁₆″)
All designed by Pieter de Bruyne, Belgium

Howard Raybould has developed traditional colouring techniques to enhance his carvings, allowing the natural colour and grain of the wood to show through. He uses watercolour, gouache bound with PVA emulsion, pastel, water soluble coloured pencils, oil and spirit stains, and pigment mixed into wax, which are applied with brushes, rags or fingers and then partly rubbed out with wire wool or solvent. The finished carving is then sealed with white polish and beeswaxed.

227
Graffiti 1977: vertical mirror frame. Quebec pine, coloured with mixed media and waxed.
54cm × 50.5cm
(21¼″ × 19⅞″)

228
Carpet 1977: vertical mirror frame. Quebec pine coloured with pastels and crayon, sealed and waxed.
73.5cm × 52.5cm
(29″ × 20½″)

229
Waves Spiral and Interlacing 1977: mirror frame. Quebec pine, coloured with pastels and emulsion, sealed and waxed.
90cm × 74cm (35½″ × 29″)

All made by Howard Raybould, England
Photography David Cripps

Sergio Asti has produced a series of designs on the theme of trees, clouds and rain, for screenprinting on standard ceramic tiles. The designs can be used in combination with each other and with plain tiles, as in the composition *L'Albero*, illustrated here.

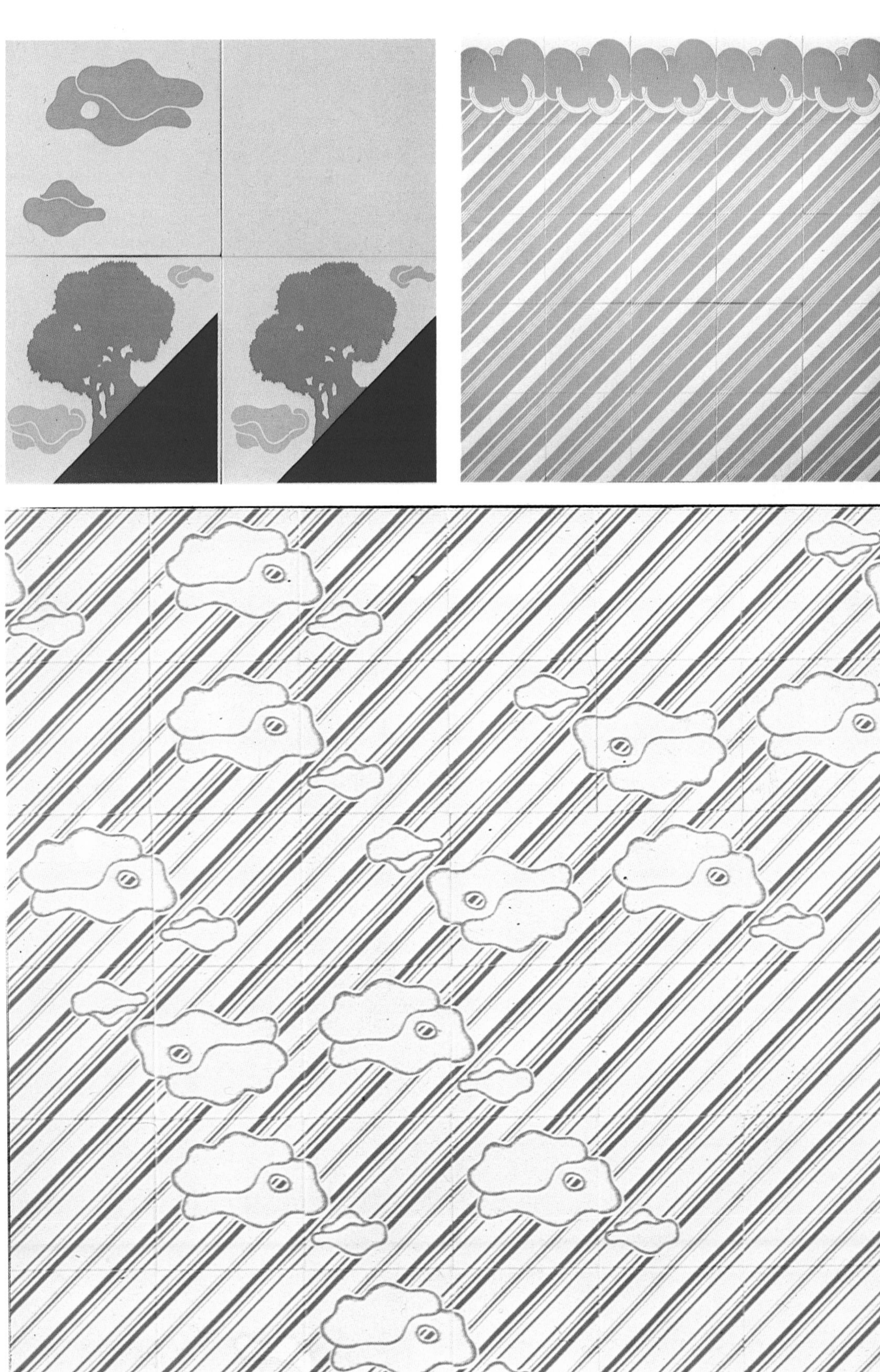

30
'Albero: composition in-
uding plain standard
es.

31
louds and Rain No. 1:
is design should be par-
cularly suitable for a
anel.

32
'louds and Rain No. 2

ll designed by Sergio Asti
or Cedit, Italy

233
Low Table, 1979: Bombay rosewood inlaid with ebony.
120cm × 120cm × 30cm
(47¼″ × 47¼″ × 11¾″)

234
Bridge Table, 1979: American black walnut and steamed pear, simulated suede top.
100cm × 100cm × 71cm
(39⅜″ × 39⅜″ × 28″)

Both designed and made by Martin Grierson, England

235, 236, 237, 238
Cabinet, 1978: by means of a mitred junction between the edge of the doors and the sides of the cabinet and through the use of a specially designed hinge, the black doors can be folded flat against the sides of the cabinet revealing the pale sycamore interior. English sycamore base and drawers, cabinet veneered with black stained sycamore, ebony drawer handles.
54cm × 36cm × 141cm
(21¾" × 14¼" × 55½")
Designed and made by John Coleman, England

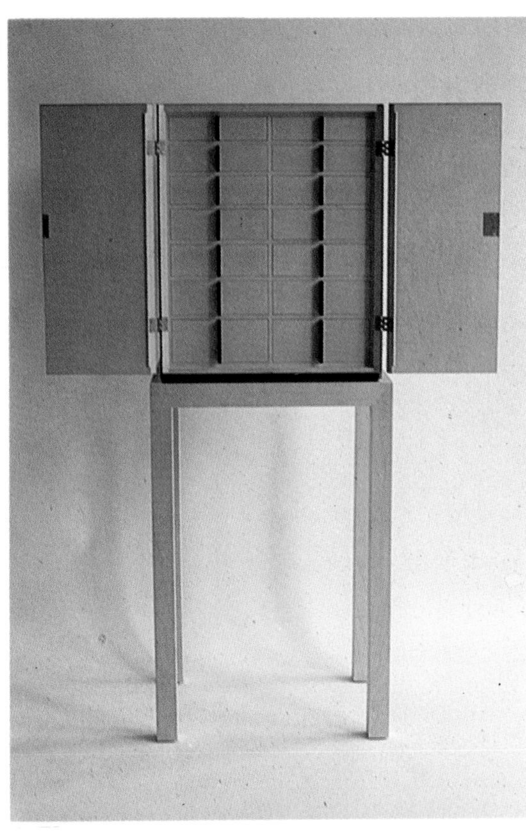

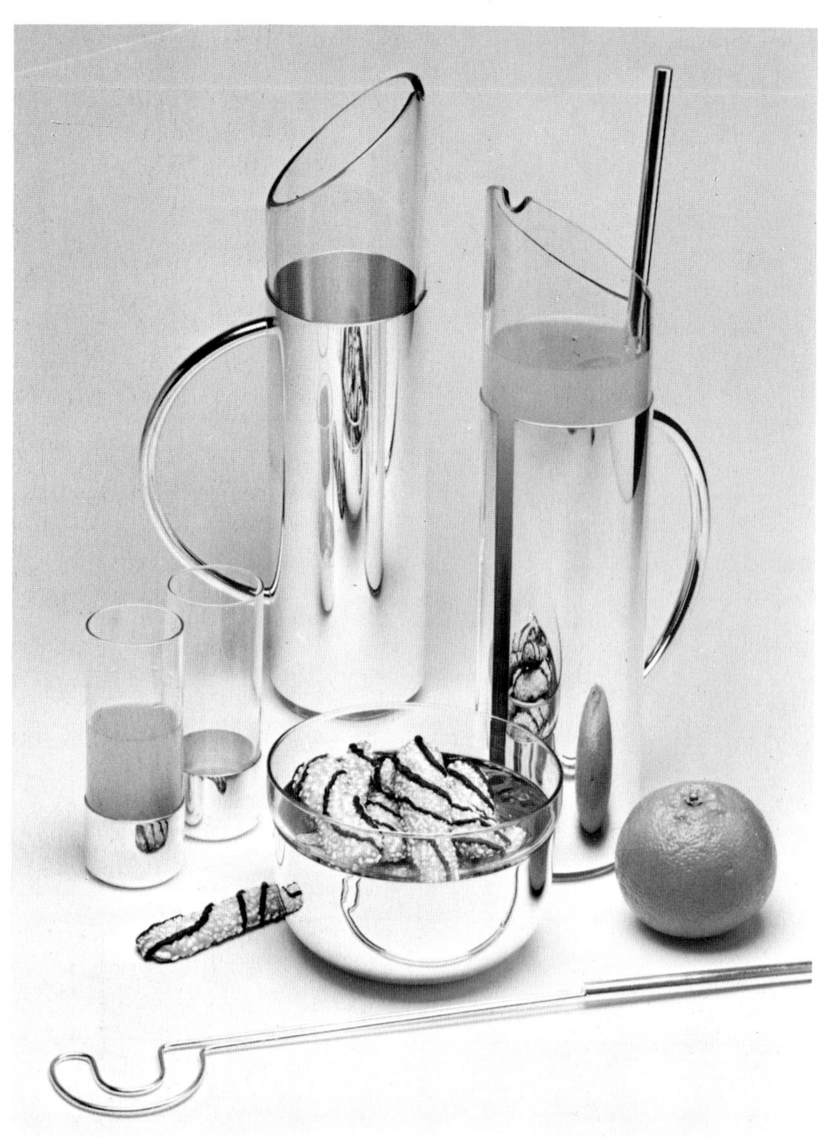

239
Bar set: silver plate on heavy gauge brass alloy, crystal containers.
Designed by Lino Sabattini for Argenteria Sabattini, Italy

240
Cutlery set from a range of tableware: 18/8 nickel steel, dishwasher safe, or silver plate on 90gr. Alpaka.
Designed by Carl Pott for C. Hugo Pott, West Germany

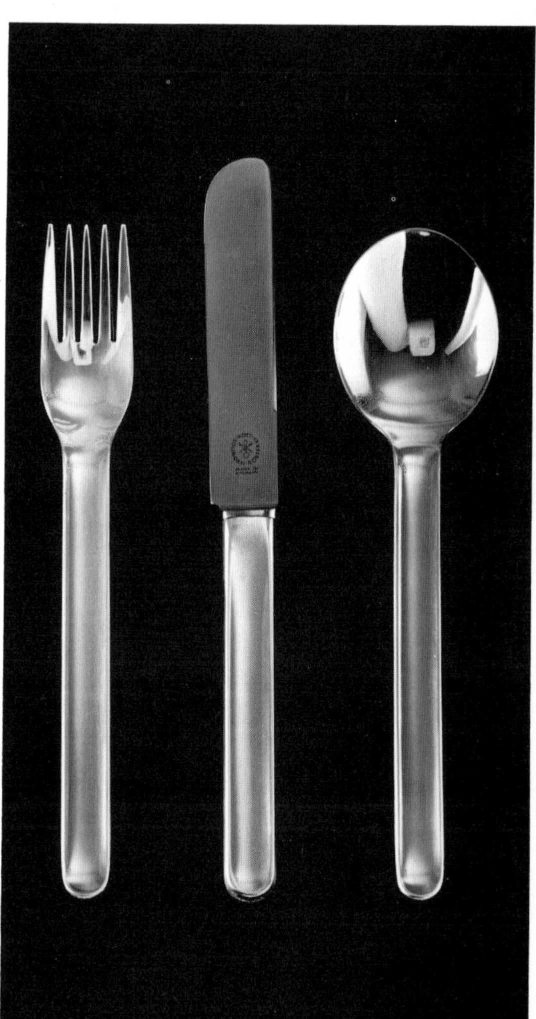

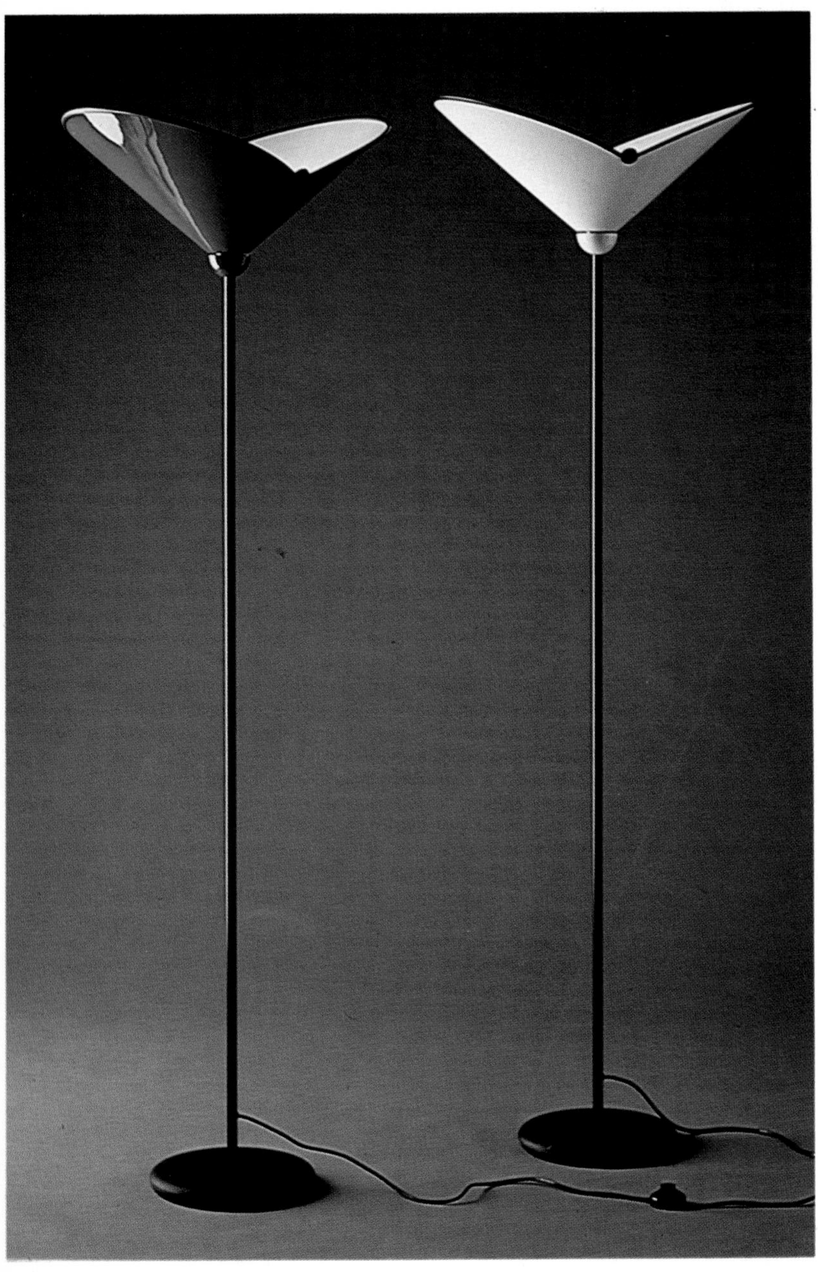

241
Fiore, Mod. 3603: floor lamp. Steel plate reflector lacquered white, green or maroon; black lacquered stem. 184cm (72″) high 60cm (23⅝″) diameter. Designed by Adalberto Dal Lago for Stilnovo, Italy

242
Mezzaluna: series of floor, wall and ceiling lamps. The lighting units, adjustable on 180 degrees, have a protecting glass on the side not shown by the illustration. Semicircular diffusors of pressed steel, stove enamelled black or white, hold halogen bulbs of 250 or 500 Watts, 110 or 220 Volts, which can be electronically controlled in the floor and wall models. The stems of chrome tubing adjust telescopically in height and rotate on a base of white, grey or black marble. Designed by Bruno Gecchelin for Skipper, Italy

The pots illustrated here were made by Jacqueline Poncelet between 1978 and 1979 in the USA, where the artist spent a year after being awarded a Bicentennial Arts Fellowship. During her stay, Jacqueline Poncelet studied the landscape and architecture of America, particularly the landscapes of Utah and Arizona and the skyscrapers of New York, and developed her new technique.

In her earlier pots the shape was created first and pattern was then superimposed on the shape. Now it is the pattern which influences the shape. At first the artist allowed the pattern to take direct control over the form but, as her study year wore on, informal patterns imposed on formal ones, such as the wavy reflections on the facade of a skyscraper, began to fascinate her. Thus in the later pots the relationship between pattern and form has become more fluid and indefinite.

Jacqueline Poncelet uses clays coloured with oxides to build up a patterned block. The block is then cut through and the slices rolled out into sheets of clay from which the sections of the slab pots are cut. To highlight the pattern, only certain colours are glazed, others being left as matt clay.

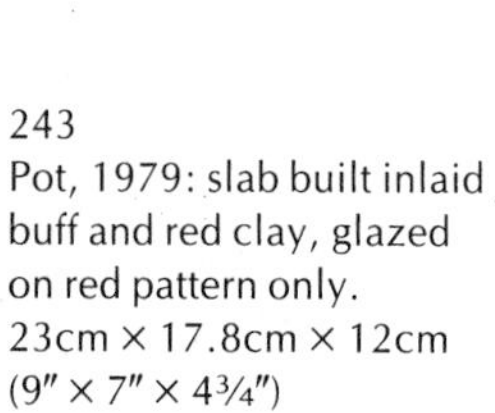

243
Pot, 1979: slab built inlaid buff and red clay, glazed on red pattern only. 23cm × 17.8cm × 12cm (9″ × 7″ × 4¾″)

244
Pot, 1979: slab built inlaid clays, glazed. 30.5cm (12″) high.

245
Pot, 1979: slab built inlaid clays of various colours, partially glazed. 21.5cm (8½″) high.

246
Pot, Seattle 1979: slab built inlaid clays, glazed. 25.4cm (10″) high.

All made by Jacqueline Poncelet, England

Ronald Pennell presents a particular view of the British way of life in his series of glass engravings. He finds that Britons take their leisure activities very seriously: he himself spends his own spare time building a stone wall in his garden. In the vase 'Butterflies and Pigs' a young farmer feeds a smug sow with nuts in his free time: a sublime form of the day to day toil of farming. Man and beast exist in complete harmony with the butterflies symbolizing the peace which reigns between them. However, in Pennell's more satirical engravings, Man is perpetually mocked by Nature. In 'Jubilee Beans', the beans proudly nursed by one of Pennell's neighbours in celebration of the Queen's Silver Jubilee, were eventually eaten by a rabbit which is depicted on the other side of the glass. In 'Oarsman', a man stands like a warrior, his oar clutched as a spear symbolizing the ritualized combat of sport, while a formation of ducks mocks this perfect specimen of man at his attempt to take to water. In 'Topiarist' a bird derides man's attempt to form Nature in the image of himself.

Pennell's satire even extends to the British institution of 'Tea Time' which is transformed into a parody of the Japanese tea ceremony.

247
Butterflies and Pigs, 1979: square glass container, wheel engraved on a fixed head lathe. 10cm (4″) high.

248
Jubilee Beans. 1977: engraved whisky glass. 8cm (3⅛″) high

249
Tea Time, 1979: engraved container 15cm (5⅞″) high.

250
Oarsman, 1979: engraved container. 15cm (5⅞″) high

251
Topiary I, 1979: engraved cylindrical container. 8.5cm (3⅜″) high.

All made by Ronald Pennell, England
Photography Cliff Guttridge

252
Crocodile mother: articulated body, hand carved Quebec pine coloured with mixed media, waxed.
Designed and made by Howard Raybould, England

253
Bird's tree: birds of different types of wood fit into a tree shape.
Designed and made by Shigeo Fukuda, Japan
Courtesy of Victoria and Albert Museum, London

Opposite

The work of Clare Murray and Mathew Warwick evolves from and relates to nature in a unique, very personal way. Clare creates her jewellery designs out of childhood recollections of a fantasy world of animals and from the scenes and landscapes of the rural English village where she and Mathew now live. In her work, she uses sheet steel, silver and coloured golds, with occasional semi-precious stones. Her technique consists mainly of piercing the outline of her design out of the metal sheet and then punching in the details. Colour is very important to her, but she obtains it only by using differently coloured golds in combination with silver and steel. Thus the *Cherry* earrings illustrated have silver flowers (with a gold centre), green gold stalks and red gold fruits.

Mathew Warwick shapes his boxes to develop the idea expressed by the jewels. He does this by adding his own ideas and also by echoing some jewellery details which interest him, often using the pattern of the wood in a figurative manner. Take for example the ebony box with a sycamore 'moon' inset which picks up the gemstone in one of the two interlocking rings contained in the box. Mathew has added to this detail an ebony 'hill' of his own, with three minute 'trees' on its top: the hill serves both as a stand for the rings and as a complement to Clare's work.

The boxes are of precious, often rare woods, turned on a lathe. They are structurally complex, often having tiny secret compartments activated by wooden springs, which intrigue and sometimes baffle their owners.

254
Ebony box with sycamore moon inset; inside the box is a ring stand in the shape of a hill supporting two interlocking rings, one of silver with a gold elephant, one of silver with a moonstone 'moon'.

255
Box in the shape of a pebble with lid surmounted by a tiny stylised tree: laburnum wood.

256, 257
Box of African blackwood with plaited linen cord. When open, the box reveals a pair of *Cherry* earrings inside one half and a mirror inside the other.

258
Orchard bangle: silver with gold inlays of different colours to represent the ladder, apple basket and various animals.

All made by Clare Murray and Mathew Warwick, England

259
Flat jugs and winged cup. Mould blown glass, hot tooled handles and wings. One of the jugs is sand-blasted and measures 25cm (9⅞″) the other, clear, is 20cm (7⅞″) high. The cup is lustred and measures 10cm (4″) high.

260
Flat decanter, mould blown and sandblasted, 35cm (13¾″) high.

All made by Steven Newell, England

261
Variation Spatiale: two blocks of crystal cut and polished by hand, one partially acid-etched. Each 6cm × 25cm (2″ × 10″)

262
Relations: two blocks of crystal cut and polished by hand, one partially acid-etched. 25cm × 10cm (10″ × 4″) and 13cm × 12cm (5″ × 5″)

263
Stress: optical glass cut and polished by hand. 10cm × 10cm × 20cm (8″ × 4″ × 8″)

Unlike the majority of contemporary glass artists, Yan Zoritchak does not work in a glass studio or workshop. The actual making of glass does not interest him: he uses the material as if it were stone or steel, in blocks which he cuts from the solid, acid etching and polishing them by hand afterwards. This is perhaps why his pieces have a distinct individuality, their heaviness expressing a controlled strength rather than the weighty quality of the original glass mass.

But where the artist depends on the characteristics of the material is in his need for light as an essential part of his work. Hence his preference for crystal and optical glass, partly etched to enhance textures and reflections.

All made by
Yan Zoritchak, France

Architects, Designers, Manufacturers

Gunnar Aagaard Andersen
c/o Den Permanente
Vesterport
DK-1620 Copenhagen V
Denmark

Eero Aarnio
c/o Asko-Upo Oy
15101 Lahti
10 Finland

Bohlin Powell Brown
182 North Franklin Street
Wilkes-Barre
Pennsylvania 18701
USA

Per Borre
Møllegade 16
2200 Copenhagen N
Denmark

Pieter de Bruyne
16 Stationsstraat
9300 Aalst
Belgium

Callister Payne and Bischoff
1865 Mar West, Box 377
Tiburon, California 94920
USA

K.D. Cannon
8313 Dewberry Street
Anchorage, Alaska 99502
USA

Lucian A. Cassetta
835 9th Street
Anchorage, Alaska 99501
USA

John Coleman
5 Alderville Road
London SW6
England

E.B. Crittenden
835 9th Street
Anchorage, Alaska 99501
USA

A.J. Diamond
322 King Street West
3rd Floor
Toronto, Ontario M5V 1J4

John Dinkeloo
20 Davis Street Hamden
Connecticut 06517
USA

Georges Evano et Jean-Luc Pellerin
28, rue du Calvaire
4400 Nantes
France

Foster Associates
12, Fitzroy Street
London W1
England

Shigeo Fukuda
c/o Victoria and Albert Museum
('Japan Style' Exhibition)
South Kensington
London SW7

Bruno Gecchelin
c/o Skipper S.p.A.
14, via S. Spirito
20121 Milano
Italy

Martin Grierson
Barley Mow Workspace
10, Barley Mow Passage
Chiswick, London W4
England

Johannes Hansen Møbel-snedkeri A/S
Design Forum
Gladsaxevej 311
2860 Søborg
Denmark

Hellmuth Obata & Kassabaum
Rockefeller Centre
1270 Avenue of the Americas
New York NY 10020

Søren Horn
Birkedommervej 33 I
2400 Copenhagen NV
Denmark

Kisho Kurokawa Architect & Associates
Aoyama Bldg. 11F,
1-2-3 Kita-Aoyama
Minato
Tokyo

Adalberto Dal Lago
c/o Stilnovo S.p.A.
8, via F. Ferruccio
20145 Milano
Italy

Clare Murray and Mathew Warwick
Shephards Bakery
Station Road
Tydd Gote
Wisbech, Cambridgeshire
England

Barton Myers Associates
322 King Street West
3rd Floor
Toronto, Ontario M5V 1J4

Steven Newell
The Glasshouse
65 Long Acre
London WC2

Steen Østergaard
c/o Den Permanente
Vesterport
DK-1620 Copenhagen
Denmark

Pearl Dot Furniture Worskshops
2 Roman Way
London N7
England

Jean-Luc Pellerin
28, rue du Calvaire
44000 Nantes
France

Ronald Pennell
2 Lower Bibbletts
Hoarwithy, Hereford
England

Jacqueline Poncelet
33 Santley Street
London SW4
England

C. Hugo Pott-Bestecke
Ritterstrasse 28
D-5650 Solingen
West Germany

Howard Raybould
36 Monmouth Road
London W2

Arley Rinehart Associates
2345 Seventh Street
Denver, Colorado 80211
USA

Kevin Roche, John Dinkeloo and Associates
20 Davis Street Hamden
Connecticut 06517
USA

Niels Roth Andersen
c/o Den Permanente
Vesterport
DK-1620 Copenhagen
Denmark

Lino Sabattini
Argenteria Sabattini
via Volta
2207Bregnano/Como
Italy

Senkowski Sakellarios
103 Deinokratous Street
Athens 601
Greece

Robert Sobel/Emery Roth & Sons, Inc.
1980 South Post Oak Road
Suite 1550
Houston, Texas 77056
USA

Skipper S.p.A.
14, via S. Spirito
20121 Milano
Italy

Stilnovo S.p.A.
8, via F. Ferruccio
20145 Milano
Italy

Hugh Stubbins and Associates
1033 Massachusetts Avenue
Cambridge, Massachusetts 02138
USA

Tadao Ando Architect & Associates
6F Domus Blds., 5 Chome
8 Minamihonmachi
Higashi-ku
Osaka
Japan

Jim Warren
128 Dunstans Road
East Dulwich
London SE22

Mathew Warwick and Clare Murray
Shephards Bakery
Station Road
Tydd Gote
Wisbech, Cambridgeshire
England

Oy Wärtsilä Ltd
Helsinki Shipyard
SF-00150 Helsinki 15
Finland

Hans J. Vegner
c/o Den Permanente
Vesterport
DK-1620 Copenhagen
Denmark

R.L. Wilkin
322 King Street West
3rd Floor
Toronto, Ontario M5V 1J4

Wørts Møbelsnedkeri
v/Holger Nissen
Hadsundvej 7
2610 Rødovre
Denmark

Bernard H. Zehrfuss
9, rue Arsène-Houssaye
75008 Paris
France

Yan Zoritchak
Bluffy
75290 Veyrier du Lac
France